Common Differences

GLORIA I. JOSEPH received her B.S. degree from New York University, her M.S. from the City College of New York and her Ph.D. from Cornell University, and has written for many periodicals, including *Journal of Afro-American Studies*, *Educational Opportunity Forum* and the *Bill of Rights Journal*. She has contributed to two books, *Women in Revolution* and *Comparative Perspectives of Third World Women*, and was the producer of the photographic essay *Caribbean Women: Impact of Race, Sex & Class*. Dr. Joseph currently holds the position of professor in the School of Social Science at Hampshire College.

JILL LEWIS has been involved in the Women's Liberation Movement as a socialist feminist since 1972. She graduated with a degree in Modern Languages from Newnham College, Cambridge, England, in 1971. Since 1975 she has held a regular spring semester position as Assistant Professor of Humanities and Arts at Hampshire College. The rest of each year Ms. Lewis resides in Brighton, England, where she is completing a doctoral thesis on the French writer Paul Eluard as well as working on a book on feminism and motherhood. She is the mother of a two-year-old boy.

Common Differences

Conflicts in Black and White
Feminist Perspectives

By Gloria I. Joseph and Jill Lewis

ANCHOR BOOKS
ANCHOR PRESS/DOUBLEDAY
GARDEN CITY, NEW YORK
1981

This Anchor Press edition is the first publication of *Common Differences*.
Anchor Press edition: 1981

Library of Congress Cataloging in Publication Data

Joseph, Gloria I
   Common differences: conflicts in Black and White feminist perspectives

   Includes index.
   1. Feminism—United States—Addresses, essays, lectures. 2. United States—Race relations—Addresses, essays, lectures. 3. Afro-American women—Addresses, essays, lectures. I. Lewis, Jill, joint author. II. Title.
HQ1426.J67   305.4′2′0973

ISBN: 0-385-14271-4
Library of Congress Catalog Card Number: 79-6885

Gloria I. Joseph gratefully acknowledges the following for permission to reprint:

Chris Albertson for excerpts from his interview with Ruby Smith from the recording *AC-DC Blues*. Reprinted by permission of Chris Albertson.

Anchor Press/Doubleday for "It Is Deep" and "Slave Ritual" from the book *How I Got Ovah* by Carolyn Rodgers. Copyright © 1969 and 1975 by Carolyn Rodgers. Reprinted by permission of Doubleday & Company, Inc.

Basic Books for excerpts from the book *Worlds Apart* by Sara Lawrence Lightfoot. Reprinted by permission of Basic Books, Inc.

Mari Evans for excerpts from the book *I Am a Black Woman* by Mari Evans, published by William Morrow & Company, 1970. Excerpted by permission of the author.

Harper & Row for excerpts from the book *All Our Kin* by Carol Stack. Reprinted by permission of Harper & Row, Publishers, Inc.

Winifred Oyoko Loving for "Crazy Granny" by Winifred Oyoko Loving. Printed by permission of the author.

Monthly Review Press for "Black Feminist Statement" from the book *Capitalist Patriarchy and the Case for Socialist Feminism*, edited by Zillah R. Eisenstein. Copyright © 1979 by Zillah R. Eisenstein. Reprinted by permission of Monthly Review Press.

The writing of this book necessarily involved collaboration in its structure. From that point, each author had to create her own way of gathering materials and presenting information. We employed different methodologies which resulted in distinct sections on each topic. Each author bears the responsibility for the sections she has written and their interpretations.

Acknowledgments

My appreciation and thanks—immensely—is extended to the many Black women from all parts of the nation who made this book possible—by being Black women. A special thanks to those who earnestly participated by responding to questionnaires and by engaging in discussion sessions and dialogue.

And to the fine network of Black women with whom I interacted during the process of writing this book: the mutual respect, inspiration, and encouragement (always supplemented by humor) provided a natural high for me as I wrote and rewrote. These include Toni Cade Bambara, Dorcas Bowles, Audre Lorde, Roseann P. Bell, Winnyoko Loving, Zala Chandler, Andre McLaughlin, Carmen Capadavilla, and Shirley Green. Adrienne Rich must be included in this network. She was a constant source of support and encouragement, and offered critical advice.

And to the women students at Hampshire College, Amherst, Massachusetts, for their help in gathering data and providing their particular perspectives on feminism and sexuality. Specifically, I would like to mention Carroll Oliver, who was my student assistant and an outstanding worker, as well as Ann Hackler, Leslie Schwalm, Ada Gay, Sylvia Rubin, and all the other "Insurgent Sisters." Not to be overlooked is my great appreciation to Bob Moore for his perspicacious editing during the early stages of writing, Marylee Taylor for her expertise in the data analysis, and, of course, to the typists—Bobbie

Rosenau, Lennie Bowen, and Fran Duda. Finally, to our editor, Marie Dutton Brown, who consistently provided us with guidance and reassurance and instilled a sense of confidence needed for the production of the book.

—GLORIA I. JOSEPH

My thinking has been shaped out of the range of readings and experiences enabled by women in the women's liberation movements, particularly in Britain, the United States, and France. I am grateful for the significant support and encouragement that came when most needed from Margaret Cerullo, Lisa Lightman, Nina Payne, and Mary Russo. I am indebted to Shirley Prendergast, Jane Flax, Clare Mundy, Jean Gardiner, Josefina Cupido, Nancy Goulder, B. Campbell, Tricia Langton, Julia Casterton, Helen Roberts, Nicola Murray, Carol Bengelsdorf, Sally Koplin, Ros Delmar, Lisa Gaughran, Michelene Wandor, and Wendy Mulford; to Mary, Margaret, Nina, and Lisa; and to Colin Mercer, Richard Schofield, and Dan Smith, for important and influential discussions over the months and years. Inspirational words of Toni Cade Bambara, Roseann Bell, Johnnetta Cole, Oyoko, Adrienne Rich, Michelle Russell, and Barbara Smith have in different ways urged me to shake and dislocate static areas of my white feminist anger and caring. I am indebted to them all for the nature and strength of their political energies. The students I have worked with at Hampshire College over the last five years have helped me dynamically in the questioning and articulating of problems woven into this book. Discussions with and critical feedback from Michele Roberts, Cora Kaplan, Margaret Cerullo, Beatrix Campbell and Lol Sullivan were of invaluable help to me in my own process of formulating my ideas for the feminism and sexuality section. Thanks to Sister Write Bookshop, London, for sharing their facilities with me during the production process. Finally a tribute of thanks to Ali, Mon, Adrian, Clare, Nicola, Cynthia, Martha, Peter, Annie, Ros, and Dan—who physically and emotionally enabled me to *write* while becoming a mother.

And without Gloria, I never would have dared.

—JILL LEWIS

Contents

Introduction

A well-known phrase of a song popular during the Civil Rights Movement of the Sixties was, "Blacks and Whites together, we shall overcome." The dream was that Blacks, Whites, males, females, the young and the not-so-young would all join forces to overcome injustices, discrimination, and segregation. All would organize and unite in a fight for equality and integration.

This was not the first time in United States history that a disgruntled, dissatisfied, angry people protested against blatant racial inequalities in the society. There had been protests in the form of organizations like Marcus Garvey's Universal Negro Improvement Association in the 1920s and the NAACP (National Association for the Advancement of Colored People), founded in 1910. There also had been periodic "race riots," which sometimes featured garbage cans filled with ashes thrown from tenement roofs and snipers with zip guns. More recently, there has been open warfare between police and other forces against the "rioters," with the "rioters" using shotguns, rifles, and handguns in retaliation. The major race riot that occurred in Miami, Florida, May 17–19, 1980, was an example of a serious confrontation, with a great deal of violence, stemming from racial injustices.

Regardless of what kinds of strategies and procedures—or lack thereof—were employed in these historical battles, the conflicts stemmed from a justifiable desire for improvement in the daily lives of Black folks.

The landmark differences between the civil rights movement of the Sixties and the previous pursuit of Black freedom were several. In the Sixties there was a nationwide emergence of new Black organizations and a redirecting of focus on the part of old organizations—all aimed toward Black liberation. Granted, they never coalesced into a powerful Black liberation movement aimed at the restructuring of American society, but they were responsible for Black consciousness-raising, and many important Black leaders emerged. The Civil Rights Movement of the Sixties was also earmarked by the support and co-operation of numerous White groups, organizations, and individuals, many of whom were students. There were the Freedom Riders, volunteers for the Southern Voter Registration Project, members of the American Civil Liberties Union, White members of the NAACP and of SNCC (Student Non-Violent Coordinating Committee) before the White purge in the latter group, and individual lawyers, teachers, priests and nuns, doctors, and wealthy liberals who gave funds, services, and support to the cause.

A courageous feature of the Sixties' movement during its later stages was the emphasis on uniting all the downtrodden regardless of race. Thus Native Americans, poor Whites, Asian-Americans, Hispanics—all who were suffering from some form of discrimination—were engaged in the struggle. It was Black leadership's articulation and analysis of Third World struggles that was responsible for the multiracial alliances within a movement in which the overwhelming majority of protesters were Black.

In 1979, a look at the record of Black and White cooperation and at progress made by Blacks showed that Blacks and Whites were not closer socially or politically, nor had the overall economic picture for Blacks improved.

Actually, the social and economic gap between Blacks and Whites has widened since the Sixties, when the dream began its march into the manifestation stages. It was a little over thirteen years ago when thousands of Blacks responded to the murder of Martin Luther King with riots and rebellion. Today the rights demanded by the protesters are still out of reach. Living conditions, jobs, and education levels for the vast majority of Black people have not improved; in some cases, they have worsened. Joblessness among Black youths is near 60%. The gap between White and Black incomes has widened.

Black medical doctors comprise only 2.2% of their profession, Black lawyers 3.4%, and Black engineers 1.0%. Nationwide, Blacks comprise close to 50% of the prison population, even though Blacks comprise less than 20% of the total United States population. The death rate for minority preschool children is approximately 50% higher than for White children.

Today the Black liberation movement has lost its news-making attraction and the women's movement has emerged as the current popular social movement in the United States. As yet, we do not sing "Women and men together, we shall overcome." On the contrary, many people believe that the women's movement implies a severe separation of men and women.

This book is a committed attempt to examine the ways in which racial and sexual factors interact in the oppression of women. This will be done by discussing the oppression that women have faced collectively, and the relationship of gender to power. The different ways that racism has affected how Black women and White women are oppressed in United States capitalist society are of crucial importance in the project of building radical coalitions. This collaboration is necessary in ending those oppressions. The coalitions depend, however, on the *recognition of differences* in the territory that Black women and White women of different classes and of different sexual preferences occupy as they enter the struggle against exploitation and oppression.

This does not mean that we will ignore class and cultural differences that exist among White women and among Black women. We have tried to recognize the varying political postures and points of view found in the Black liberation movement and in the women's movement. We can no more speak of White women as one amalgamated body than we can refer to Black *and* White women in such a manner. There are sharp differences among White women in terms of wealth and ancestry; these account for some serious problems in understanding and coalition-building. In many ways, a poor, White, Appalachian female may have more in common with the wife of a Black sharecropper than with a suburban homemaker. There is nonetheless a dominant White culture whose racism affects the lives of *all* Americans. The contrast between this dominant White culture and Afro-American culture figures importantly in our analyses.

Our aim is to open up, through discussion, some of the features of oppression peculiar to Black women in contrast to White women. This discussion will take place within the framework of a society where privilege (race, class, or sex) means power—and inequality is integral to the organization of society. Through dialogue, discussion, and criticisms, the book intends to stimulate its readers to develop a political understanding of the importance of formulating realistic strategies that are both anti-racist and anti-sexist. These strategies are aimed at fighting oppression, power, and exploitation—fights which are at the center of the women's movement and the Black liberation movement. Having engaged in extensive dialogue and long collaboration, the authors know that the questions they raise are only a start.

We are hoping to bring together the different perspectives of the liberation struggles fighting racism and sexism by exploring the myths and prejudices, assumptions and misunderstandings that encompass and separate Black and White women. The White women's movement has had its own explicit forms of racism in the way it has given high priority to certain aspects of struggles and neglected others, and it has often been blind and ignorant about the conditions of Black women's lives. It was bound to do so—given that the movement did not begin with women who had some all-encompassing political and historical knowledge, but with women who responded to the forms of immediate injustices crossing their own lives. These injustices, though related to the oppressions known to Black women and men, were within the specific White realities which these women experienced daily and which embodied all kinds of discriminatory and exploitative situations and emotions. Yet as a political movement, women's liberation did and does touch on questions which in different ways affect *all* women's lives—and men's lives too. It shines a brilliant spotlight onto the whirlpool of power and antagonism which surfaces in relationships between men and women because of the profound inequalities which sexism sustains in societal institutions and ideology as well as in economic and psychological relationships.

These are not abstract or invented problems. The women's movement gave and gives emphasis to examining the undercurrents and evidence of women's daily lives, such as looking at the causes and effects of sexual division of labor. Men are expected and trained to perform those kinds of activity that are given higher social status, are more highly paid, and are therefore powerful, while women are expected and trained to do other kinds—which have secondary status, result in lower earnings, and reflect the powerlessness they are meant to signify. The assertion that sexuality and everything that goes along with sexuality is political was the explosive impetus of the surfacing of the women's movement. It was manifested in concerns with power, exploitation, and inequality in the struggle against the damage caused by discrimination, contempt, and hatred based on sex. It was an assertion that made it possible to analyze the patterns of behavior, work, and identity that gender determines in our society. This meant focusing a spotlight on all the formal injustices—the lack of rights and equality—that women confront in their survival day by day. It also meant looking at the nature of relationships between men and women, women and children, men and children, women and women, men and men—and questioning all the assumptions about "what a man is" and "what a woman is," which make the injustices and their resulting antagonisms seem "natural." Such injustices and antagonisms, deriving from a heterosexual definition of what is "natural," create a denial of the legitimacy of the lesbian and homosexual experience. The feminist incentive has been to raise questions about more and more areas where sexual politics affect women's lives—whether this means looking at contraception, abortion, forced sterilization, rape, wife battering, pornography, or inequities in law, health care, welfare, work conditions, and pay. It involves even sexual practice itself and the politics of orgasm, penetration, monogamy, marriage, and the patriarchal erotic.

However, because of the inherently racist assumptions and perspectives brought to bear on these questions in the first articulations by the White women's movement, Black women's lives were not taken into account. Accordingly they were rejected by Black women as irrelevant, when in fact the same problems, seen from different perspectives, can be highly relevant to Black women's lives. Too frequently, participants in the struggles of parallel liberation movements are blinded to each other and have only a limited understanding of each other's priorities. There are valid reasons for this, but the results are often deleterious to both groups. Capitalist society and the racism and sexism it institutionalizes are strengthened by antagonisms. Think how advantageous it would be, for capitalist society, to have Black women watching news coverage or talk shows about "libbers," or advertisements about "liberated" professional White women, or about the White housewife/mother in a modern, glistening home. Or, on the other hand, think of White women perceiving Black struggles through reports of crime and imprisonment rates among Blacks (as if these were intrinsically related to race rather than to the unavoidable Black poverty endemic to racism in the United States), or the sexual stereotypes of Black women and men in television shows and advertisements, or the inadequate representation in the media of the complexities behind "race riots" and the confrontations in Black political protest. The media helps promote superficial and stereotypical images of political movements and thereby influences activists to direct their energies against each other. However, radical political movements emerge out of real social problems and structure their priorities according to what they see as most important based on the contradictions most acutely felt by those who make up the movement. The Black movement has viewed White analysis of class with well-deserved suspicion, given the frequent failure to adequately include an analysis of racism under advanced capitalism in the United States. Yet the violent and insidious dispersal of socialist, labor, and communist movements is dramatically paralleled in United States history by the systematic violent suppression enacted against Black movements of resistance. A most recent case in point is the United States government's decimation of the Black Panther Party. The Black movement scorns feminism partially on the basis of misinformation, and partially due to a valid perception of the White middle-class nature of the movement. An additional reason is due to the myopic ways that White feminists have generalized their sexual-political analysis and have confirmed their racism in the forms their feminism assumed. On the other hand, the Black movement too often neglects to adequately consider the effects of class and sexual oppression. Its tendency is to stress those priorities for struggle that stem most clearly from racial oppression, at the expense of class and sexual considerations, as if these were totally separate issues that could be resolved on their individual terms.

The White women's movement righteously criticizes the organization and strategies of the White male left—which emphasized class struggle and anti-imperialism while perpetuating attitudes about women and gender roles that reproduced and reinforced male power and male superiority. The left was guided by socialist and Marxist analyses which attempted to delineate the structure and functions of capitalism—of how it worked to expropriate and exploit people's labor and sustain a wealthy ruling class, while vast numbers of people remained poor and powerless. However, the analyses centered on the "workplace" and only minimally and selectively dealt with the role of the family or of reproduction and childrearing. What was important and what was not important was defined in terms of sexist attitudes, and the relationship of gender to power and democracy was absent from the main agendas.

In contrast, the White women's movement tilled the "anti-patriarchal" ground. It attempted to challenge the organization of power around sexual (not just class) divisions—which, from the most intimate to the most formally instituted levels of society, create and reinforce male domination and female oppression. Yet with increasing alertness, bafflement, or self-righteous indignation, the White women's movement wondered "why more Third World women don't get involved" in this struggle. Indeed, they barely did at all. So in the women's movement recently there is developing a critical and self-critical process which has begun—only begun—to explore the racist reasons for the movement staying mostly White. This process has been urged on by the autonomous voices of Black women, who insist that this process of questioning must be undertaken if the feminist movement is to have any integrity for them. Thus the White women's movement in the last few years has become increasingly alert to the significance of the absence of Third World women in the movement and a self-reflective process of examining the reasons for this has begun. White feminists are having to deal directly with the far-reaching implications of their own racism. The political reassessments and new dimensions of critical understanding generated by this questioning cannot be underestimated.

At the same time, a growing number of Black communities are experiencing the phenomenon of emerging Black feminism. In most cases the process of Black women expressing their priorities as women has evoked negative to hostile responses. The question of sexual politics has been ignored for far too long in Black communities. Heterosexual and homosexual relationships and the power structures they inscribe need to be seriously analyzed. The element of humor, which is often present when Blacks refer to or discuss sex, has its place, but we must not allow the sexual jokes of Richard Pryor—genius though he is—to be the basis for Black sexual politics. This issue of sexual politics is a key aspect of this book.

Overall, however, Black women are raising important questions concerning sexual politics. In Black communities one more frequently hears the phrase "the women are beginning to get it together." Black and White men's responses to the women's movement have been both negative and positive, but the men have been alerted to the fears, anxieties, and anger that sexual politics evokes in them. The racial centering of their politics has taken its toll elsewhere.

These concerns have been important for us as we formulated our discussion. As a Black woman and a White woman, neither one of us can entirely escape from the racial and sexual biases of political movements in which we have been involved. Rather than deny these biases, we have used them as springboards to set in motion a process which has enabled us to move away from a self-centered, moralistic belief that "our" posture/position is the correct one, as we confront, explore, and better understand the different political movements. We have had to struggle against blindfolds and surface labels. We have recognized the essential importance of autonomous political movements, yet believe that political interaction is necessary in order to make possible the collaboration and alliance needed for change. It is crucial for political movements to allow for the development of unified liberation struggles which are not riddled with contempt based on gender, race, or other factors.

Throughout the preparation of this book, our process has been the persistent encounter of our political histories. The culturally shaped resilience, strategic coping, and defense mechanisms in the heritage of Black women have met the cultural heritage of White women's struggle for autonomy, as well as our self-doubts and the different defense mechanisms in our daily conversations and arguments—whether over films, political events and our responses to them, looking after the baby, people we met or heard, the weather, our social connections, our families. None of the ideas were just *there* for us to lay out side by side. Our selections and choices, our emphases and juxtapositions took shape during three years of dialogue and struggle. Our differences made our own perceptions clearer in unexpected ways, and what we felt we had to or wanted to talk about emerged differently during the process of our collaboration, criticism, and caring. Often this meant reformulating to each other things that each of us took entirely for granted on her own territory. This, in turn, shifted the actual ground we had originally hoped to cover—since a fabric of cultural and ideological limits and insights informed differently not just a *content* of what we thought important but the very means we had of understanding the political significance of *any* of the content of what we had to say to each other. So larger political discourses were lived out—painfully or with amusement—in our personal political discourse. That discourse is still, of course, ongoing, and has only begun to break certain ground.

The histories and conflicts we brought together were endlessly specific. The flaming buildings of the Black Studies program at Cornell University, Ithaca, N.Y., where Gloria watched her office burn in the night, hovered against the student movement occupations and Women's Liberation Movement disruptions in Cambridge, England, while the miners' strike and left-wing struggles brought a Conservative government to its knees. A network of family and relations from St. Croix to Yonkers was talking through to the voices from postwar, nuclear-family Northern Ireland. So our series of priorities always had to be qualified by the other's re-vision of the importance from *her* perspective. Jill recalls the interest she felt on reading Nancy Chodorow's book, *The Reproduction of Mothering*—and the frustration of trying to make Gloria "see" some of its political importance—to be met by an initial resistance and unwillingness to enter into controversies it raised, since they did not seem relevant to the Black experience of family and gender Gloria's culture knows. Only much later could the conversation be reformulated, with Jill beginning again: "This book touches on some crucial questions for *White* feminists concerning their personal/political gendered history and organization of the family . . . and raises ways of thinking about them which, in the categories it uses, could *differently* and *tangentially* spark off interesting insights into the specific ways gender is organized through Black family experience." Or again, Gloria's firm assertion of the powerful affirmation and importance of heterosexual sexuality that Black women could bear witness to (and the implicit triumph over White women's inability to give account of something similar) moved from initial shared humor into Jill's sulky resistance and defensiveness, on to a dynamic continuing exploration and discussion of the specific racial histories and their articulation into male and female sexuality.

It was not just a question of spelling out what we each felt we knew, not just a matter of revealing to each other what we thought important, but a reevaluation of how race was specific to the agendas and vision that each of us had developed. This in turn threw new light on each of our perspectives as well as opening up new avenues of political thinking which had been closed off through the racial isolationism of our political histories. For example, certain White feminist modes of talking about "men," their implicit or explicit ways of naming "men" as the oppressors and challenging or condemning heterosexuality had to be, in our dialogues, made specific to the economic, political, and daily realities in which White men and White women meet and interact. For Afro-American men there are *no* easily equivalent categories for the feminist rhetoric about "men." On the other hand, the humor, anecdote, resilience, and relishing with which Black women often give account of their alliance with men could—by interaction with the kinds of (if not the same) problems White feminists raise about sexuality and power—be opened up into more complex ways of understanding the intersection of racial solidarity, community sustenance and personal support with the fears, abuses and humiliations which a racist and sexist capitalist society infuses into them.

Another dimension of the dialogue of our lives was lived out in our working lives. We became aware of the choices which oriented us into different options—what we went to or participated in, how we were situated in certain events on the campuses confronting racist and/or sexist practices in the institutions. And this escalated our critical self-perceptions and critical interaction with each other. The overlapping of the edges of our political interests and personal friends enlarged for each of us a scope of discussion and challenge by initiating each of us into political and personal discussions and accounts which we would not otherwise have found ourselves in. Jill recalls urging a reluctant and suspicious Gloria to come with her to a reading by Adrienne Rich. Rich's poetry was of key cultural and political significance in White feminist circles, but had not been publicized (at that time) on Black political horizons, though her poetry was already addressing dilemmas related to racial oppression as well as sexual.

The recurrent experience of being involved in activities, intimate discussions, laughter and anger with Gloria's friends revolutionized for Jill aspects of thinking and understanding. Without these experiences, the more abstract or theoretical discussions between Jill and Gloria would have taken *years* to open up; they nourished and challenged the site of our collaboration in immeasurable ways. Yet we had always to sustain our different and separate rootings—knowing we could never appropriate a complete knowledge of each other's history and political impetus, we only could deal problematically and dynamically with the clashing parameters delineated by our racial and class positions and our consciousness, which circumscribed our meeting and working together as women.

Our work on this book has been a process of serious arguments, spontaneous gut laughter, quiet fears, and anger. These and many other reactions have been and still are triggered by the revelation of deeply rooted biases, ignorance born of too much academia, strikingly different responses to similar questions, recognition of the need for new questions, and qualifications upon qualifications. Having engaged in extensive dialogue and long collaboration, we know that the questions we raise are only a start. Our hope is to begin to construct and illustrate questions and point the direction to answers.

We have begun to explode generalizations about White feminism and Black politics to which we were previously attached as with an umbilical cord. The joint utilization of a particular analysis helped to significantly lessen the gap between the politics of the Black liberation and women's liberation movements. That analysis is based on a recognition that this society is organized economically and socially around privilege and profit for a few; that people do not control their conditions of work or what they produce, nor have any real collective or democratic power to determine the kind of society in which they live; and that United States-dominated multinational corporations extract profits, at whatever social and human cost, from any part of the world into which they can get their tentacles.

Our students were invaluable in opening many new avenues in our thinking. They often refused to take our political points of reference for granted, and insisted on reexamining the implications of our political language. "We must examine the concept of relative deprivation and its implications for resistance movements," we would say. "Relative deprivation?" they would query. Lengthy discussions would ensue. "Then," a student would retort, "we need to examine the politics of poverty under capitalism." And so we did.

The process of collecting materials and gathering data proved to be a constructive and enjoyable learning process for all involved. The students helped to administer questionnaires, collate data, conduct interviews, tape conversations, videotape group discussions, and write biographical accounts of the lives of women who were considered to be insurgent sisters. Our diversities in race, ethnicity, age, and class provided a neat system of checks and balances and exemplified "learning by doing" and "learning from one another." In many cases what we, the authors, considered to be self-explanatory was not so at all. The concepts of working-class women and older women yielded an illuminating range of responses. The students' definitions of rape, sexual harassment, racism, homosexuality, and unemployment reflected the depth and complexity of racial and sexual perspectives.

This book is the product of the beginnings of our explorations. It does not claim definitive answers. Nor does it contain specific analyses, for example, of the ten possible pairings of Blacks and Whites, males and females, in sexual relationships. It is an exposure of the kinds of problems and conflicts endemic to liberation struggles and how they are reproduced in daily life. It may sound as if this book should be titled *The Blues Politics of Women's Liberation*, because so much of the content concerns problems, troubles, and tribulations —but "gospel singing" would be more appropriate in the title in the sense that, although troubles are spelled out, there is a real feeling of hopefulness. It is a hope born out of the belief that oppressed groups will be important historical agents in bringing about the major changes needed in our society. We live in a society that has mastered advanced technology and productivity beyond our dreams. Yet because it is a system based on poverty and oppression, discrimination and exploitation, it is seen by its victims as being barbarous and unnecessary.

The rising consciousness of Black and White women and men is encouraged by the tide of revolutions against exploitation across the world. The root causes of spiraling prices for food, energy, housing, and medical care, cleverly camouflaged under the chicanerous title of "inflation," are increasingly being understood by the public. The increased consciousness about domestic and international exploitation can be effectively translated into action through the recognition of key political questions and challenges posed by both the women's movement and the Black liberation movement. This book is the beginning of a long but vital journey into the political lives of Black women and White women, highlighting the racial and sexual politics involved. Only by undertaking such a journey can the problems surrounding racial and sexual politics be surveyed and understood and dealt with. This process is necessary to identify the possibilities for collaboration—not in male, or White, or middle-class terms, but encompassing varied relevant meanings for the different groups of people whose interests necessitate fundamental change in the society as we know it. This book is intended to stimulate readers to begin to make such connections.

Throughout the book, with a few exceptions, reference has been made to Black women rather than to Third World women or other specific nonwhite women. This was due to the respect that we hold for different cultural and historical backgrounds among Third World women. We are fully cognizant of the fact that in many cases what is applicable to Black women would also be applicable to other non-white women in America.

Common Differences was imagined out of the understandings and determination which this introduction touches on, but we did not aim to produce a seamless piece of rounded analysis and argument. We feel that to have done so would be closing rather than opening important areas of debate and changing vision, both for us and for the posing of questions related to the political issues we are concerned with.

The book has evolved structurally and stylistically out of our process of dialogue. Its intent is not to synthesize "obvious" conclusions, nor to argue for "true," "correct" positions beyond existing contradictions and differences—but to actually examine side by side, dynamically, those very differences and conflicting visions, in the form of dialogue itself. This does not presuppose the eventual outcome of an understanding that is "beyond" racial and sexual conflict and oppression. Rather, it expresses the cultures and histories out of which grow the political differences, and allows for new forms of recognition as we look *at* each other, as we try to imagine viable ways of joining our strengths.

So, in that we speak as Black, as White, as Black woman, as White woman, we are not a homogenized unit of coauthors, blending and harmonizing our knowledge and perspectives. We speak from our own histories and cultures. But we also speak *to each other* from those histories, cultures, and political experiences. The book itself posits a process of learning how to hear each other's histories and learning what we need to spell out to make our own understood.

So we begin by Gloria examining the different attitudes and responses expressed by Black women concerning their ideas about the Women's Liberation Movement. Then, with those responses setting the pace, Jill talks about why and how the movement is significant for White women—what real political problems it explores, exposes, and struggles against. We found that to understand the way we imagine ourselves *as women*, certain key features of the mother-daughter relationship raised fascinating questions and contrasts, enabling far-reaching understanding of our economic, ideological, cultural, and historic roots. So Gloria examines how Black women view their mothers, and the messages transmitted from Black mothers to their daughters. Then Jill looks at the White feminist understandings and explorations of the mother-daughter conflict, which White patriarchal contexts necessitate in certain forms. Next, in turn, we think about the media and question the way the capitalist imperative produces and capitalizes on certain sexual images charged with racial overtones and systematic violence. Last, but not least, we look at sexuality itself. Gloria, through research, interviews and taped conversations, allows Black women to define and describe their sexuality in terms of their socialization as Black women in American, capitalist society. They discuss how this sexual socialization affects their relationships with men and with each other, and they provide and highlight highly relevant data for historical and political reevaluation of the role of sexuality in the lives of contemporary Black women. Jill explores how White feminists have come to understand and talk about forms and problems of sexual oppression. She looks at the sexual dilemma that White patriarchal oppression has generated and continues to generate for White women, the political nature of this dilemma, and some of the strategies that are significant in the Women's Liberation Movement for struggling against the sexual negation, repression, and abuse that patriarchal structures institutionalize in the White dominant culture.

We conclude by recapitulating the losses experienced when Black women and White women view their oppressions through parallel, monolithic, yet disconnected lenses. We argue for the importance of Black women and White women connecting their specific understandings of oppression to an understanding of the political totality that thrives on these oppressions. Through such connections, we believe, both groups can reevaluate and restructure their strategies for liberation in the most effective ways possible.

NOTES

In the stagnant economy of 1975–76, the economic gap between Black and White families widened in absolute as well as in relative terms.

Year	Income of White Families	Income of Black Families	Gap
1975	$14,268	$8,779	$5,489
1976	15,557	9,262	6,295
1977	16,740	9,563	7,177

Education and Income:

1975 Median Earnings of Full-time Workers

	Less than High School	High School Only	College (4 years or more)
White men	$10,544	$12,473	$17,351
Other men	8,413	10,325	13,801
White women	5,932	7,133	10,575
Other women	5,384	7,265	10,061

SOURCE: *Fact Sheet on Institutional Racism*—compiled, published, and distributed by the Council on Interracial Books for Children, 1841 Broadway, New York, NY 10047, October 1978.

Black men—only half of Black males can expect to live to age sixty.

Black Women's and White Women's Liberation

I

White Promotion,
Black Survival

> White skin is to racism,
> As the penis is to sexism,
> As class, profit, and corruption are to capitalism.

Three women are standing before a covered mirror. At a given signal the cover will be removed and the following question will be put to them:

> Mirror, mirror, on the wall,
> what is the greatest oppressor of us all?

The mirror is unveiled and all three see their reflections bouncing back.

Woman number one sees her Blackness. "It is my Blackness that is most dominant. That is what makes for my oppression. And who oppresses Blacks? Whites. So it is White racism that is the greatest oppressor. Yes, racism oppresses!" So thinks woman number one.

Woman number two says, "I see myself as female, and as such, dominated and controlled by men. Men and their sexism oppress women, so sexism is the greatest oppressor of us all."

Woman number three observes her reflection and sees her gender, race, and class. "My femaleness, my color, and my class are sources of exploitation. Who is exploiting me? The question deserves serious consideration. An immediate response will not do."

The mirror reflects images, but cannot show the experiences which have shaped the perceptions of these three women. The racism, classism, and sexism associated with each woman's experience of being Black and female in the United States are the critical measurements of their oppression.

Many factors contribute to the institutionalization of racism, classism, and sexism. These include what kinds of work are available and to whom the wages are paid; the meaning of volunteer labor; assumptions about the family; mutual dependence in marriage; access to education; images of women and men, Blacks and Whites, in the media; availability of health care; the distribution of wealth; laws and law enforcement. All of these and much more define how privilege, exploitation, and powerlessness are distributed among women and men, Blacks and Whites. Underlying all of this is the profit motive, which perpetuates racism, sexism, and classism.

The debate about whether race or sex is the major source of oppression has separated Black and White women in both current and past liberation struggles. The analogy that leads off this chapter indicates that both White skin and the penis, as "biological determinants," are false measures of superiority and, like most false things, are maintained and supported by systems that are corrupt, unjust, and fused with ignorance and prejudice. Women, all women, must begin to look for the root causes of their oppressions. As a first step, they must take a good look at themselves and discover where their present attitudes came from, as well as where they now stand on certain issues. Then, and only then, can they begin to make a concentrated and effective effort toward change.

In Chapters I and II, we will hear and discuss Black and White women's feelings and attitudes toward the women's movement. It is important for Black and White women to recognize the widespread beliefs and opinions that each group holds about itself and about the other. We will also bare certain assumptions and some of the misunderstandings that have developed as a result of ignorance, prejudices, surface labeling,[1] and blindfolds. Such misunderstandings are harmful to both groups and interfere with the mutual respect necessary to the development of effective collaboration.

A look at selected verbatim responses of fourteen Black women will give a strong sense of how and what they think about the women's movement. These women represent a variety of historical and social experiences and their comments will strike familiar chords in the orchestra of Black expression. While the names are fictitious, all other information is accurate. An analysis of their responses follows. The question asked was: "How would you define the women's movement in the United States today?"

ANN: *age 45, eleven children, separated, born and raised in Mississippi, income minimal, low socioeconomic level.* "They just a bunch a women that don't know what they want. One while it's this and the next it's that. It's a whole lot of gibberish about nothing. If they so tired of staying at home, let them change places with me for a while and see how tired they get."

BARBARA: *age 37, no children, married, divorced, born and raised in the Midwest, income $15,000, professional counselor.* "I see it as cyclical in the sense that almost 100 years ago the women's suffrage movement was started. Now, let's see, about this women's movement, as a Black woman I don't know which issue comes first. Third World women view the feminist movement with suspicion and mistrust because it is primarily a White women's effort. The feminist issues are not relevant to the needs of Third World people in general or Third World women in particular. Feminist issues revolve around sexism and it's a laudable cause. However, they do not confront the effects that racism or economic exploitation have on the Third World communities throughout the world. As a Black woman who is concerned with the impact of the feminist movement in American society, it is obvious to me that feminists have not analyzed any of the historic conditions of Black people or Black women and consequently have ignored a genuine ally in terms of the struggle for equality in all walks of life. Black women, on the whole, recognize that Black men are not as 'sensitive' to the needs of Black women and their quest for justice or their fight against discrimination. However, we are cognizant of the 'divisive' tactics which alienate Black people from the continuous struggle against our existence, and that includes the feminist movement. Black women perceive that the feminists will want to alienate themselves from men, and Black women will not participate in that effort."

CARRIE: *age 65, no children, married twice, living with husband, born in Jamaica, W.I., raised in the Bronx, N.Y., income $9,000.* "Women's liberation? Not for me! A woman should get equal pay if she is equally qualified as a man, but a woman is supposed to be a woman. She must not let herself be pushed around, but she must be feminine. Where most colored people are concerned, it should be fifty-fifty. Both have to share the responsibility equally. They both have to go out there and do the do. These women liberationists just want to get in the same position as men so they can do the same incorrect things like men. It's wrong for Black women to get in the women's movement. A relationship will only work if there is care and trust."

DOROTHY: *age 27, no children, unmarried, lesbian, raised in the Midwest, college teacher, income $12,000.* "The White women's liberation movement is basically middle class. Very few of these women suffer from the extreme economic exploitation that most Third World women are subject to day-to-day. The economic and political and social realities of the Third World woman's life are not an intellectual persecution. It is not a psychological outburst. It is tangible, present in every endeavor we choose to undertake. The problems are realities of day-to-day living which affect the well-being of all Third World people. A common bond cannot exist between White women and Third World women if there is no realization on the part of the White groups that they are fighting racism and capitalism. The realization must come that their condition stems from a debilitating economic and social system and not from the exploitation of their bodies. There is no logical comparison between the oppression of Third World women on welfare and the suppression of the suburban wife and her protests about housework. This is exemplified in the situation of the welfare mother who does not know where the next meal is coming from and the suburbanite who complains about preparing and serving meals."

EVELYN: *age 53, divorced, seven children (one adopted), husband deceased, worked as domestic, waitress, shipyard worker, cigar factory worker, postal clerk, born and raised in the South, lower income bracket.* "I'm old-fashioned enough to want a man to carry my heavy load and open doors, but a woman should have control over her own body. I couldn't even get a diaphragm without my husband's consent. I like the way women are demanding more for their bodies and for better jobs. The man has nothing to do but listen. Things will change."

FLORENCE: *age 35, one child, divorced, author, college teacher, currently self-employed, born and raised in the South, living in the Caribbean, income below poverty level—$6,000 per year.* "As with many things in the United States, the women's movement has been, I feel, adulterated and bastardized largely because of the input and impact of the media (the buying and selling of an idea) and because of the ever-present opportunists who find in each 'new' thing yet another opportunity to display and exploit the thing within them which can only be labeled *dilettante*. Ideally, the women's movement in the United States is a rapidly growing and organized network of conscientious women who realize that change in many areas—politics, economics, etc.—must and will take place, but that these changes, these women feel, can take place more rapidly when persons of the same ilk join together for progress. Note, I said *ideally*. Realistically, I have no idea what the goddamn movement is all about, since I have very little contact with White women and the Blacks with whom I have immediate contact do not express much interest."

GERTRUDE: *age about 60 (not sure because she has no birth certificate in either Georgia or Connecticut), started working at age 13 as a fruit picker, widowed, three sons, low income level.* "Women's lib? It's fine for a woman to have a career. In fact, I love the idea, but it would be nice if the mother could be home with the kids when they are young. If a husband doesn't want his wife to work and the issue is threatening the marriage, the woman should give up her job. I think this going dutch business is crazy. If a fellow takes me out on a date and I have to pay my own way, I'd just as soon go out with a girl. Men have to pay for the pleasure of our company."

HULDA: *age 24, no children, single, college graduate, temporarily unemployed, part-time waitress, born and raised and living in Washington, D.C., low income bracket.* "I see the women's movement in the United States today as a struggle for (1) self-identity, (2) an uplift in the social strata, and (3) a unification of females to fight and ultimately change the sexist and racist laws that run this country. As a member of NOW, I feel that Black women should be an active part of a movement that is fighting for women's rights. Who else is doing that for us?"

IRENE: *age 96, living alone, twice married (both husbands deceased), born and raised in North Carolina.* "If God wanted that, he would not have made Adam and Eve."

JANET: *age 42, three children, married, born and raised in the Southeast, college professor, upper middle-income level.* "It seems to me that we can see a general awakening or sensitivity to the issues of women's inequality —ranging all the way from the Madison Avenue corporate world's hustle of one more genuine people's concern, to various expressions of political activism. But I'm not sure there is a women's movement in the sense of a sustained, organized, and in some sense mass-based program directed toward gender equality. What we clearly have are many groups, factions, interests, ideological persuasions regarding the woman question. Which is the women's movement, or are they all: Equal Rights advocates; National Organization for Women members; militant separatists; lesbians; Coalition of Labor Union Women; Women for Racial and Economic Equality; National Council of Negro Women?"

KATE: *age 19, single, no children, first-year community college student, working-class parents, born and raised in suburb of New York City.* "I don't want no part of those women libbers. I don't know what they're about and neither do they."

LILLIAN: *age 35, one child, divorced, author, college professor, living in the South, income irregular, times of scarcity and times of plenty.* "I view the overall phenomena in five ways: (1) a recently reactivated sector of the movement for democratic rights; (2) as part of the demystification of the Western process, challenging the assumptions that inform orthodox history, anthropology, medicine, science, arts, psychology, etc.; (3) a mass consciousness movement affecting women, men, challenging children, institutions, systems, public policy, national images, popular culture, etc.; (4) an informal network of like-minded women deliberately/consciously working on behalf of women's economic, political, social, spiritual, psychological freedoms, as defined by the communities they most closely identify with (racial, ethnic, religious, political, feminist, lesbians, etc.); (5) a network of formal organizations who have assumed responsibility (or appointed themselves as guardians and most appropriate people) for fashioning the ideological, organizational/political guidelines with which to harness, shape, direct that mass energy released within the last decade and a half by the civil rights movement and subsequent movements."

MARY: *age 25, high school graduate, working as a cleaning (domestic) aide in Washington, D.C., income poverty level.* "I know nothin' about the women's movement."

Mary says she "knows nothin' about the women's movement," and Lillian shows sophisticated knowledge about the meaning of the movement. Can we say that one is in the know and the other isn't? Mary is saying many things when she says she knows nothing about the movement. She is really saying that the movement has played no part in her consciousness; is irrelevant to her; hasn't been explained to her; is simply not a part of her reality; and is a rather meaningless phrase. She knows, of course, that it has something to do with women and that there is a lot of talk about certain things like men and jobs. But she doesn't know from her own experience what the movement is really about. Her reality is cleaning those urine-smelling bathrooms on a daily basis, looking forward to that weekly paycheck to keep herself together and spending time with her boyfriend.

Florence, who is college-educated, views the movement with similar disinterest and some derision as she says, "Realistically, I have no idea what the movement is." Florence has limited contacts with Whites, and her Black peers, friends, and acquaintances show little interest in the women's movement. Florence knows little about the movement, cares less, and really couldn't give a damn!

Ann, age 45, and Kate, age 19, understand the women's movement in a manner similar to Mary's. Their consciousness has not been invaded by the realities of the movement. It's something out there that is "going on," like the United Nations is "going on." It exists, has been going on for some time, but has no tangible or direct bearing on the material conditions of their lives.

The responses of Carrie, Evelyn, Gertrude, and Irene imply that the primary goal of the women's movement is "to make women become like men." Irene says it most directly: "If God wanted *that*, he would not have made Adam and Eve [italics mine]." Paraphrased, she's saying, "If God wanted everyone to be alike, he wouldn't have made two sexes." Carrie explicitly says, "These women liberationists just want to get in the same position as men so they can do the same incorrect things like men."

Evelyn, age 53, expresses a similar concern to the one above (not wanting to be treated the same as men) when she says that she wants men to help her "carry her heavy load and open doors." She fears that the women's movement's concern about male/female relationships will be expressed at the expense of obliteration of role/gender differences. On the other hand, in advocating that women should have the right to control their own bodies, she is supporting a major goal of the women's movement.

The response of Gertrude (age about 60) is more complicated. She refers to the movement as "Women's Lib." She would like to see a balance between having a career and doing the "motherly" duties of raising children. However, she takes a giant step backward by saying that "a woman should give up her job if the husband doesn't want her to work and the marriage is threatened." Her final comment, "Men have to pay for the pleasure of our company" throws women into the arena of being sexual objects for the pleasure of men, bartering their bodies in the exchange. How far is that from prostitution? And how far is it from traditional marriage, wherein the woman receives room, board, and possibly spending money in exchange for keeping house, bearing and raising children, providing sex, and caring for the family for her spouse?

Carrie, Evelyn, Gertrude, and Irene have a perspective on the women's movement that is based on their past experiences. Their statements are directly concerned with the oppressive conditions of their lives. The fact that many of their concerns are similar to those expressed by the White, middle-class women who are rejected and criticized by the Black respondents exemplifies the complex and contradictory nature of Black/White coalition-building. This congruence of concerns includes women having control over their bodies, an end to labor exploitation, and the development of sexual politics putting men and women on an equal footing for negotiating sexual involvement.

The blanket rejection of the movement by several of the Black women, coupled with their firm belief in ideas that are central to the women's movement, is a curious combination. Examine Carrie's response. There is an emphatic, categorical rejection of women's liberation, followed immediately by a statement about "equal pay for equal work," a central tenet of the women's movement. Carrie then says, "But a woman is supposed to be a woman. She must not let herself be pushed around, but she must be feminine." That sentence seems to be loaded with inherent contradictions. What does it mean for a woman to *be* a woman? The images and roles of women in the United States are associated with status and characteristics that allow women limited access to an array of jobs—for example, bank presidents, lawyers, doctors, engineers, maître d's, electricians, carpenters, firefighters, and production line supervisors. However, on the other hand, to be feminine in the traditional mode is to be dainty, fragile, cute, and/or unable to perform simple mechanical tasks, to wear sexy-looking clothes, to smile and act ignorant even when knowledgeable, to refer to Joe DiMaggio as a boxer and Wilt Chamberlain as a prime minister, and to raise your voice only when screeching at a two-inch mouse. These characteristics are an invitation to be "pushed around" and advertise a need to be directed, protected, managed, and aided at practically every turn. It is the very rare woman who can be "feminine" and not be "pushed around." She would have to have a cold, calculating interior accompanied by razor-sharp sarcasm, and even then she would probably be referred to as a "cold bitch."

In a less direct way, Evelyn, Gertrude, and Carrie allude to the interpretation that the women's movement is about a separation of men and women and aims to have women become "like" (equal to) men at the expense of "losing their femininity." Stereotypical feminine characteristics are considered to be at stake and the idea of their loss is disconcerting.

Black women have historically defied the Western images of femininity in so many ways that it seems an ironic twist for them to express concern and fear about losing those characteristics (see Chapter IV for a discussion of this point). However, the important point is that the so-called feminine characteristics do not carry the same meaning and messages for Black women as they do for White women. As the Black feminist and abolitionist Sojourner Truth so aptly said in 1851:

That man over there says that women need to be helped into carriages and lifted over ditches and to have the best place everywhere. Nobody ever helps me into carriages or over mud puddles or gives me the best place. And ain't I a woman? . . . I have borne thirteen children and seen most of 'em sold into slavery, and when I cried out with my mother's grief, none but Jesus heard me, and ain't I a woman?[2]

Most Black women still do not receive the respect and treatment—mollycoddling and condescending as it sometimes is—afforded White women. So when these Black women complain about not wanting to lose their femininity, they are referring to something quite different. The difference has to be understood in an analysis of how the classic "feminine characteristics" are viewed in relation to Black women.

On the most basic level, Black women in many situations are treated as non-females. The ghost of Sojourner Truth's haunting question is still with us today. Consider the crime of rape, which is punishable by death in many states. According to the Federal Bureau of Prison reports, in Florida during the years 1940 to 1964, of 125 White males who raped White females, 6, or about 5 percent, received death penalties, of the 68 Blacks who raped Black females, 3, or about 4 percent, received death sentences; of the 84 Blacks convicted of raping White women, 45, or 54 percent, received the death penalty; not one of the 8 White offenders convicted of raping Black women was sentenced to death. This pattern varies little throughout the country. It must be considered an impossibility for White men to rape Black women in the eyes of justice and in the minds of many. Black women apparently are considered as something other than "women." The statistics also say a great deal about the double standard for punishment applied to Black and White men.

While many people would consider certain menial, laborious jobs as being "unfit for women," they fail to notice if Black women hold them. The jobs may be unfit for women, but not for Black women. In work situations such as the laundries, factories, and kitchens where Black and White women sweat, the worst, most abhorrent jobs are reserved for Black women. Society views Black women in stereotypical images, among them being the stereotype of strong, tough-minded, sharp-tongued women, or, as the Black writer Zora Neale Hurston said, as the mules of the world.

Many Black women affect male-defined feminine characteristics in much the same manner as do White women. They can act cute, dainty, helpless, demure, nonaggressive, and sexy. Within the Black communities these characteristics are "appreciated," accepted, reinforced, rewarded, and perpetuated in a typical Western tradition. The conflict or psychological drama for the Black woman occurs when she moves into the dominant society and these same behaviors and characteristics are received and interpreted in a different manner because they hold a different interpretation for White society. The Black female is either unnoticed or overnoticed and misinterpreted. (For a fuller discussion of self-concepts and media images of Black and White women, see Chapter IV.) Among Black women, feminine characteristics play a unique and peculiar role and thus must be interpreted on the basis of particular historical grounds.

Black women have been working women since their arrival in the Americas and from the beginning have been denied job equality in every conceivable way. Simultaneously, they have struggled—individually and collectively—against oppressive conditions and job discrimination. History—at least available "his-story"—tells us little of the numerous attempts by Black women to organize for job equality. Black women, first and foremost, are workers. Most of the Black women in service work (approximately 49 percent of Black women workers) do not profit from unionization. This is further compounded by the fact that the median wage or salary income for Black women is less than that of White females and both Black and White males.

The emphasis of the women's movement on eradicating the "helpless female" stereotype has a different meaning for White women than it has for Black women. The image has a debilitating effect for White women; rejecting it and ultimately eradicating it is necessary for the structuring of new self-images. However, a different set of dynamics operates for Black women. The Black woman has to develop her political struggles in keeping with her personal consciousness, while at the same time maintaining her ties with the Black community. Her role in the Black community is as central to her survival as is her personal political development in sexual areas.

As Barbara said in her response, ". . . it is obvious to me that feminists have not analyzed any of the historic conditions of Black people or Black women and subsequently have ignored a genuine ally in terms of the struggle for equality in all walks of life. . . . Black women perceive that the feminists want to alienate themselves from men, and Black women will not participate in that effort."

The extent of participation and involvement of Black women in the movement will largely depend upon recognition, understanding, and acceptance by White women concerning Black patterns of male/female personal interactions and relationships. Black women cannot operate with a philosophy whose dynamics include separation, rejection, or exclusion of men. Carrie said it well in her response: ". . . where most colored people are concerned it should be fifty-fifty. Both have to share the responsibility equally. They both have to go out there and do the do . . ."

In this country, Black men and women have to share the task of making a go of life while constantly being confronted by racism and other oppressions. Carrie is introducing a loaded dictum when she says, "A relationship will only work if there is care and trust." Our society is not set up to allow or to encourage or to facilitate an equal sharing of responsibilities between men and women, be they black, brown, red, tan, pink, or white. The ingredients necessary for care and trust in a relationship simply are not that readily available. Individualism, consumerism, competitiveness and winning at any expense, and the drive to maximize profits regardless of the cost to people, do not create an environment conducive to or encouraging of trust and care.

The Black woman's socialization process ceremoniously includes the parameter of a distrust for men. (See Section Two, "Mothers and Daughters.") Men are socialized to not demonstrate tenderness, caring, and gentleness. These are conditions that Blacks are aware of. Barbara points out that, "Black women, on the whole, recognize that Black men are not as 'sensitive' to the needs of Black women and their quest for justice or their fight against discrimination. However, we are cognizant of the 'divisive' tactics which alienate Black people from the continuous struggle against our existence, and that includes the feminist movement. Black women perceive that the feminists want to alienate themselves from men and Black women will not participate in that effort."

The issue of male/female relationships is only one of several important areas in which disagreement, misunderstanding, and alienation exist between Black and White women. Other perspectives about the movement are seen in the comments of other respondents. Lillian, Janet, and Florence reflect a panoramic but idealistic view of the movement while at the same time distancing themselves from it. That is not to say that they do not involve themselves in issues that pertain directly to the women's movement, but there is a lack of direct identification. These women take part in women's conferences and workshops and they participate in demonstrations protesting rape and supporting abortion rights or advocating child-care centers, but their basic opinion of the movement represents a dubious distinction. Janet sees the movement as a general awakening and sensitivity to the issues of women's equality, but she questions it for not being a sustained, organized, mass-based program directed toward gender equality and views it as consisting of many groups, factions, ideological persuasions. This view is in line with Lillian's description of the movement as "a network of formal organizations as well as an informal network of like-minded women deliberately/consciously working on behalf of women's economic, political, social psychological freedoms, as defined by the communities they most closely identify with (racial, ethnic, religious, political, feminists, lesbians, etc.)."

Hulda represents a Black woman who has joined a formal organization of those associated with the women's movement. She sees the organization as a vehicle for attaining self-improvement (self-identity) as well as a means for bringing about changes in the laws to help eliminate racism and sexism.

Black women's attitudes toward themselves have changed considerably within the past five years. The majority still do not identify with *the* women's movement, but ask if they are in favor of women's rights and you will receive an overwhelming number of "damn right" responses.

Since the day-to-day problems of survival are the immediate concerns of Black people, most of Black women's involvement in political organizations has emerged out of crises or issue-oriented conflicts. Those Black women who are affiliated with groups whose central concerns are abortion rights, sterilization abuse, genocide, health care, day care, or welfare and prison reforms can be recognized as a part of the overall movement. However, Black women in these types of organizations are among those who disclaim involvement in the women's movement and vehemently object to being called feminists. When asked, "Do you consider yourself a feminist?" Black women responded as follows:

1) No, because I don't get involved in political issues.
2) I consider it at times. It is not, however, a term that readily springs to my lips when asked to identify myself, unless I am in the company of people talking specifically, usually narrowly, of the women's movement, which is rare. It is not a term readily used by the community of women in whose presence I generally am—"good sister," "productive sister," "hip sister," "righteous sister," have more currency.
3) Yes and No. I want to be a "person" regardless of age, sex, or race —Yes. I am trying too hard to keep my own family intact to be radical—No.
4) Well, I wouldn't march with them but I would vote for ERA.
5) No, in the same way I don't consider myself a nationalist. I strive to be a socialist in the acceptance of a given analysis *and* in my everyday practice. So, rather than describing myself as a socialist, nationalist, feminist—I will put my energies into being a socialist.
6) No. I have dedicated my life to struggles with Third World people's problems, inclusive of women. However, my major thrust of emotional support goes toward the Black movement, both male and female.
7) I consider myself a low-profile, feminist-inspired Black woman. I cannot lock myself into a category of "feminist" because I've not seen a definition which is wide enough for all the qualifications I have attached to "feminist." I'm sure this doesn't satisfy you, but that's tough.
8) No way! Those women don't know what they want and I ain't marching for "nothing."

We have seen that many concerns of Black women coincide with the concerns of various issue-oriented groups and organizations which make up the conglomerate called the women's movement in the United States. Black women's concern for improvement in their daily lives serves as a genuine motivation for their involvement with issues of job opportunities, day care, sterilization abuse, abortion rights, and sexual harassment and abuse. But since Black women represent the most oppressed group in the United States as compared to White men, White women, and Black men and have the most to gain from many of the formal demands of the women's movement, their apparent underrepresentation in the movement is a seeming paradox.

A factor in this paradox is that, if "the movement" is defined with strict reference to the current movement that began in the late Sixties or by means of membership in formal organizations, then there are very few Black women involved. If, however, the current movement is defined in its broadest sense as ". . . a recently reactivated sector of the movement for democratic rights," as Lillian said, then Black women are definitely involved. While traditional historians and the media have historically denied Black women recognition of their roles in history—a denial that continues today—numerous female freedom fighters were involved as central figures in the struggle, and Black women as a whole have always played an active role. In the fight to end slavery, Harriet Tubman was a key part of the Abolition movement. Sojourner Truth was another warrior in the antislavery struggle as well as an early fighter in the women's suffrage movement. Mary McLeod Bethune was a pioneer in the struggle for education for Blacks. Ida B. Wells was a tireless fighter for antilynching laws and an organizer for women's clubs. Frances Ellen Watkins Harper, the first Black female novelist, was an early reformer and speaker for temperance and women's rights. Assate Shakur was a fearless activist; Rosa Parks's refusal to move to the back of the bus ignited the early 1960s drive for civil rights. This is to name but a few of the thousands of Black women who sustained the struggle against racism from slavery to the present day.

Black women should not allow a movement to be defined by others and then allow themselves to be subsequently judged, criticized, and condemned on the basis of a definition that never considered their reality. Black women should define their role in social movements in terms that are consonant with their own motives and goals. Only then can they be judged fairly. Blacks today are still involved in a fight for freedom and the issue of race is still prominent in their society. In the fight for freedom, it makes little or no difference if one is male or female—if one is Black. Rosa Parks had to sit in the back of the bus because she was Black. Her sex had nothing to do with the denial of her rights nor with her response to the denial.

If Black women are interested in equal rights for themselves and their race, as they are, it is impossible for them not to relate to feminist ideas and demands. It is Black women who are more likely to suffer and die from botched abortions and sterilization abuse. A high percentage of Black women are in the labor force and thus suffer more from lack of child-care centers and unequal pay for the same work. Thousands of Black women *suffer* from brutal family relations and Black women are more often rape victims than White women. These and many other valid reasons exist for Black women to be concerned about women's rights and there is a growing consciousness among Black women focused on these kinds of issues, manifested by their involvement in a number of major women's organizations in the 1970s.

The Coalition of Labor Union Women (CLUW), begun in 1974, was an ambitious attempt to establish a national framework for the struggles of women workers. CLUW had its problems, largely due to its close ties with established union leadership, but it does represent a mass organization of working women. Nearly half of all Black women are in the labor pool and their presence is visible in this organization. At the founding conference of the CLUW in Chicago in March 1974, 20 or 25 percent of the 3,200 women present were Black and several Black women assumed leading positions.

The National Black Feminist Organization, NBFO, was one of the first and more important of the formal feminist organizations that emerged in the Seventies. It was founded in 1972 by approximately thirty Black women from the New York City area. The NBFO opened chapters around the East Coast and in major cities throughout the country. New York City remained the national headquarters and base of the organization and in 1973 was the site of one of the most important events in contemporary Black feminists' organizing—the Eastern Regional Conference on Black Feminism. The purpose of the Black Feminist Organization was to "address the specific needs of the Black female who is forced to live in a society that is both racist and sexist." A feminist was rather ambiguously defined as "one who believes in feminism and works to eliminate the inequality of men and women."[3]

This rather ambiguous definition and the bureaucratic tone of the conference disillusioned a large number of the participants. Referring to the perspective and philosophy operative in NBFO, Michelle Russell, a Black Marxist feminist active in the organization for a short period, reportedly stated that "It was like a White woman's conception of what a Black feminist organization should be." A Black woman lawyer in New York City said of NBFO's failure to perceive and articulate the conflicts in the community, "After a while they might as well have been White girls, all the shit they were talking."

The NBFO failed as a viable Black feminist organization because it could not address or support the women of the Black community in any visible, concrete manner. Despite the conflicts that were to develop and the failure of the organization to become an effective organ for Black women's participation in the movement, the NBFO was one of the most influential organizations of the early 1970s. It introduced large numbers of Black women to the concept of Black feminism and raised many essential questions and problems that Black women are still trying to answer and solve. Margaret Sloan, National Director of the NBFO; Brenda Eichelberger, Chicago regional director; and scores of other women must be recognized for their insight in seeing the need for a feminist perspective among Black women from all economic backgrounds. The NBFO enabled a number of Black feminists to clearly define what they wanted in terms of organizational structures and leadership.

Black women were also quite active in the Campaign for Wages for Housework, an organization whose theory represented an important step in challenging the concept that child care and home maintenance are not considered "real" work in this society because of the false assumption that nothing is produced. However, a study by the Chase Manhattan Bank estimated that an upper-middle-class housewife should earn $257.63 a week for the work she regularly does in her home. Women of lower income should earn substantially more since they have less access to child care and other services and spend more of their own time shopping, sewing, and maintaining their homes in order to stretch each dollar as far as possible. It has been estimated that if women were compensated for housework, it would cost between $500 billion and $650 billion annually—the government's total budget. This unpaid and underpaid labor of all women, especially Black women, sustains the economy.

Women in the Campaign for Wages for Housework demand "more money for the work we do as women, all women." Sister

Davine, a Black woman involved in the campaign, contends: "The only time that we'll have a choice is when we have our own money . . . The more clearly we define what it is we're after and struggle for the money that will give us power to define and discover our own possibilities, the more powerful we will become."

This perspective seems to ignore other crucial dynamics that make up the psychosexual, cultural, societal, and economic dialectic of oppression. While admittedly based on survival, the campaign tends to strive to legitimize capitalistic privileges for women. The power dynamics of capitalism require a much more profound solution than the one the campaign advocates.

However, the fact that large numbers of Black women have joined the Campaign shows that they have begun to understand their exploited position in this society. Given that our society is capitalistic, the Wages for Housework Campaign must be recognized for the concern extended to women, both housewives and domestics, for the injustice and lack of appreciation doled out for their unpaid, and in the domestic's case, minimally paid, housework.

The Campaign argues that housework is free labor. For example, concretized in economic terms, the housework Canadian women perform equals roughly one-third of the Gross National Product. "Unpaid housework is the single largest industry in Canada. An army of five million women work as full-time housewives in the nation's homes for no pay, no benefits, no holidays, and no pensions. Most housewives never retire, they just tire."[4]

The Wages for Housework Campaign, although it has become a very effective and worthwhile organization, must eventually seek to concretely transform the relationships to each other of capital, work, production, consumption, and the distribution and accumulation of income.

It is significant that Black lesbian groups have been forming. The Black community's negative attitude toward the current wave of Black lesbianism is frightening, outrageous, and founded on taboos which are bred out of ignorance. These deeply ingrained attitudes serve to keep the Black community ignorant and divided. They perpetuate male chauvinism, encourage scapegoating, and alienate lesbians from nonlesbian women. Given the strength and magnitude of the homophobia directed against lesbians in Black communities, the emergence of even a relatively few lesbian organizations and individuals must be considered remarkable. Organizations in this vanguard include: the Combahee River Collective, which originated in the Boston area; the Lesbians of Color (LOC), a caucus formed in Los Angeles in 1977 to meet the needs of Asian, Black, Latin, Native, and other lesbians identified as "wimmin" of color; and the Salsa Soul Sisters, based in New York City. This group formed the Jemima Writers Collective to meet the need for creative/artistic expression and to create a supportive atmosphere in which Black women could share their work and begin to eradicate negative self-images.

A Black lesbian writers' conference, sponsored by the Jemima Writers Collective, was a historic first. Among those attending were Audre Lorde, an exceedingly fine poet whose renowned artistry is matched by her political astuteness; Barbara Smith, an energetic, prolific writer and speaker on the political and sexual politics of women; Lorraine Bethel, a literary critic who has produced the finest work yet done on Zora Neale Hurston; Mary Watson, a brilliant pianist and member of the Varied Voices of Women, a predominantly Black group of lesbian musicians.

At the 4th Annual Conference of Afro-American Writers in 1978, sponsored by Howard University's Institute for the Arts and Humanities, both sexual and racial politics were discussed by most of the participants. In his keynote address, Dr. Nathan Hare, a well-known Black sociologist and clinical psychologist, echoed the as-yet-unproven but widely accepted belief among Blacks that the ". . . bourgeois White women's movement was threatening unity between the Black male and female."[5] During a later interview, while explaining his interest in male/female relations, he said, ". . . everywhere I went people were crying the blues. Black women say they have no strong Black men to stand beside them. On top of this, White women don't have enough White men to go around, so they are moving over to deplete the vanishing Black male supply."[6] A highlight of the conference was a speech given by Barbara Smith, a lesbian-feminist advocate. Her remarks, likewise, pertained to sexual and racial politics and the women's movement, but her perspective was an enlightening one. She concluded her speech by appealing to Blacks and Whites in the audience to examine all their thoughts about feminine culture. "I want to encourage in White women, as a first step, a sane accountability to all the women who write and live on this soil. I want most of all for Black women and Black lesbians somehow not to be so alone."[7] The audience raised questions as to how far a lesbian-feminist position could take her. The Black psychiatrist Frances Cress Welsing was said to have best summed up this reservation when she said, ". . . but if we endorse homosexuality, then we have endorsed the death of our people."[8]

Comments such as those of Nathan Hare and Frances Cress Welsing come from Black scholars, but parallel the type of comment sometimes heard in street talk in ghetto communities. The words are different, but they convey the same attitude and contain similar misconceptions.

Street talk: "Women going with women is plain freakish." (This remark reveals homophobia.)

"Having babies is natural for women. If they don't have them who's supposed to?" (This statement is based on the belief that lesbians do not desire or have children. They do both.)

"That's another trick the Man pulled out of his genocide trickbag." (What is implied here is that the White women's movement as a part of the White man's system encourages homosexuality so there will be fewer Black babies.)

"The more Black bulldaggers, the more Black men for the White women." (The implication here is that the White women's movement encourages homosexuality among Black women so there will be more Black men available to the nonlesbians.)

Remarks such as these reflect a lack of analysis of Black male/female relations and a general ignorance about lesbians. Further, they raise some serious questions. Are Black male-female relations so fragile that the much maligned and discredited women's movement can destroy them largely with words? And what is the nature of the unity between Black males and females that is supposedly being threatened? The emphasis should be on analyzing, studying, and improving Black male-female relations rather than on reacting to the opinions of the White women's movement.

As with any minority group, Black lesbians have developed a subculture. The subculture is important to them in terms of survival and nurturance, empowering lesbians by insulating them from the mainstream of society and Afro-American culture. However, isolation and protection from the dominant male culture are not in and of themselves political action—and, unfortunately, by making Black lesbian politics a closed political system, they contribute to dividing Black women. Such tactics isolate lesbians from contact with Black women who have not been exposed to Black feminism or have had only limited contacts and constricted relationships with Black lesbians. It also limits their contact with women who have not chosen but still respect lesbian lifestyles, and are committed to the Black liberation struggle. Black feminist analysis suffers from the limited experiential basis and isolationist tendencies that result.

Society cannot afford to waste the human resources and talents of any group of people by causing them to remain hidden or unexpressed. These talents and resources are necessary and beneficial and should be appreciated, utilized, and respected. No person's talents should be discredited, despised, or rejected, nor should the human dignity of any individual be degraded on the basis of sexual preference. Unfortunately, the homophobic fear and/or dislike of lesbians all too often serves to discredit their contributions.

The Black liberation struggle and the Women's Liberation Movement are two separate entities based on their own distinctive realities. However, an individual cannot be two separate entities. Yet an analysis of the two movements indicates that this is the idealistic role expected of Black women participating in both struggles. Black women face the dilemma that Siamese twins would face if one were to wholeheartedly devote her energy, time, and labor to the women's movement as her top priority, and the other were to devote equal time, energy, and labor to the Black liberation struggle as her top priority. Neither twin could participate fully in both movements. Nor can the Black woman. Her choice lies between two equally unsatisfying alternatives, for to choose one and omit the other is detrimental to her well-being as a Black woman. She cannot afford to ignore either movement.

For the survival of family, kin, and self, the Black woman must necessarily be concerned with and involved in the Black liberation struggle. At the same time, for the sake of her own sanity and a self-expression uninhibited by self-denial and second-class sex/gender behavior, she must be a part of the women's movement. There should be no question about the need to be concerned with both. Pauli Murray summed it up well in her article, "The Liberation of Black Women," in *Voices of the New Feminism*. The Black woman's fate in the United States is inextricably bound with that of the Black male. The history of slavery suggests that Black women and men shared a rough equality of hardship and degradation. With dignity, Black women have shared with Black men a partnership as members of an embattled group excluded from the normal protections of the society and engaged in a struggle for survival during nearly four centuries of a barbarous slave trade, two centuries of chattel slavery, and a century or more of illusive citizenship. Black women cannot and will not end this partnership either during the continued struggle for liberation, or on the utopian grounds of equality where male/female relations would be on egalitarian grounds. As a matter of sheer survival, Black women have no alternative but to insist upon equal opportunities without regard to sex in education, employment, and health. These concerns are equally as important for Black men. The multiple jeopardies that Black women face make it clear that they can neither postpone nor subordinate the fight against sex discrimination to the Black revolution. Since they have crucial stakes in both, they are key figures at the juncture of these two movements.

The major question is how to deal with the two movements at the same time. Black women are once again called upon to play a central role in helping to resolve one of the most pressing problems facing our society.

In the end, it is a question of priorities, and given the nature of racism in this country, it should be obvious that the Black liberation struggle claims first priority. In understanding this position, one of Malcolm X's wisdoms should be helpful. Let's imagine that a White and a Black woman are both struggling to get water because they are dying of thirst. "Let's join forces," says the White woman, "then we will be able to get the water." The Black woman responds with, "Yes, we can both get the water, but you have your foot on my neck!" That foot, of course, represents racism, and the water is of no benefit without a visible or even long-range guarantee of being able to drink it. If the collective struggle was women's right to job equality, both women would have to fight to get the foot of racism off the neck of one in order that both can share the waters of job equality.

The commitment to the Black liberation struggle should not result in alienation from the women's movement. The importance of both movements has been articulated and the similarities in goals have been recognized. What has not been so clearly understood is the need for coalescing around these goals while clarifying the distinct differences that exist for both groups on the same issues. The need for coalition and collaboration is necessary for the ultimate success of both movements. The divide-and-conquer tactic has been employed successfully for centuries by those in power as a means of keeping oppressed people in a state of powerlessness.

Yet when Black and White women coalesce around an issue, it is important for both groups to recognize the crucial differences in the ways in which the oppression each suffers is manifested. For example, both groups are undeniably concerned about abortion rights, yet Black women have even more at stake, since it is they who suffer more from illegal and abusive abortion. Additionally, death and injury from abortion is only one of many aspects of the inadequate and incompetent health care that Black women and their families receive. It must be realized that the death rate for minority preschool children is approximately 30 percent to 50 percent higher than for White children. In 1975, for children under one year, the mortality rate was 18 per thousand for White children, whereas for Black children it was 27 per thousand. The death rate among Black women from hypertension is 17 times that of White women. Thousands of Blacks die in emergency rooms (clinics) and thousands more from neglect while in hospitals. Consider the case of the Black youth in the South who received a serious cut on his hand while working. He went to a doctor and had his hand stitched. In her haste to get the child to the doctor, the mother had neglected to take any money. When the doctor heard there was no money, he pulled the stitches out of the boy's hand! The only reprimand the doctor received was a fine, which equaled the cost of replacing the stitches. Given these realities of health care seen by Black people, White women must understand why Black women do not devote their full energies to the abortion issue. The emphasis has to be on total health care.

Another important area of differences is the history of experiences. Black women must recognize that in the same manner that they have developed a perspective on the liberation movement based on their past and present experiences, so too have White women developed their perspective. It is incumbent upon both Black and White women to become familiar with each other's history and the ways in which their sexual oppression has been felt and has influenced their present concerns and priorities. It is incumbent upon White women to understand that this is both a sexist and a racist society and that, as social beings, they too participate in inhumane social conditions. White women's position in United States society as the benefactors of racism has allowed them to ignore their Whiteness. Some of them tend to accept the mystical belief that the category "women" is the most natural and basic of all human groupings and can therefore transcend race division. It is further argued that this common root should lead directly to Black/White coalition. This type of thinking is shallow and myopic, in that it fails to realize that being women is only part of their identity and that they are also White. These women must begin to understand the nature of their own oppression within the context of the oppression of Blacks. Black women must use the shortcomings of the women's movement as part of the process of analysis which will lead to overcoming those shortcomings. The possibilities of a Black/White alliance can only be found within such an understanding.

Who Said
It Was Simple

There are so many roots to the tree of anger
that sometimes the branches shatter
before they fall

Sitting in Nedicks
the women rally before they march
discussing the problematic girls
they hire to make them free
An almost white counterman passes
a waiting brother to serve them first
and the ladies neither notice nor reject
the slighter pleasures of their slavery.
But I who am bound by my mirror
as well as my bed
see causes in color
as well as sex

and sit here wondering
which me will survive
all these liberations.

—Audre Lorde[9]

*   *   *

I have drawn on Carroll Oliver's research on lesbian women's and Black women's feminist organizations in writing this chapter.

Patricia Armstrong's unpublished paper, "Racism in Feminism: Division Among 'The Oppressed'" was helpful in suggesting perspectives on this issue.

NOTES

1. "Surface labeling" refers to the careless use of terms, regardless of whether the lack of care is deliberate or unthinking. For example, the term "women's libber" has been applied to an enormously wide spectrum of women. These range from a woman who is totally "apolitical" and who is sexually and racially biased, but happens not to wear a bra (or is flashily successful in the White male professional world), to a serious, progressive-minded woman who is presenting a well-documented thesis on sexual politics and who engages in political struggles to change the social conditions of women's lives.

Another type of carelessness is the assumption that all White women have the same history. Their individual experiences, including those of class or race privilege, must be taken into account in analyzing their current behavior.

2. William Loren Katz, *Eyewitness: The Negro in American History*. New York: Pitman Publishing Corp., 1967, p. 186.

3. An interview with Ginny Apuzzo and Betty Powell, "Confrontation: Black and White," in *Quest: A Feminist Quarterly*. Special issue on Race, Class and Culture, Vol. III, No. 4, Spring 1977, p. 34.

4. Judith Ramirez, "Immigrant Domestics: Modern-Day Slaves," in *Wages for Housework Campaign Bulletin*, Vol. 4, No. 2, Winter 1979, Toronto, Canada, p. 1.

5. Hollie I. West, "Sexual Politics and the Afro-American Writer," the Washington *Post*, May 8, 1978.

6. Ibid.

7. Barbara Smith, "Towards a Black Feminist Criticism," in *In the Memory and Spirit of Frances, Zora and Lorraine: Essays and Interviews on Black Women and Writing*, ed. Juliette Bowles. Washington, D.C., Institute for the Arts and Humanities, Howard University, 1979, p. 40.

8. Frances Welsing, "Black Women Writers and Feminism," from a question-and-answer session in *In the Memory and Spirit of Frances, Zora and Lorraine: Essays and Interviews on Black Women and Writing*, p. 53.

9. Audre Lorde, "Who Said It Was Simple," in *From a Land Where Other People Live*. Detroit: Broadside Press, p. 39.

II

Sexual Division of Power: Motivations of the Women's Liberation Movement

Generalizations and stereotyping of the Women's Liberation Movement among Black women (aided by the media and by the ways Black men and White men have projected the movement) are prevalent. It is crucial to clarify certain questions about White feminists' incentive to participate in a women's movement, if we are to prevent antagonisms, misunderstandings, and dismissals from becoming further rigidified.

What dimensions of struggle and oppression that lie behind the contemporary women's movement need to be understood? What motivated White women to form the movement? Why have White women had to struggle against White men and what was and is at stake in that struggle? What realities of their lives did they have to question? What were the issues and experiences which necessitated that they fight *as women*? What do they have to confront in their liberation movement?

The clichés which cling to the Women's Liberation Movement —clichés portraying privileged women acting on a whim, hysterically raising "side" issues of little import to most people, indiscriminately seeking to activate hostility toward men—need to be directly challenged. They blind us to the daily realities that have caused women throughout U.S. history to confront, in a myriad of ways, the oppres-

sion of women, the domination of women by men, and the forms
that male privilege assumes.

A cursory overview of U.S. life reveals a society that has systematically institutionalized male power in its legal, economic, political,
educational, and cultural structures. This has been true since earliest
colonial history, when various immigrant groups imported value systems, beliefs, and attitudes from several parts of Europe. The imported assumptions of class privilege and racial superiority were
institutionalized as the U.S. society and economic system developed.
The assumption of male dominance, with concomitant female powerlessness and social devaluation, is intrinsic to the historical development of this country. Cultural and ideological norms were constructed and retained in all areas of social and productive life as
the gendered polarities were institutionalized—from laws and norms
of marriage, to the conditions of pay (or bondage) for female domestics, factory workers, and nurses; from the social existence of
mothers and daughters, to prevailing conceptualizations of education
and the family.

If, for a moment, we were to indulge in an alluring yet illusory
fantasy that racist mechanisms and attitudes could be eliminated by
a struggle focusing *only* on racial oppression, we would see that a
complexity of sexist inequalities, hierarchies, and forms of exploitation would remain. This sexism involves the use of gender to de-
value, control, and limit women's abilities, while it enhances male
privilege and power. Sexism has been and is a constant factor in the
lives of White women, determining their status throughout personal
and public spheres.

The realization of what this has meant and continues to mean to
White women in different classes is not easy for Black men and
women to recognize. The advantages of "skin privilege," which White
women profit from in terms of their Whiteness, can blur the complexities of exploitation and oppression sustained within the "White"
camp. This lack of understanding is nurtured by the fact that there
are no easy parallels to make between the historical experiences of the
Black and White communities. The relationships of Black men and
women have developed and been sustained in a context of survival
and struggle. They have been allied against White domination and
the savage brutality it has entailed. The history and culture of Black
men and women have therefore evolved in large part in opposition to
the dominant culture and its codes and laws. The struggle for sur-

vival and for the most elemental human rights has meant a collaborative opposition to and disruption of the structures "White" culture valued. The different conditions, tactics, and collaboration experienced within Black history created forms of support, collusion, mutual respect, and reliance between men and women in the Black community. Against all the violence, separation, and dehumanizing conditions imposed by White controllers, Black women have been and are involved in a history and a present of shared resistance with the men of their community.

While millions of White women from the various White ethnic groups have shared the consequences of exploitation with the men in their communities, their immediate experience was not as victims of the extreme and brutal forms of racism that the conditions of slavery produced and continued to sustain even beyond abolition. Although many White women were directly exploited economically, their lives were still experienced within the cultural forms that dominant White society legitimated. This White reality affected their daily experiences at work and at home in complex ways. Yet, their lives were and still are dominated and shaped by particular conditions of discrimination, inequality, injustice, and oppression based specifically on their gender.

Whatever local power women may have experienced in organizing families and homes, at the individual, legal, economic, and political levels women were assumed to be dependent creatures, relying on male authority, decisions, protection, and support. Women's paid work was always seen as secondary to the central role of men in providing for family financial needs. Women who were forced to work outside the home, usually at menial and ill-paid work, also had to fulfill specific "woman" roles inside the home. Men, however, did not equally participate in what were seen as the "naturally feminine" tasks of domestic labor and the nurturant processes of child care. These tasks were defined and "taken for granted" in terms of their being done by women. Even women with class privilege suffered discrimination and exclusion from training, employment, education, or political responsibility. Sexist prejudice has proliferated in all areas of all White women's lives—though to differing degrees and in various ways relating particularly to their class positions in U.S. capitalism.

The emergence of the Women's Liberation Movement in the 1960s led to a substantial and expanding scholarly investigation of women's experience throughout U.S. history, which focused on the oppression and struggle involved. Under the rhetoric of democracy and equality—which rings with familiar hollowness on Black folks' ears—White women have been oppressed and exploited *as women*. They have been affected in specific ways by that oppression and they must wage various struggles to confront the complex means by which that oppression operates. For oppression—as Black men and women know only too well—is sustained not only in easily identifiable ways, but also by attitudes, prejudices, and psychological mechanisms which affect the oppressed as well as the oppressor.

In White culture, power is still systematically controlled by White men. Even with the changes of the last twenty years, women are still perceived as inferior in their economic capacities, intellectual abilities, and political acumen. The struggles of White women are inscribed in, and emerge from, a history in which women have been degraded and humiliated by the persistent celebration of male control and dominance. Women have had to fight for every human right they have been able to wrest from the Constitution and legal system of this country. That fight continues at many levels. For example, while the Equal Rights Amendment (which deals with sexual equality and formally affects the status and rights of *all* women in the United States), was first proposed in 1929, it still faces an uphill battle fifty years later. But the struggle for liberation faced by White women is not just at that formal level. It is a fight against assumptions about the "natural" roles of men and women, resulting in attitudes of contempt and patronizing superiority in men and feelings of humiliation, powerlessness, and paralysis in women. These assumptions and attitudes affect daily reality, from the workplace to the most personal of relationships, from media to the law. They result in a conditioning of the oppressed that disables and undermines self-image and silences and disempowers political response. How interesting that the educated, "privileged" women who founded NOW should feel compelled to assert:

We are . . . opposed to all policies and practices—in church, state, college, factory, or office—which, in the guise of protectiveness, not only deny opportunities but also foster in women self-denigration, dependence, and evasion of responsibility, undermine their confidence in their own abilities and foster contempt for women.[1]

And how central an imperative behind the White Women's Liberation Movement were these ideas spoken from the radical sector of the movement in 1970:

We have to try to imagine what we could have been if we had not been taught from birth that we are stupid, unable to analyze anything, "intuitive," "passive," physically weak, hysterical, overemotional, dependent by nature, incapable of defending against attack, fit only to be the housekeeper, sex object and emotional service center for some men or men and children.[2]

Many of these attributes have similarities with the reductive, racist attributes with which Blacks have been labeled in American society. The sexual politics which inform these categorizations are intrinsic at all levels of the lives of White women. While the privilege of Whiteness anesthetized the majority of White women from their awareness of the implications of racist oppression, the "privilege" of female Whiteness disabled them in other key ways. The struggle for women's liberation becomes for them a struggle into activity and consciousness itself. It is a political fight to be engaged in at many levels simultaneously, a fact that makes the Women's Liberation Movement so diffuse, contradictory, diverse, and—potentially—so revolutionary. The movement is about people who have been discriminated against, devalued, and excluded from coming into consciousness of their oppression and challenging the forms that oppression takes. That process ultimately exposes many other dimensions of inequality, privilege, profit, and exploitation that have been intricately woven into the social and economic fabric of United States society.

A wide range of material and information is now available concerning the background, origins, and various strategies of the current Women's Liberation Movement. However, in light of the continuing myths and misleading assumptions, it is important to summarize briefly some of the key features and concerns of the women's movement, the contradictions that have motivated it, and the diversity of questions it addresses.

We come into women's liberation out of our specific predicament as women.[3]

World War II dramatically affected the nature of work women in the United States did, the extent of married women's employment, the provision of child care for working mothers, and the negotiation for pay in the diverse areas of employment where women undertook jobs and responsibilities formerly considered "men's work." After the war, government, business, and unions tried to bring things "back to normal." A massive media onslaught in the 1950s pushed images of the mother-housewife as a loving, demure, consumer-woman, fulfilling her femininity through domestic roles. However, the realities facing most women conflicted dramatically with the images held up to women as role models. Many women had a stronger sense than ever of their capacity to earn, their abilities in various areas of work, and their economic responsibility in the home. Since one income was insufficient to provide for the majority of families, women *had* to work. The full-time mother-housewife image related to a minority.

By the mid-1970s, 40 percent of the United States labor force was female. More than 45 percent of the women of working age worked outside the home; of these, 65 percent were married and two-thirds had children under 18 years of age.[4] Yet these "official" statistics do not register the wide range of part-time or full-time menial, isolated jobs women have held and hold. Since World War II, women have joined the work force at five times the rate of men.

In particular, more married women are entering the labor force than ever before. Yet women have remained primarily responsible for domestic labor and child-care responsibilities while men have only minimally increased their work responsibility in the home. Thus, the lives of millions of women are under a double work pressure. This reality is vividly at odds with the images of women projected in the media as charming and radiant girl friends, wives, and mothers maintaining spotless, idyllic homes and sensitive to the needs of men and children. These images only aggravate the discrepancy between the realities of daily life, which involve both domestic work and outside employment, and the escalating ideals of "true" femininity, wifedom, and motherhood.

Simultaneously, developments in technology, drugs, and health education have enabled more women to control their reproduction. This, along with economic problems which discourage large families, has meant for many women that fewer years of their lives are taken up with family responsibilities. So, more women are available and willing to engage in paid labor and have increasing need to do so for their survival. Also, since the early 1960s, more and more women have opted not to structure their lives in the conventional marriage/family situation.[5] There has been a marked increase of women of marriageable age not marrying; also, the number of families headed by women has increased as the divorce rate rose. Yet, despite the higher percentage of women who have full or shared economic responsibilities in supporting themselves and their families, and in spite of the passing of the 1963 Equal Pay Act, women's earnings have dropped in relation to men's over the last twenty-five years.[6]

At the same time, access to educational development and training has greatly opened up to women over the last thirty years or so. The greatest proportion of women to take advantage of this, given the racist nature of society, was White women. But the "opportunities" and jobs supposedly available to them following education are undercut by the sex discrimination which pervades the job market. To be male counts and earns more than any "objectively" rated skills or abilities. Women of all classes experience this reality, though educated women encounter the contradiction with particular severity, since their expectations for employment are higher.

These very general observations evoke the complex contradictions in the material conditions of White women's lives, which over the last decades have become more evident in terms of the *sexual* oppression and discrimination reflected in them. When Betty Friedan wrote *The Feminine Mystique* in 1963, she said that gradually, without seeing it clearly for a while, she came to realize that something was wrong with the way American women were trying to live their lives. She created the term "the feminine mystique" to describe the strange discrepancy between the reality of their lives as women and the image to which they tried to conform. And these contradictions are among those which millions of working mothers, union women, white-collar women, female students, and housewives have all experienced to a greater or lesser extent. As the women's movement erupted and raised questions that addressed real problems in women's lives, it touched the lives of many women not "in" the movement as such. The images of movement women as bored housewives or professional women playing men's roles only scratch the surface of the unrest experienced by White women in different communities. By themselves, those two groups could never have unclenched the movement and the myriad demands and confrontations forced into the open during the first ten years of it.

The women's movement is not a monolithic, homogeneous or centralized organization representing one set of attitudes or one set of struggles. It includes a wide range of groups operating in different contexts, with differing priorities and political visions. The movement is constantly changing, expanding the scope of its struggles and producing new groups with new priorities as different women become involved and expand its sometimes narrow initial demands. It also changes in relation to the changing political contexts and urgencies that the development of U.S. capitalism and imperialism throws in its path. The movement itself represents a multiplicity of confrontational activities and organizational strategies which address different aspects of women's oppression and stress different dimensions of male domination. Because the movement as a whole challenges the unjust distribution of power, rights, and privileges, as well as forms of oppression and exploitation, it is constantly having to deal with dimensions of all of these which cannot be explained by sexual oppression alone.

For example, different sectors of the women's movement have engaged in the fight for abortion rights since the early 1960s. While initially focusing merely on a woman's legal right to decide whether or not to have a baby, thus challenging the efforts of state, church, and male professions to maintain control over the decision, the issue was to explode in many directions. Third World women confronted the privileged bias of isolating abortion from other forms of control imposed on women's reproductive rights and demanded that the fight against sterilization abuse be as integral to the struggle as the right to abortion itself. This, in turn, raised the issue of population control and the funding of programs in Third World countries by the Western capitalist countries, raising questions of imperialist political control and economic exploitation. Closer to home, it meant looking at the barbarous practices of the U.S. health system for millions of women with no access to health insurance, raising questions about whose interests were served by a health care system run for the profit of big business, the medical profession, and drug companies. At the same time, the movement gave birth to many women's health collectives and clinics and published information on women's health which had never before been widely available, and also generated wide debate over women's control of their bodies within "normative" heterosexual practices.

Another example of the broader dimensions of political issues raised via women's concerns is to be seen in the formal women's commissions and advisory boards which were created at local, state, and national levels. They were accepted by the establishment as long as they passively pointed to specific women's problems on a formal or legal level. However, Bella Abzug was fired from the National Advisory Committee for Women (NACW) when the members opted to deal with broad economic issues and their impact on women, and Governor King of Massachusetts peremptorily dismissed the forty women comprising the state's Commission on the Status of Women when they were determined to confront him on his economic policies concerning welfare, abortion, day care, and displaced homemakers. These developments demonstrate that even an eclectic grouping of educated women operating as a state or federal "women's" advisory body is quickly drawn to connecting specific women's issues to the larger political and economic organization of U.S. society. The threat posed to capitalist organization of profit and its necessary class hierarchies, by women charged with "bettering women's conditions," came into focus.

Because people in capitalist society are organized into separate and competing groups and classes, no one segment of the women's movement represents all the interests and concerns of all women. Even among White women, different groups confront different social and economic experiences and encounter oppression and injustice in different ways. All of these oppressions need to be recognized as valid oppressions to be struggled against. Just as racism manifests itself in a multiplicity of ways, so sexism, too, has its range of manifestations—from brutal physical and economic manifestations to subtle psychological mechanisms. The confrontation with male dominance, sexual exploitation, and injustice takes many forms in the women's movement, according to the economic and cultural realities and the political visions of different groups of women.

The term "women's movement" thus refers to a myriad of groups which are not connected by formal definitions, structures, or organizational ties. Rather, the connection results from the refusal, from different perspectives, to accept discrimination by sex, to be bound by male definitions for women and men, or to allow women—because they are women—to be degraded and exploited economically, culturally, legally, educationally, politically, or psychologically by individual men or by male-controlled institutions. In the face of male domination and control and the assumptions that go with them, the movement emphasizes the need for women to consciously resist the roles and definitions that male-dominated society imposes and to struggle to understand the processes that reproduce them. The movement provides the political space in which women organize themselves and others to fight for equality, to confront oppression and to demand reorganization of society in order to meet the needs of women in more democratic and caring ways.

What emerged in the Sixties was a surge of radical movements which applied new emphasis and approaches to issues with long histories in the United States. It is within the wider context of this phenomenon that the Women's Liberation Movement erupted and crystallized. With conditions and varying contradictions faced by women in all walks of U.S. society, the radicalizing energy of the Sixties and the New Left provided the political ground on which a wave of mostly younger women became politically conscious and active feminists. While the more traditional feminist organizations continued their momentum in the older feminist traditions, the impetus of the Women's Liberation Movement came from the catalyst of the other movements that exploded during the Sixties.

The contradictions and confrontations, violence, and repression faced by thousands of activist women and men in the civil rights movement, the Black liberation movement, the White student movement, and the anti-Vietnam War movement created critical consciousness and political awareness. From the different perspectives of these struggles, thousands and thousands of young people were led to analyze and question the basic assumptions and logic of U.S. society: "The value of law and order, the truth of 'American democracy,' the legitimacy of private business, the rightness of 'normal' sex roles and sexual relations—all came up for questioning."[7] It was a time of rejecting the structure and boundaries of U.S. society. From different points and levels of struggle, the movements indicated various consequences of U.S. capitalism.

Published accounts by activists of that time highlight the questions that emerged from these movements. Bernice Reagan, Black activist and singer, notes that: "The Civil Rights Movement exposed the basic structure of the country which, as it's set up, cannot sustain itself without oppressing someone."[8] From analyses and realizations that developed out of endless confrontations and organizing, the civil rights movement "created new room for politics in the U.S., it inspired other movements by example, and it served as a training ground for many of the future activists in other movements . . . and not just Black power and Black revolutionary movements, but every progressive struggle that has occurred in this country since that time."[9] Later, the Black Panthers, in their education and community projects, stressed that the enemy was not "Whites in general" but the capitalist system and demanded Black self-determination, decent living conditions, adequate employment, and an end to exploitation and state violence.

Meanwhile, the White student movement blossomed nationwide on college campuses over issues such as education reform, disarmament, community organizing, and resistance to the Vietnam War. This movement developed critical indictment of U.S. institutions and values, linking the profit-mongering and oppressive U.S. foreign policy in Vietnam, Cuba, and later Chile with oppression and exploitation in the United States itself. As Dick Cluster, a White male activist during the Sixties, emphasizes, the White student movement brought about a realization for many students that "both the values and the policies we opposed had their roots in an economic and political system whose motivating force was private profit . . . Where corporations had a right to produce napalm, but poor people had no right to decent housing . . . Through our involvement in specific struggles, then, we came to understand that what we were opposed to was a system."[10] The antiwar movement expressed vehement opposition to the U.S. intervention in Vietnam and mobilized millions of people from all sectors of U.S. society in vast demonstrations and widespread acts of resistance.

The movements dramatically altered the attitudes of a significant number of people toward U.S. society and its government, corporations, and other institutions. The women who were to activate the Women's Liberation Movement came from these radicalizing struggles.[11]

When people are unhappy, no one can tell them their pain is unimportant.[12]

When the fog before our eyes began to lift, the movement for women's liberation came of age.[13]

Women who had been actively involved in these struggles experienced continuous difficulty with the men with whom they worked. They were involved in struggles for equality, human rights, justice, and freedom, but in different organizations; and in personal relationships the women found themselves slighted, harassed, patronized, and treated as inferior helpers or sex objects. There was a legendary antiwar rally at which one of the women activists got up to speak and was met with cries of "Take her off and fuck her." This typified the atmosphere of ridicule, contempt, and sexual reductionism which pervaded the radical movements. In many ways, the sexist degradation that women became acutely conscious of in their workplaces, campuses, radical organizations, and personal relationships with men was too much to bear. Affected by the Black movement's affirmation of dignity and power against the pervading reality of racist degradation, women began to assert themselves by demanding equal treatment, collaboration, and recognition. Political White women had a lot with which to contend and, as their antagonism grew, women's groups sprang up, both inside and outside the male-dominated radical groups. The women criticized the way men categorized politics, the way men behaved, and the way they themselves were conditioned to see reality through men's eyes. As the anger mounted, so too did the refusal among many radical women to accept "their own exploitation in the name of some larger justice."[14] The tone and momentum of the clashes, effectively expressed by White author and poet Marge Piercy with these words in 1969, was as follows:

The movement is supposed to be for human liberation: how come the condition of women inside it is no better than outside . . . It is true some oppression kills quickly and smashes the body, and some only destroys the pride and the ability to think and create. But I know no man can tell any woman how to measure her oppression and what methods are not politic in trying to get up off her knees . . . We are told that our sense of oppression is not legitimate . . . Nowhere on earth are women free now, although in some places things are marginally better. What we want we will have to invent ourselves. We must have the strength of our anger to know what we know.[15]

The attitudes and perspectives of the White male Left were objectionable because, as Robin Morgan, White political activist, speaker, and author, pointed out, they resulted in organizations with hierarchical power distribution—with men at the top. These men refused to recognize the problems of women's lives, saw women's issues as secondary to their own priorities, and used women sexually. Morgan wrote:

We have met the enemy and he's our friend. And dangerous . . . Women's Liberation is to cost men a lot of privilege.[16]

There was a call for an autonomous Women's Liberation Movement in which women could define and analyze the means and causes of sexual oppression and develop strategies for combating and transforming that oppression. In diverse and divergent ways, women formed the movement, radiating out from the radical movements of the Sixties and adapting the consciousness developed by those movements into new forms of political theory and action. In 1970 Robin Morgan described the Women's Liberation Movement in these terms:

You *are* women's liberation. This is not a movement one "joins." There are no rigid structures or membership cards. The women's liberation movement exists where three or four friends or neighbors decide to meet regularly and talk about their personal lives. It also exists in the cells of women's jails, on welfare lines, in the supermarket, factory, convent, farm, maternity ward, street corner, old ladies' home, kitchen, steno pool, the bed. It exists in your mind and in the political and personal insights that you can contribute to change and shape and help its growth.[17]

The Women's Liberation Movement stressed noncentralized, nonhierarchical organization, collective and experimental processes, and diversity of perspectives. The movement was to be women in action —at work, in their homes, among themselves—questioning, challenging, and changing, refusing to let men dictate the terms of their lives and the lives of other women, from the most publicly political to the most personally political arenas.

There were two main trends in the Women's Liberation Movement which were to diversify and snowball in multiple directions over the first twelve years. On the one hand, the radical feminist tendency vehemently identified men as the agents of oppression and argued that "all other forms of exploitation and oppression (racism, capitalism, imperialism, etc.) are all extensions of male supremacy."[18] The radical feminist onslaught created a fertile space in which many women could articulate the hostility and resentment they experienced toward men on personal, social, political, and economic levels. It created a space for women apart from men and in conflict with men. It stressed the need for cultural and structural alternatives to be developed by and for women apart from White male domination. Radical feminism has been inspirational in various ways to most White feminists, even those who would not define themselves as politically in agreement with the premises on which radical feminism is based.

On the other hand, the socialist-feminist tendency was to refuse to prioritize sexual oppression as the "origin" of other oppressions. It moved more cautiously into analyzing the complex ways capitalism interacts with male dominance and stressed a "commitment to a basic change that included all oppressed groups, not just women."[19] It argued that "in contemporary America the reality is that sexism cannot be pulled out from the nature of capitalist hierarchy."[20] Socialist-feminism was to become concerned not with indicting "men" as a universal category of enemies, but with trying to understand the complex ways in which, in different societies and cultures (specifically in capitalist and socialist contexts), with different historical traditions, the sexual divisions of power were rationalized into patriarchal institutional forms and shaped the terms of real, everyday social relations. Its aim is to elaborate ways of understanding the connective processes that produce *men and women* into gendered beings embodying different powers and possibilities, in order to make the struggle to transform the social construction of gender integral to radical struggle to end all forms of oppression.

These trends have resulted in development and proliferation of a wide variety of priorities, questions, and issues. Whatever the trends, the Women's Liberation Movement represented a "movement by, for, and of women, one that would analyze women's condition in the context of a broader struggle for revolutionary change in the society."[21] The demand was not merely for equal rights for women, but for a radical transformation of U.S. society into one based on different terms, structures, processes, and values.

Before examining the strategies, issues, and demands of the Women's Liberation Movement, it is important to consider other dimensions of feminist and women's struggles within the wider women's movement. These have a dialectical relationship to the motivating energies that led to the emergence of the Women's Liberation Movement. The Women's Liberation Movement was concerned with complete restructuring of power, institutions, personal relationships, and all the socially constructed gender divisions these involved. The White women involved had been politicized by their involvement in struggles over race, imperialism, and capitalist institutions. The more traditional channels of feminism, which date far back into United States history, had very different roots.

This older tradition of feminism struggled for formal legal, economic, and "citizenship" rights for women, stressing recognition of women as "equal" in terms of federal and state law. Women in this tradition have fought for the vote, equal pay, the Equal Rights Amendment (E.R.A.), and endless changes in laws and institutions which denied women equal rights and basic "freedoms." These struggles have been, and still are, led by relatively privileged and educated White women. These women did not work to create a broad grass-roots movement, but instead tended to organize in small groups that dealt with issues at the state and federal (rather than community) levels. This tradition of feminism was—and still is—concerned that certain changes be won and implemented within the framework of the U.S. "democratic," capitalistic state. Women in this tradition fought for rights and privileges for *women* without questioning the rights and privileges they already enjoyed from the class and race oppression endemic to the capitalistic system. It is often only the more educated, professional women who are able to take advantage of the reforms for which this tradition has fought. Yet the political reality feminism faces does demand that single-issue struggles be fought at all levels of reform. Faced with the inequalities that capitalism depends on sustaining, many feminists of the Women's Liberation Movement have channeled their energies—within traditional organizations or through their own parallel groups—to fight for these same rights and changes.

Although the traditional feminist organizations reinforce the cliché that the Women's Liberation Movement is bourgeois and middle class, their struggles have been significant in several ways. The questions they pose and the problems they address concern the institutional and legal framework that denies certain rights to all women and reinforces sexual discrimination in endless situations. They fight to remove obstacles in the state structure that realistically and symbolically embody women's exclusion and oppression. The battles won "in principle" by these feminist groups provide other women in the movement with important support and encouragement. The crucial point is that although these feminist groups represent White, middle-class perspectives and priorities, they are fighting in principle for *all women* and not just for themselves. They are the only groups that have engaged in and won concrete struggles that potentially open up new terrain for *all* women—and they must be given due credit. None of the White male radical or revolutionary organizations have engaged effectively in these struggles over the status and rights of all women, nor have any sectors of the Black movement as such. Black struggles to win the vote, access to education, and to end legally enforced segregation within American capitalism were crucial in real and symbolic terms for all Black people and in turn strengthened other more revolutionary struggles. Attainment of formal rights reinforces political struggles at grass-roots levels and highlights more fundamental contradictions and less overt forms of exploitation and injustice that people face.

The more traditional feminist organizations include a variety of groups.[22] For example, the Women's Equity Action League, formed in 1968, was primarily involved in fighting sex discrimination in education through the courts. It was also concerned with divorce reform, taxation, credit and banking practices, and the promotion of women in sports. It published a monthly newsletter/bulletin on pending legislation that concerned women and worked to insure implementation of such legislation once it was passed. The Women's Lobby, Inc. was formed as a congressional lobby for women's issues which worked especially to insure passage of the E.R.A. A group that provided legal and financial information and assistance for women fighting sex discrimination and abortion cases was Human Rights for Women, formed in 1968. The Women's Action Alliance, formed in 1971, was an information and resource center that dealt with a range of feminist activities. The National Black Feminist Organization also ranked among the more moderate groups in the women's movement.

The largest and best-known feminist organization is the National Organization for Women (NOW). NOW was formed in 1966 by a small group of professional, middle-class women in order to win equality and justice for women under the law. It did not question the overall economic and social structure of the United States. Rather it was to be an action organization designed "to bring women into full participation in the mainstream of American society now, assuming all the privileges and responsibilities thereof in truly equal partnership with men."[23] Rather than emerging from the radical mass movements of the Sixties, it was structured "from the top" by a group of women whose feminism was rooted in traditional bourgeois perceptions of "human justice," giving priority to sexual equality to the neglect of class inequality and racial oppression. NOW fought and won specific battles over such issues as including the category of "sex" in certain legal rulings guaranteeing nondiscrimination, and the end to segregation of job advertisements on the basis of gender.

In contrast to the radical sector of the Women's Liberation Movement, NOW was organized conventionally with formal structures and with definite hierarchies and notions of membership. As NOW grew, there were several split-offs by conservative and special-issue sections of the organization—and heated internal disagreements occurred over support for issues such as the E.R.A., abortion, and lesbian rights. In 1970, a NOW-organized women's strike to mark the fiftieth anniversary of the Nineteenth Amendment was well publicized by the media and NOW membership boomed. By 1974 there were over 40,000 members in 700 chapters—consisting mainly of educated, clerical, and white-collar White women. A survey that year of members showed that 5 percent were Black, 60 percent had B.A.'s, and 30 percent had advanced degrees.

NOW flourished particularly in suburban areas, where many "housewives" became involved. The aims of the organization reflect the priorities and political perspectives of the kinds of women who joined NOW. Its ideology stresses individualistic approaches to women's oppression, with selectively organized strategies to win rights through formal channels. It can be argued, however, that NOW has been significantly affected in the 1970s by the more radical perspectives of the Women's Liberation Movement, expanding its political discussions and activities to include a much wider range of questions and issues.[24] If the E.R.A. is ratified, it will be due in large part to the concerted efforts of organizations like NOW and other traditional feminist groups. And the E.R.A. "[writes] sexual equality into the constitution," making "literally hundreds of discriminatory state laws invalid." The issues it addresses will be fought out and will be the focus of organizing at many levels by women of all classes: "The record suggests that working-class women will use it energetically if passed."[25] Nevertheless, the emphasis of the E.R.A. remains on rights for women within *established* institutions and social structures.

In the 1960s and 1970s the momentum of struggles related to women's oppression and exploitation flowed from many sectors of women with perspectives far different from those of the more traditional feminist organizations. As the Women's Liberation Movement emerged and expanded into a diverse range of struggles and activities, it impacted on the lives of women of different classes and generated questions that were spotlighted in all kinds of overt struggles not specifically associated with the Women's Liberation

Movement. It is worth emphasizing briefly these dimensions of struggles generated by the Women's Liberation Movement, since the "elite nature of the movement has been exaggerated by the greater publicity commanded by the spokeswomen of the more conservative feminist organizations and projects."[26] This distortion led many Blacks, as well as many White radicals, to dismiss the significance of the struggles which the Women's Liberation Movement has helped activate. What follows are examples of women's struggles which have stressed not only the exploitation by class and race which many women workers have to fight, but also the specific nature of the *sexual* oppression and discrimination they confront at the workplace, in the very nature of their political struggles.[27]

The National Welfare Rights Organization, founded in 1963, has increasingly spread the message during the 1970s that there are more than 3 million women on welfare and that 44 percent of all poor families are headed by women. The United Farm Workers strike, while strengthening the labor movement as a whole, also strengthened the *women* in the Chicano communities that were involved. It posited a "challenge to male chauvinism among the union members themselves," as the women refused to be excluded from the struggle and protectively kept at home in what they called the "middle-class way."[28] The case of job and pay discrimination won by the Equal Employment Opportunities Commission in 1973, against the American Telephone and Telegraph Company, resulted in equalizing back pay and new pay rates for thousands of women workers in the company. Women in unions such as the United Steel Workers have been engaged in actively pressuring for an end to sex discrimination, which the unions themselves have actively perpetuated. Gay workers—such as the Gay Nurses Alliance, formed in 1973—have organized against sex discrimination in some areas of employment. And, significantly, a conference of 3,200 women from 58 different unions founded the Coalition of Labor Union Women (CLUW) in March 1974.

Although the CLUW has since been weakened by the bureaucratic, conservative, and sexist functioning of many of the unions, the coalition succeeded in focusing for women workers the issues raised by the Women's Liberation Movement. Its purpose was for women in various unions to collaborate in the struggles for gaining union involvement by organizing for affirmative action in the workplace, engaging more women in union politics, attacking discriminatory job classifications and wage differentials, and, as the first CLUW statement of purpose claimed, taking ". . . aggressive steps to more effectively address ourselves to the critical needs of 30 million unorganized sisters and to make our unions more responsive to the needs of all women, especially the needs of minority women."[29] The effect that the Women's Liberation Movement had on the development of the CLUW's focus on issues affecting millions of women employed as secretaries, sales clerks, school teachers, factory workers, waitresses, sewing machine operators, nurses, cleaners, etc., cannot be underestimated. "The growing economic crisis, the bankruptcy and male chauvinism of traditional unionism, the expansion of women's employment, especially in the service and clerical sectors of the economy, all contributed to the birth of the CLUW; but its single most critical cause was the Women's Liberation Movement. The ideas that the movement spawned, though diffuse, created the consciousness essential for CLUW's beginning . . ."[30] The Women's Liberation Movement also spurred the formation of women's caucuses within the ranks of many radical and socialist organizations in the United States and emphasized dimensions of women's oppression that had been theoretically and strategically neglected by those organizations.

All of the information summarized in this chapter stresses the context in which the Women's Liberation Movement emerged, its relationship to other political movements, and some of the key questions and activities it generated. Against the myths and clichés which ridicule, dismiss, or categorize the movement for many Black women, it is crucial to briefly establish a sense of the place from which the movement comes, why and how certain questions came to be asked, and what some of the key political influences were in its development. The last part of this section will be concerned with the political questioning, perspectives, and activities that the Women's Liberation Movement uniquely brought to bear on political activism. It is, as mentioned before, a new movement and contains different groups with different emphases and contrasting analyses and priorities. The White women who initiated it emerged from other radical movements in which they did not have the stakes of *racial* unity or solidarity with White men that the Black women had with Black men. The Women's Liberation Movement formed *against* the experience and consequences of White male power and *against* the kind of subjective experience of being women which this power necessitated. Because of the privileges of education experienced by many of the women involved in the Women's Liberation Movement, they were free of the survival struggles that are priorities for minority and working-class women. The White feminists of the Women's Liberation Movement brought their own priorities and limits to their political demands and visions. These were to shift as the movement advanced, and the repercussions of their struggles, confrontations, and demands hit home in the minds of many women who did not see themselves as actually belonging to the movement. During the decade of the 1970s, the Women's Liberation Movement did not remain statically attached to certain ways of defining, criticizing, and organizing around women's oppression. Different segments of the movement dynamically responded to criticisms and developed analyses of women's oppression with new perspectives and emphases.

To deny that you are oppressed is to collaborate with your oppressor.[31]

Many of the questions and realizations concerning sexual politics that were catalysts for the Women's Liberation Movement arose from the process of consciousness-raising (CR). Small groups of women met together and talked about their lives—families, work, relationships, experiences, and feelings. From this exchange of "personal testimony" came the realization that many experiences thought to be "personal problems" were ones that many women recognized and shared. The process became one of trying to understand in political and social terms the ways individual women, and women as a whole, experienced their lives within society. The CR process dismantled the resistance, defenses, and fears that kept many women from thinking about the politics of their daily lives and personal experiences. It shattered certain illusions and myths and necessitated that participants confront politically the mechanisms sustaining forms of oppression, privilege, and social organization. For many White women, CR was an experience of emerging from isolation, silence, and paralysis. The understandings they gained from engaging in criticism and questioning led many to various levels of activism. The CR process involved a collective recognition that sexual oppression is systematic, not a random or chance feature in just *some* women's lives; is evidenced in mechanisms beyond those of formal institutions; and requires strategy, commitment, and collective political struggle if it is to be successfully fought.

The Women's Liberation Movement seeks to address the reasons for and processes of male domination and female subordination at every level of experience, from the most obvious to the most subtle. Although this means struggling against legal and institutional forms of discrimination, such struggles are relevant only in relationship to the understanding, challenging, and restructuring of relationships between women and men in every area of social, productive, and personal life.

We looked at our present lives and realized how we were perpetuating unequal power relationships between ourselves and men.[32]

In the process, hostility and resentment toward men often exploded violently, and indictments of men and male behavior were prolific. Some sections of the movement focused on men as the causal oppressors and withdrew political alliance or personal interaction with men. Others tried to explain the complex economic, ideological, and psychological factors which structure women and men into different roles, invested unequally with power and powerlessness. These sections of the movement worked politically with men to engage them in criticism and activism. There was, however, initial consensus that men were a problem. This emerged from shared experiences of treatment at the hands of men in personal, social, and work situations. Although recognizing, at least superficially, that class and race differentiated men from one another, the Women's Liberation Movement asserted that:

All men enjoy male supremacy and take advantage of it to a greater or lesser degree depending on their position in the masculine hierarchy of power.[33]

More recently, socialist-feminists and others within the women's movement have begun to discuss the complex problems involved in understanding the social construction of gender—the socialization of women into certain "feminine" characteristics and roles, which parallel and complement the social construction of "masculine" identity. The social construction of gender identity, requiring specific psychological forces related to the process of reproduction and the historical organization of the family, as well as economic and institutional factors, is now being examined in its historical and cultural contexts. Also, the relationship of language and culture to patriarchal oppression is encountering a new wave of feminist scrutiny.

The women's movement dramatically questioned the whole area

of sexuality itself (from White women's perspectives, of course—although often ideas were generalized and universalized in very inadequate ways), attacking the myth of the vaginal orgasm, questioning the power and manipulation involved in sexual intercourse with men, and rethinking the actual experience of sexuality within a capitalist culture which obsessively flashes certain images of sexuality at people every way they turn. Women discussed fears and problems they experienced having intercourse with men and their dissatisfactions with heterosexual rituals—from penetration, romantic love, and marriage to the property rights involved in monogamous commitments, the double standards surrounding female and male sexual freedom, prostitution, pornography, rape, and the institution of heterosexuality itself. All these issues, and more, were most often seen as socially produced phenomena (rather than normal and to-be-taken-for-granted practices) which needed political examination. In a society where 1 of every 3 marriages ends in divorce, where wife-beating and family violence are not uncommon, and where the image of the ideal "housewife" is not accessible to most women (and is devastatingly destructive, demoralizing, and neurosis-forming where it *does* exist), the love-marriage-sex pattern did not make sense. Marriage—the public institution organizing sexuality—had to be analyzed historically and economically in order to understand the power relationships traditionally invested in it and to posit alternatives. The economic, ideological, and psychological development of family structures in White dominant culture, with the consequences and causes of the sexual divisions they embody, were to be reexamined and questioned.

The issue of violence against women—particularly the soaring incidence of rape and wife-battering in a society with a thriving pornography industry—and questions about the absence of viable legal protection or social alternatives for abused women surfaced as the movement gathered momentum. The Women's Liberation Movement organized rape crisis centers and battered women's centers to help victims recover from the attack and fight for their rights. Feminists organized "Take Back the Night" demonstrations to publicize and counteract the fear of violence women experience daily on the street. Halfway houses were established for women who were separated, divorced, or widowed and needed help restructuring their lives after years of dependence on men. Women's legal aid centers were set up to provide legal advice and help for women who did not have easy access to male-controlled legal systems to fight cases of sexual discrimination and to alter laws that were oppressive to women. These efforts were based on recognition of the fact that victimization was not the exceptional experience of a few women, but was the inevitable, visible eruption of the violence institutionalized in the way gender is organized in this society.

Nothing connected with sexual division of roles has been allowed to pass unquestioned. There were heated debates over the role and function of the family under capitalism: the aim was to try to understand how the family, and the power roles of men and women in it, have been acted on historically by economic and political forces. Housework and childrearing were lifted out of the invisibility and neglect to which they had been relegated by White, male-dominated perspectives—whether bourgeois or revolutionary. The women's movement saw them as crucial to the social construction of what were conventionally seen to be "natural" and "normal" sex-role activities. At the movement's insistence, the institutional reinforcement of sex roles came under scrutiny. The sexist biases of the education system, children's books, and the media were brought into question with the argument that no roles or behaviors could be proved universally natural and that "women, like men, are 'basically' anything that society makes them."

Women affected by the movement began reexamining the way history was written, noting which parts of society had been deemed worthy of recording or neglecting, and criticizing male biases and selectivity. Women writers and activists were rediscovered and brought out of the silence and obscurity to which patriarchal culture had relegated them. New women writers were encouraged to address the newly alerted feminist constituency and feminist publishers, printers, magazines, newsletters, and journals began to appear in considerable numbers. A reevaluation of the assumptions that male supremacy and sexism had "normalized" has been occurring in medicine, art, music, law, religion, and every aspect of education, as well as in the fields of literature, history, psychology, sociology, anthropology, etc. In all of these areas the contradictions, misrepresentations, and distortions related specifically to the *sexual* axis are being critically examined.

Reexamination and reconstruction have been complemented by a spirit of reconnection and solidarity among women as they met and engaged around political issues. The White community, especially in more "mobile" urban or industrial sectors, is fragmented. Many White women live their lives far from any family network or any known or supportive community. For many of these women, the women's movement meant, for the first time, constructing networks of relationships among women engaged in political questioning or struggles over specific issues—relationships which were not mediated or centrally defined by their relationships to men. It was in this atmosphere of connection, informal friendships, and "sisterhood" that many women came to value (often for the first time, since White culture cultivates antagonism and competition among women) relationships with all kinds of other women.

In spite of the initial resistance, violence, and hostility that the lesbian presence generated in the Women's Liberation Movement, and the continuing ghosts of homophobia, the momentum of gay liberation opened up new spaces, understandings, and means of relating among women. Lesbian sexuality and connections came to be affirmed and celebrated in the movement, though not without strong residual traces of ambiguity and homophobia. The lesbian space in the women's movement has been shaped by many different elements: by strong criticisms of the stakes involved in heterosexual relationships, the power structures within them that undermine women, and the forms of abuse that exist in them; by the movement's assertion of women's right to define themselves rather than be defined by male-controlled images of women; by the caring and collaboration of women politically and socially; by the challenges to every kind of socially reinforced dependence of women on men, from the economic to the sexual; and by the affirmation that women can love women and do not necessarily need men in order to survive emotionally, sexually, or economically.

The lesbian momentum has played a crucial role in illuminating many of the humiliating forms of women's dependence on men and in showing how the patriarchal structuring of gender and of social activity sabotages women's potential personal relationships with men. The lesbian momentum has also generated tremendous cultural creativity among women—gay and nongay—and opened up new ways of thinking about sexual oppression and of imagining alternatives. While the lesbian voice sounds clearly in the women's movement, it is nonetheless false to see the movement as predominantly lesbian. Women are living out all kinds of relationships with men and women; they are questioning and struggling to define all relationships to eliminate violence, inequality, power abuse, possessiveness, and dependence, while stressing the need for both nurturance and autonomy in meaningful personal connections.

A final dimension of the Women's Liberation Movement is the engagement of many women in examining different cultural and historical aspects of women's experiences. From the early generalizations about "all women," feminists are recognizing the need to understand the specific nature and conditions of women's oppression in differing cultures, societies, and economies. The similarities or curious recurrences of certain patterns of male supremacy in cross-cultural views are being questioned, especially from the socialist-feminist perspectives, in relation to the particular historical and economic factors and cultural customs evident in women's lives. From early celebration of universality and sameness, the movement is more and more concerned with the implications of differences among women's experiences and understanding the political factors at work in those differences. From its beginnings, the movement turned to Chicano, Puerto Rican, and Black women to give account of *their* particular experiences of oppression, though the movement as a whole has had difficulty digesting the implications of these and shifting its central perspectives away from the perspectives of its White majority. Inquiry into the lives and histories of women in revolutionary struggles and in socialist societies has also activated discussion and debate about what must be changed and restructured if sexual equality is to become real.

It is important, in conclusion, to recognize the continuing shifts within the women's movement as political understanding of sexual oppression becomes more developed, and as the class and race biases of certain thinking become more and more evident to women in the movement. Thus the "anti-housewife" trend of the late Sixties rapidly moved into a more class-oriented analysis of the "house-wife" phenomenon, the role of domestic labor under capitalism, and the "double load" of paid and unpaid work that the majority of women face. Even more recently, this has shifted into considering the social and psychological conjuncture which rigidifies women's and men's relation to the organization of parenting and domestic work. Similarly, the earlier rhetorical attacks on the "family" (which the media often simplistically present as symbolic of the thinking of "women's libbers") have developed into more tentative and careful questioning of the historical changes in the role of the family in different economic and cultural contexts. The revulsion experienced by many White women in the Women's Liberation Movement toward the isolating, competitive, and antagonistic relations predominant in the White "ideal" nuclear family (separated from kin and any vibrant community), is shifting to an understanding of the complex economic, legal, psychological, and ideological structures that have historically defined the family and the gendered rituals it embodies.

The ongoing shifts and developing positions in the movement concerning the abortion rights struggle provide significant examples of this process. When formulated in the mid-Sixties by traditional feminist groups and later, in the early Seventies, by the radicalized Women's Liberation Movement, the issue of abortion stood alone and was seen in terms of "women's right," "self-determination," and "freedom of choice." Criticisms of these perspectives, as well as problems encountered organizing on the basis of them, profoundly affected the way active feminists now struggle on the issue. One of the main abortion-rights organizations to emerge from the radicalized Women's Liberation Movement was CARASA—the Committee for Abortion Rights and Against Sterilization Abuse. CARASA was formed in 1977 in the face of rightwing backlash against the hard-won progressive abortion legislation and judicial rulings of previous years. CARASA developed a political perspective around *all* issues affecting women's choices in reproduction, not just the "right to abortion." While energy was directed toward legislation, emphasis was placed on the educational role of meetings in hospitals, unions, colleges, and neighborhood organizations. CARASA works with other groups involved in reproductive issues at a local, national, and international level. However, it is critical of methods used by traditional feminist organizations, such as the way they formulate their goals, isolate the abortion issue, and use population control arguments. CARASA's specific goals for all women are: abortion services regardless of income; available, safe birth control; sex education in schools; access to good prenatal, postnatal, and maternal health care; and an end to all sterilization abuse. CARASA's political analysis can be understood from the following extract from the booklet "Women Under Attack."

No government, court, religious group, social services organization or doctor, no parent or husband should have control over a woman's reproductive decisions. No category of women, poor, young, handicapped— should be excluded from reproductive freedom . . . Reproductive freedom depends on equal wages for women, enough to support a family, alone or with others; welfare benefits for an adequate standard of living; decent housing . . . reliable skilled childcare . . . an end to toxic working conditions which cause sterility and birth defects . . . Reproductive freedom is incompatible with forced sterilization . . . incompatible with cutbacks in abortion funding which force poor, minority, and working women into unwanted childbirth, back-alley or self-induced abortions, or unwanted sterilizations . . . REPRODUCTIVE FREEDOM DEMANDS A RADICAL TRANSFORMATION OF SOCIETY AND THE QUALITY OF LIFE.[34]

I am not trying to suggest here that the Women's Liberation Movement is without problems and conflicts, or that it is in every way a progressive and dynamically revolutionary movement. No political movement under capitalism is immune to contradictions in perspectives and strategies that are shaped by the contradictions and ideologies of the larger society. Nor is it immune to having its impetus coopted, absorbed, and institutionalized into actual state structures and ideological forms. Before analyzing more specific questions of the contrasting sexual politics of Black and White women and ultimately men, it was important to recognize the women's movement and the historical importance of the movement as a whole, even with its limits and difficulties. Because of the prevalent myths and stereotypic images of "women's libbers," "spoiled housewives," or simply "men-haters," it was crucial to provide a glimpse into the actual problems the movement has addressed, the new and highly important areas of political struggle it has opened up, the motivations and demands of the women involved, and the diversity of activities and questions it has initiated as it has moved into new political contexts. As one feminist stated: "We learned there is no one key to liberation. We must fight on many fronts at once." The sexual politics of the Women's Liberation Movement has inspired revolutionary analyses and strategies with connections to the struggles of women of different classes and races in a way that no feminist movement has ever before done.

I must emphasize, in conclusion, that here I merely have dipped evocatively into the currents and energies generated by the women's movement. It is important that readers turn to more adequate and detailed accounts of the histories and politics involved in it, sources for which are suggested in the notes for this chapter and in the bibliography.

Notes

1. This passage from the NOW statement of purpose was quoted in Jo Freeman, *The Politics of Women's Liberation*. New York: Longman, 1977, p. 74.

2. Meredith Tax, *Woman and Her Mind: The Story of Daily Life*. Boston: New England Free Press, 1970, p. 3.

3. Sheila Rowbotham, *Woman's Consciousness, Man's World*. Harmondsworth, England: Penguin Books, Inc., 1973, p. 125.

4. Freeman, op. cit., p. 24; Ros Baxandall, Linda Gordon, Susan Reverby, eds., *America's Working Women*. New York: Random House, Inc., 1976, p. 405.

5. Freeman, op. cit., p. 25.

6. Carol Hymowitz and Michaele Weissman, in *A History of Women in America*, New York: Bantam Books, Inc., 1978, note that in 1956 women's salaries averaged 63% of men's salaries, but by 1973 this had fallen to 57%. Freeman, op. cit., notes that Third World women's income in the U.S., though the lowest category of income altogether, has risen relative to Third World men's income over the last forty years; she therefore argues, p. 34, that sex discrimination in earnings over this period has been felt most dramatically among White women.

7. Dick Cluster, ed., *They should have served that cup of coffee*. Boston: South End Press, 1979, p. xii.

8. Bernice Reagan et al., "The Borning Struggle: The Civil Rights Struggle," in Dick Cluster, ed., op. cit., p. 25.

9. Ibid., pp. 35 and 37.

10. Cluster, ed., op. cit., p. 116.

11. Ann Popkin, "The Personal is Political: The Women's Liberation Movement," Dick Cluster, ed., op. cit., p. 184.

12. Marge Piercy, "The Grand Old Coolie Damn!" in *Sisterhood Is Powerful*, ed. Robin Morgan. New York: Random House, 1970, p. 491.

13. Ann Popkin, op. cit., p. 187.

14. Marge Piercy, op. cit., p. 490.

15. Ibid., p. 473 and 490–91.

16. Robin Morgan, op. cit., p. 13.

17. Ibid., p. xii.

18. Red Stocking Manifesto, in Morgan, ed., op. cit., p. 109.

19. Ann Popkin, op. cit., p. 193.

20. Leslie Cagan, "Something New Emerges: The Growth of a Socialist Feminism," in Cluster, ed., op. cit., p. 256.

21. Ann Popkin, op. cit., p. 196.

22. These references are drawn, illustratively, from Freeman, op. cit., and Baxandall, Gordon, and Reverby, eds., op. cit.

23. Freeman, op. cit., p. 55.

24. Mary Thompson, ed., *Voices of the New Feminism*. Boston: Beacon Press, 1970, p. 233.

25. Baxandall et al., eds., op. cit., p. 374–75.

26. Ibid., p. 384.

27. The examples mentioned here, along with many others, are discussed at greater length in *America's Working Women*, edited by Baxandall, Gordon, and Reverby, and in A *History of Women in America*, Hymowitz and Weissman.

28. Baxandall et al., eds., op. cit., pp. 363 ff.

29. Hymowitz and Weissman, op. cit., p. 366.

30. Baxandall et al., eds., op. cit., pp. 390–91.

31. Robin Morgan, op. cit., p. xviii.

32. Hymowitz and Weissman, op. cit., p. 352.

33. Roxane Dunbar, "Female Liberation as the Basis for Social Revolution," in Morgan, ed., op. cit., p. 537.

34. CARASA, *Women Under Attack*. New York: CARASA, 1979, pp. 59–60.

SECTION TWO

Mothers and Daughters

III

Black Mothers and Daughters: Their Roles and Functions in American Society

Introduction

In the present feminist movement, women's relationships are being given serious and much-needed consideration. Much attention has been given to the mother/daughter relationship in books like Nancy Friday's *My Mother/My Self: The Daughter's Search for Identity*, which sold more than 2.6 million copies. Nancy Chodorow's *The Reproduction of Mothering* sold out in four months a printing that was expected to last two years. Other leading sellers that are concerned with this theme, such as Dorothy Dinnerstein's *The Mermaid and the Minotaur*, Adrienne Rich's *Of Woman Born*, and Maxine Hong Kingston's *The Woman Warrior*, do not specifically address Black mothers and daughters, although Adrienne Rich's comments about Black mothers in her book are insightful, valid, and welcomed.

Initially, this section of the chapter was entitled "Relationships Between Black Mothers and Daughters." It was intended to be patterned along the lines of the current popular wave of mother/daughter writings. It soon became apparent that it would be dysfunctional to engage in a discussion of Black mothers and daughters which focused on specific psychological mechanisms operating between the two, the dynamics of the crucial bond, and explanations of the explicit role of patriarchy, without also including the important relevancy of racial oppression as a critical factor for consideration. To follow such a pattern would necessitate forcing Black mother/daughter relationships into pigeonholes designed for understanding White models, thus ignoring the reality of their situations.

Far too often, research on Black families, child-rearing practices, discipline, rewards, and aspirations follow patterns of research that are based on middle-class White values. To discuss Black mother/daughter relationships in terms of patterns of White mother/daughter relationships would be to ignore the explanations and interpretations of Black women regarding their own historical and cultural experiences as Black women.

The effects of racial and economic oppression figure largely in the structure and functioning of Black families. Black women play integral roles in the family and frequently it is immaterial whether they are biological mothers, sisters, or members of the extended family. From the standpoint of many Black daughters it could be: my sister, my mother; my aunt, my mother; my grandmother, my mother. They are daughters all and they frequently "mother" their sisters, nieces, nephews, or cousins as well as their own children. As women "We are, none of us, 'either' mothers or daughters; to our amazement, confusion, and greater complexity, we are both."[1]

In discussing Black mothers and daughters, it is more realistic, useful, and intellectually astute to speak in terms of their roles, positions, and functions within the Black society and that society's relationship to the broader (White) society in America. In discussing these roles and functions, the mother/daughter interaction must be described within the context of the Black family network. That is not to say that Black mothers and daughters do not have ties that are peculiar to them as compared to the mother/son, mother/husband ties, but to view the mother/daughter relationship as an entity in and of itself, divorced from other family members and family responsibilities, would be misleading and dysfunctional. It would be like trying to discuss the importance of the relationship between the thumb and the pinkie, when both have been detached from the palm of the hand. Therefore, the ensuing discussion will concentrate on Black women (some of whom are mothers and all of whom are daughters) and their positions in society; attitudes toward mothers;

socialization of daughters; and messages that are transmitted from one generation of women to another (not specifically mother to daughter, but also grandmother to daughter and mother to mother). Specific attitudes toward men and marriage will also be major points of discussion.

CRAZY GRANNY

When crazy granny told me
All men is dogs, I was nine.
I said, "Are granny. You have to say, all men *are* dogs."
She just chuckled, dried her hands,
And said softly,
"Don't talk back to your Granny, cheekie. Just believe
what I told you."
It's 22 years later and I Believes in granny's wisdom:
Some are lap dogs, and some are huskies,
you got yr well-groomed poodles
and those that are trained to sniff before they eat.
Some are all bark and no bite, panting all night.
And then you got your watch dogs.
They snarl—and sometimes attack dogs.
But they all got the same thing in common.
They all fuck out in the street
And then come home whining to be petted.

Winnie Oyoko Loving
April 18, 1978
(unpublished)

IT IS DEEP

(don't never forget the bridge
that you crossed over on)
by Carolyn Rodgers

Having tried to use the
witch cord
that erases the stretch of
thirty-three blocks
and tuning in the voice which
woodenly stated that the
talk box was "disconnected"

My mother, religiously girdled in
her god, slipped on some love, and
laid on my bell like a truck,
blew through my door warm wind from the south
concern making her gruff and tight-lipped
    and scared
that her "baby" was starving.
she, having learned, that disconnection results from
                non-payment of bill(s).
She did not
recognize the poster of the
grand le-roi (al) cat on the wall
had never even seen the books of
Black poems that I have written
thinks that I am under the influence of
              communists
when I talk about Black as anything
other than something ugly to kill it befo it grows
    in any impression she would not be
considered "relevant" or "Black"
            but
there she was standing in my room
not loudly condemning that day and
not remembering that I grew hearing her
curse the factory where she "cut uh slave"
and the cheap J-boss wouldn't allow a union,
not remembering that I heard the tears when
they told her a high school diploma was not enough,
and here now, not able to understand, what she had
been forced to deny, still—
she pushed into my kitchen so
she could open my refrigerator to see
what I had to eat, and pressed fifty
bills in my hand saying "pay the talk bill and buy
some food; you got folks who care about you . . ."

My mother, religious-negro, proud of
having waded through a storm, is very obviously,
a sturdy Black bridge that I
crossed over, on.[2]

The poems by Oyoko and by Carolyn Rodgers reflect key roles
that their (grand)mothers played in their lives. Women transmitting
messages to women, along with the capacity of women for nur-

turance and caring, are two themes that are central to this chapter. Oyoko's poem portrays the oral tradition of messages being passed from generation to generation, with the present generation giving it an upbeat. Data from my nationwide survey of Black women, conducted 1979–1980, reveal that an overwhelming number of mothers (72 percent) gave their daughters negative messages about men. Oyoko's poem graphically portrays this message. When Oyoko reads her poem, it draws resounding applause and exclamations of appreciation, approval, and sanction from women. The typical male responses are: a headshake with an utterance of "Now ain't that a bitch"; a rueful or wry smile; a chagrined grimace; or a solemn, disapproving glare. There are also a few resolute claims of "She is absolutely right."

Data from the research also reveal that daughters (age 17 and over) overwhelmingly (94.5 percent) showed great respect for their mothers despite difficulties that exist in the relationships. Carolyn Rodgers' poem reflects the theme of the centrality of mothers in their daughters' lives, even though the daughters are grown, on their own, and have a political orientation alien and foreign to their mothers'. The concept of motherhood in Black culture plays a key role in the discussion of mothers and daughters. It is the mother who constructs the sturdy Black bridges for daughters (sons, husbands, and mates) to cross over on.

Through the influence of the contemporary feminist movement, theories about the mother/daughter relationship have gained prominence. Self-avowed feminists and self-declared nonfeminists have contributed clever, controversial, and interesting analytical literature to the newly popularized topic, all of which has served to stimulate new understandings in the area of mother/daughter relationships. The subject of mothers and daughters has been largely neglected in the past; when it was considered, it was generally analyzed within a traditional psychoanalytical framework. The recent writings on the topic are largely based on critical reevaluations of Freudian and other psychoanalytical theories. Although the resulting efforts of the authors yielded important and productive publications about women, the writings contain a shortcoming similar to that of the traditional White analysts in that the writings do not embrace the Black female population.

The majority of available publications that deal with the subject of mothers and daughters follow a similar pattern of excluding Black women or including them peripherally. Black women find limitations in identifying with the content of the material in these works and with the characters and individuals being discussed. However, when materials include Black mother-and-daughter relationships, usually within the context of Black families, regardless of the socioeconomic class, Black women experience little trouble identifying personally and vicariously with the female characters and their experiences. These sources of material, available to students and the public in general, are rarely textbooks, nor are they designed to be analytical theories; rather, they are novels, short stories, fiction, biographies, and poems by an array of authors—Toni Cade Bambara, Paula Marshall, Carolyn Rodgers, Mari Evans, Gwendolyn Brooks, Toni Morrison, Alice Walker, June Jordan, Ann Perry, Zora Neale Hurston, Brenda Wilkinson, Ann Moody, Sarah E. Wright, and others.

There is an undeniable dearth of material dealing specifically with an analysis of the Black mother/daughter relationship, particularly from a Black feminist approach. The vast majority of popular literature on Black family studies and the psychology of Black behavior are the works of Black males, and these authors, to date, have not written about the mother/daughter relationship in any depth whatsoever. Resources for this chapter include the writings of Black authors, predominantly females, and Black family studies. More importantly, significant pioneering research has been conducted based on new resources in the area of Black mother/daughter relationships. The research consisted of a nationwide questionnaire administered to Black women and a small number of Whites. The data obtained provided information on the attitudes, feelings, and experiences of Black mothers and daughters in contemporary Black families as well as material for the development of analytical theory on Black mothers and daughters.

A specifically Black feminist approach is called for in discussing mother/daughter relationships in Black families. In the same way that any theory about mother/daughter relationships among Whites is incomplete without consideration of the role of patriarchy in women's lives, a theory about mother/daughter relationships among Blacks is incomplete without a consideration of racial relations and racism. This is not to imply that Blacks are excluded from being affected and influenced by patriarchy, but ample evidence indicates that relations between the races have a long and important history which cannot be exclusively reduced to an analysis limited to sex or class. Blacks respond to the sociopolitical reality of a social structure

in which Blacks are systematically dominated, exploited, and oppressed. The psychological dynamics that function within Black
families are influenced by the existing economic and racist conditions and are, therefore, qualitatively and culturally different than
the dynamics that exist in White families.

The studies of families become critical to our understanding of the
mother/daughter relationship within the context of the socialization of children and the diversified roles of family members. From
the time of slavery, Black families and communities have been the
environmental setting for the transmission of cultural values, survival
techniques, moral and religious training, role modeling, and political
indoctrination (the latter refers basically to learning who exploits
whom and why). Some patterns of socialization and adult-child relationships have survived in modified forms today. For example, it is
recorded that in the slave communities, the elderly women were left
in charge of the young children. The intergenerational distance between the children and the aged and often feeble adults created a situation wherein a heightened sense of autonomy and responsibility
was developed in the children. The interaction among the children
was earmarked by mutual responsibility and caretaking among peers.

In discussing mother/daughter relationships among Blacks, it is
important to include the role of significant others. Today, as in the
past, grandmothers, siblings, aunts, nieces are/were common mother
figures.

From the slavery period, for example, we find evidence of the critical
caretaking role performed by older siblings and peers, and the powerful
influence of grandmothers and women elders in the rearing of young children. Reflections of these more extended patterns of childrearing are
found today in Black communities where children seem to be less focused on the *adult* as the central figure for sustenance and guidance and
seem more likely to seek help and support from agemates. A comprehensive description of the educative function of families therefore would
have to include socialization and learning that are not supervised or controlled by adults; would have to document *child-initiated* interactions
with significant others; would have to reflect patterns of communication
and behavior extending far beyond the boundaries of the nuclear family
or household.[3]

These cultural continuums must be considered in analyzing Black
mother/daughter relationships.

Too frequently social scientists doing research on Black families commit a major methodological and conceptual error by ignoring these continuums. As Robert Hill comments in his critique of social science research on Black families, the fallacy is "the tendency to impute function on the basis of structure." For example, a "fatherless" home does not automatically signal disintegration of the family. It is the quality of the relationships within families that is most crucial—not the family structure. Powerful and supportive social networks and bonding patterns frequently operate in single-parent homes, with members of the extended family playing critical and influential roles. There is also a tendency on the part of social scientists doing research on Blacks to offer explanations for "deviance" when explaining the behavior of Blacks, rather than perceiving a different lifestyle based on real, material differences. This tendency is due to racist indoctrination. A case in point: Black mothers who are single have been described as unwed, irresponsible, promiscuous and ignorant, while single White mothers are referred to as liberated, experiencing an alternative lifestyle, or deliberately choosing motherhood without a husband.

An analysis of the ways in which Black family members respond to one another—the caring, sharing, animosity, rejection, fratricide, support, protection—demonstrates the interchangeability of roles within the Black family. For example, extended family members—particularly aunts, grandmothers, older sisters, cousins and nieces—frequently play major roles in the care and raising of younger children. Interestingly, the high percentage of unemployment among Black males has not resulted in Black males playing nurturance/mothering roles to any substantive degree. Sexism has severely influenced male attitudes toward roles in the home.

In discussing Black mother/daughter relationships within contemporary Black family structures, to focus on the term "relationships" can be misleading for the following reasons: (1) it brings to mind a Freudian-based description of daughters' prescribed behavioral responses at specific development stages—e.g., at certain stages of development daughters are supposed to resent their mothers; (2) it detracts from the essence of the dynamics of the Black mother/daughter dyad; (3) it detracts from the most salient feature of the dyad—that of the communication/interaction process. It is more worthwhile and valid to focus on the nature and quality of the mother/daughter interaction, because that is what distinguishes the relationship. Their relationship should not be imagined as a set pattern from which predetermined behaviors emanate. It is misleading and invalid to discuss Black and White mother/daughter relationships categorically within the framework of identical theories.

Signe Hammer, in her book, *Mothers-Daughters: Daughters-Mothers*, included mothers, daughters, and grandmothers from all classes and from a variety of ethnic backgrounds in her 75 interviews. The emphasis was on the psychological aspects of the mother/daughter relationship, stressing racial, ethnic, and class differences only when they seemed particularly relevant. This was done because she believes that the basic psychological mechanisms in the mother/daughter relationships are common to all women in our society, but the impact of racism must be taken into account initially in order to see the point at which developmental difficulties for Black women are likely to originate. Signe Hammer says that certain basic psychological mechanisms in mother/daughter relationships, such as attachment or bonding, are common to all women in our society. However, it can be strongly argued that interactions other than bonding or attachment must be viewed as resulting from societal influences. Despite certain commonalities among all mothers regardless of race or class, the concept of motherhood cannot be reduced to a biological function.

Mother, mama, mom, ma are emotional concepts as well as definitive words. The true relevancy of the words are found in the emotional ties that exist between mother and baby. The emotional feelings of the mother and those of the child have different motivational sources and intrinsic rewards. The expressions "I am her mother" and "She is my mother" spell out the closest biological relationship between two human beings, but in the psychological realm the forces flowing between the two are not always compatible or complementary. To a baby the mother is "the tree of life"; to a mother the infant is a prime responsibility.

The responsibility lessens and alters as the child approaches adulthood, but that sense of caring for an infant is forever a part of a mother's life experiences. In the baby's eye the mother figure is the protector, the one who provides comfort, security, nourishment, and warmth, the one who is depended on for unconditional acceptance and establishes a deep sense of trust in the child. To the mother the baby needs, demands, needs. The baby also provides the mother with a sense of being needed and wanted. The mother sacrifices sleep, gives of her energies, worries over the child, and fears for its survival.

As the child advances through various stages of development, its needs change and so do its attitudes toward the mother. The father, siblings, other relatives, and peers play significant roles in the child's life, meeting different needs as the child's world broadens.

So the child goes through childhood with the knowledge, feeling, or hope that in some manner or form this mother person will care for her/him. Even the battered child will continue for years to seek approval from the mother, hoping for acceptance and having faith in what used to be a sanctuary—what society has promoted as a sanctuary: Mother.

Naturally we must realize that there are variations on this theme of mother/child relationships. There will always be atypical cases stemming from organic and inorganic causes, which will result in aberrant mother/child behavior. The intervention of highly traumatic events such as emotional or physical deprivation or abuse can affect the process of the relationship. The sense of trust can be replaced with a sense of distrust. Economic poverty has a direct influence on the developmental lives of parents and child. Mothers in the lower socioeconomic brackets experience a disproportionately higher amount of anxiety and stress related to poverty. The mother copes as best she can with the oppressive conditions, but in the process experiences frustrations and anxieties. These tensions frequently cause the mother to respond to the child with irritability, impatience, and anger. The baby's reactions to this behavior are frequently negative (unpleasant, undesirable to the mother). This in turn further frustrates the mother. A vicious cycle is created and operates in its circular way.

Fortunately, with proper nurturance a child will develop a positive sense of self. According to Comer and Poussaint, authors of *Black Child Care* (1975), as quoted by Joyce Ladner, "all children develop a positive self-image mainly from the consistent love and care of their parents and other significant adults in their environment. This is especially true for the children of minority groups, since parental nurturing must offset the effects of an antagonistic society."[4]

The disproportionately high percentage of Blacks in the lowest economic categories accounts for numerous Black mothers of young children having to face difficulties in raising them that stem from economic and racial sources. Despite this fact, Black family members far more often than not supply the necessary loving and nurturance to babies.

Awareness of the difficulties their children will face socially and occupationally in a racist society causes deep concern for mothers in every socioeconomic class. The strength of the early nurturance helps carry the children through the difficult adolescent years.

The Black mother is well aware of the types of problems her daughters will face contrasted to those her sons will face. She knows this intuitively from her experiences as a Black female being raised in a White, male-dominated, heterosexual society. She doesn't have to read books to know that her daughter will have to struggle to get a decent education, a decent job, and a reliable husband. Nor does she need a book to tell her that her son will have a tough time battling to stay off drugs, out of prisons and out of women's beds (other than his wife's) and will have to struggle to provide economic stability for his family. The Black mother knows from her relationship with her husband or with the father of her children what it takes to make ends meet, what it takes emotionally to "share" her man with another woman and either pretend she doesn't know or argue and fight over the fact or scheme and/or pray to keep him. She is very familiar with feeling ambivalent about being pleased sexually and being sexually pleasing. The Black mother knows the psychological turmoil of being able to do more intellectually and professionally than she is doing and knows the psychological trauma of seeing her husband begrudgingly but resolutely working at menial, inferior jobs and taking orders from "the man," who really doesn't give a damn about anything more than profits, and the Black mother knows the strains and anxieties of trying to climb the social ladder with its ersatz rungs. But she also knows the joys and pleasures that emanate from her family, the celebrations, the proud feelings when a family member accomplishes something "big," and she has memories of and desires for the soothing, sensuous, sexual encounters from which hope springs eternal.

It is no secret to Black mothers that American society and Black culture combined have programmed their daughters for romantic love and marriage. The Black mother looks at the way Black men strut, strive, and connive in their undaunted roles. She thinks about their good intentions being sabotaged by the games they play trying to get over and be slicker than thou, and lying and jiving, and promising and profiling, just to "get a little piece." Knowing all of this, what messages will she deliver to her daughters about men and marriage and how to get ahead as a Black woman in White America?

Will it be the same messages that she as a daughter received from her mother? Have the realities of being a Black woman in America changed substantially over the past generations?

The role of the mother in the Black family and how she is viewed by her immediate family and society play a central part in mother/daughter interactions. A cultural/historical account of the concept of motherhood in Black families will shed some light on the existing patterns of interactions.

Any discussion of the topic of "mother" in the Black scheme of things definitely calls for an analysis of two outstanding phenomena: Mother's Day on the Block and the Dozens.

Riddle me once, riddle me twice.

What occurs in the month of May on a Sunday, is bigger than Easter, and more of a religious rite than Christmas? We are talking about Mother's Day on the Block in Black communities—a most important day. It's big profit time for Hallmark Cards, Gibson, American Greeting Corporation, and Contemporary Cards, Inc. Local stores will have a special display of Mother's Day cards and boxes of candy from past holidays, wearing a new "Mother's Day" wrapping. Even the little candy store with the back-up numbers room will have Mother's Day cards, some with and some without fly speckles. (You can bargain for a cheaper price if the fly speckles are too numerous.) Bars and restaurants honor this occasion with a Mother's Day discount on drinks and a special Mother's Day menu. The movie marquee carries a sign, "Half price for all mothers today," along with the announcement of the movie for the day. For this special occasion the children hustle. Sons and daughters *know* it's their ritualistic, unquestionable duty to honor Mother with a show of love, appreciation, and respect. In many homes it's a day off from cooking for Mother, so hands alien to preparing meals will earnestly prepare an extra special dinner for Mom. And the gifts—there just gotta be a gift for Mom! If you didn't save for it or if Pop didn't give you money or if you weren't young enough for your mother to give you money to shop for a gift, then the gift may come from the grace of a department store with the aid of gifted fingers. Flowers, too, play a special role on this day. Someone in the family or among her friends will send or bring Mom some flowers. It may be in the form of a corsage or a plant or a bouquet—but there gotta be flowers! The churches on that Sunday will be overflowing with flowers. Sunday school children have been busy the week before making tissue paper flowers which may or may not be worn or serve as altar decorations. Young, middle-aged, old, and ancient mothers are honored. The middle-aged and older women may wear the traditional white corsage if Mother is dead and red if she is alive.

The walls of a home, like the students' bulletin boards in college, tell what is important in the lives of its inhabitants. The walls of many kitchens in low-, middle-, and upper-income homes will reveal Mother's Day artwork made in school as well as family pictures. Shelves and the tops of cabinets, dressers, and china closets will carry an overwhelming array of Mother's Day cards. The card companies know their business well as they make cards: "To Mother from: Your son, daughter, husband, grandchild, godchild, great-grandchild, niece, nephew, daughter-in-law, son-in-law, my sister on Mother's Day, you are just like a mother to me, to the mother of my friend, and to my friend on Mother's Day."

The tradition of Mother's Day is a nationwide phenomenon, and adoration of mothers, mixed with a bit of adulation, is obviously not limited to Black families. However, the style and manner of celebration for Blacks has cultural differences and the role of honor and respect for the Black mother has its roots in African history.

The spirit among Black women has its historical roots in the mother country, Africa. Large numbers of African women carried a fighting spirit with them across the Atlantic and into their lives of slavery. This spirit was a reflection of their backgrounds of militancy and aggressiveness, great self-respect, confidence, courage, and independence.

In ancient Africa, women often ruled society with unquestioned power. During the rise of the great dynasties in Egypt, Kush, and Ethiopia, African women were great militarists and heads of state.

According to Egyptologist James Henry Breasted, Queen Hatshepsut was "the first great woman in history of whom we are informed." She was born about 1,500 years before the birth of Christ and her reign was one of the brightest in Egyptian history. This great Queen Hatshepsut ruled Egypt for twenty-one years and ruled it well. Her temple, one of the most beautiful in all Egypt, still stands and is known today as Deir el Behr. The story of her ascendance to the throne states that "she dressed herself in the most sacred of the

Pharaoh's official costumes, and with the royal scepter in one hand and the sacred crook in the other, she mounted the throne and proclaimed herself Pharaoh of Egypt." Thus the first and perhaps the greatest female ruler of all time came into power in Egypt.

The Egyptian Queen Nefertiti, the Queen of Sheba, called by the Greeks the "Ethiopian Diane," and Cleopatra, who was neither White nor Greek, played major roles in the theater of history. Queen Kahina of the Hebrew faith fought fiercely in a valiant attempt to save Africa for the Africans (in the year 705).

Extremely outstanding was Queen Nzingha, born in 1583 in Angola, an extraordinarily great head of state and a military leader with few peers in her time. She belonged to an ethnic group called the Magas, an extremely militant group who formed a human shield against the Portuguese slave traders. Nzingha never accepted the Portuguese conquest of her country and was always on the military offensive. In the seventeenth century, when the Portuguese transferred their slave trade to the Congo and the southern part of West Africa, their most stubborn opposition came from Queen Nzingha, who stood as a symbol of early Mbundu resistance. From 1620 until her death in 1668, she was the most important personality in Angola. She became Queen of Ndongo and forbade her subjects to call her Queen. She preferred to be called King and dressed in men's clothing when she led her army in battle. She possessed both hardness and charm, both of which she readily used, depending on the need and the occasion. Although Nzingha failed in her attempts to expel the Portuguese, her resistance to the slave trade was inspirational.

Other outstanding African women helped to mount offensives against the colonial system throughout Africa. Among these were: Madame Tinubu of Nigeria; Nandi, the mother of the great Zulu warrior Chaka; Kaipkire, of the Herero people of southern West Africa; and the female army that numbered more than four thousand elite, unmarried, handsome, fierce, and powerful young women who followed the great Dahomian King, Behanyin Bowelle.

The last major war in Africa led by a woman was the Yaa Asuntewa War. Yaa Asuntewa was the Queen Mother of Ejisu, and the inspiring force behind the Ashantis, a fierce and warlike people who inhabited what is now the central portion of Ghana. In 1900 the British Governor, Lord Hodgson, demanded that the Ashanti surrender the Golden Stool, the supreme symbol of the sovereignty and independence of the Ashantis. This demand was a terrible blunder and a tremendous insult to the Ashanti people. They prepared for war. During the meeting discussing war, Yaa Asuntewa saw that some of the chiefs were afraid. She stood up and made a historic speech ending with these words: "If the men of Ashanti will not go forward, then we will. We the women will. I shall call upon my fellow women. We will fight the white men. We will fight till the last of us falls in the battlefields." This speech stirred the chiefs to battle and for many months the Ashantis, led by Yaa Asuntewa, fought the British. They were finally defeated by fourteen hundred troops with large guns. Yaa Asuntewa was the last of a long line of African warrior queens that began with Hatshepsut fifteen hundred years before the birth of Christ.[5]

Historic feats of women and great respect for mothers exist among other groups of Americans of various ethnic backgrounds, and there are numerous examples that bespeak the central role of mothers in other nationalities. Among Italians was an old proverb: "If the father is dead, the family suffers; if the mother dies, the family cannot exist." In certain communities in the "old country," if a child did not obey or respect his parents he was ostracized by the entire community. For the immigrant mother it was easy to bring up the young children in the old ways and to maintain traditional relationships. However, as the children grew older and attended school, they were more apt to listen to their American teachers than to their foreign-born mothers. When parents spoke in Italian, Yiddish, or Polish, the children would answer in English. This practice, Harry Golden, the late liberal Jewish columnist, said, gave rise to the ghetto proverb: "In America the children bring up the parents."

Blacks in America did not undergo the same type of transition from their homeland to America. There was no "African language" for the children of Black Afro-Americans to continue to use, since the slaves were forbidden to use their native languages. Therefore, schools did not present the problem of causing conflict in families due to language usage. Ironically, the traditional role of mother was preserved with less conflict among Blacks due to the circumstances surrounding their lives in America. The family had to depend more on family members and roles which were preserved partially due to the enforced segregation, isolation, and insularity of Black families. Unlike the Jewish, Italian, Russian, and German immigrants, African slaves were prohibited from maintaining their traditional values and customs, class obligations, and religious beliefs. The Blacks practiced and maintained their customs to the best of their abilities, but in clandestine ways, and variations had to be made due to the very separation from Africa.

The European women immigrants were predominantly from peasant societies, which were organized along patriarchal lines. They clung tenaciously to the old values and customs. Women had no separate legal existence apart from their fathers and husbands. Most marriages were arranged in the old countries and the women's lifestyles were repeated generation after generation, like carbon copies. These women, however, in most cultures were viewed as the emotional, spiritual, and moral centers of their households and exerted varying amounts of power within their families. The children of immigrants absorbed the American culture more easily and herein lay the crux of the conflicts that developed between immigrant children and their parents. The conflicts between mothers and daughters were particularly acute, with mothers holding on to the old values and the American-born experiencing severe conflict over the old and new values.

The conflicts between Black children and their parents did not parallel those of the immigrants. Blacks had to work in concert for survival. So even though both Black and White women prior to coming to America were viewed similarly in terms of their being moral, spiritual, and emotional centers of their families and regarded as honorable, charitable souls, the American way of life wreaked havoc on family relations, pronouncedly so in the mother/daughter relationship in immigrant families. On the other hand, the moment the Black mothers were transported to American soil new roles and practices were thrust upon them. The Black family in concert developed and established new roles, combining the requisites of the new society with all that could be maintained from the old. An important point to be made is that societal conditions intensified Black mother/daughter relationships. While social factors had a tendency to fracture the European mother/daughter relationships, in an ironical way they forced the role of the Black mother in her family to persevere. Each generation of Black children will experience more pressure from the dominant society, and we can expect new attitudes to develop and new behaviors to be exhibited toward mothers. But as of 1980, Mother's Day is still ritualized in Black families with respect and reverence; the ritual's origins can be traced to Africa and the slave quarters.

This respect and reverence for mothers is further demonstrated in the phenomenon called the Dozens. Playing the Dozens is very unlike the usual childhood games such as hide-and-go-seek, Red Rover, kick the can, ring-a-levio, farmer in the dell, or even stickball or pitching pennies against a wall. The Dozens is a verbal ritual. It's a word game requiring the ability to think, feel cool, be cool under fire, and be prepared for some action. The theoretical structure behind this game is that you can go so far, and then no more. There is a stopping point, a limit, which you don't go beyond. The thirteenth is beyond. Twelve, a dozen, is all you are allowed, and if you go further be prepared to take the consequences. And who can trigger the boiling point? Mother!

A rhyme that elucidates the Dozens is: "You can talk about my father and that's a dirty shame, but if you talk about my mother, that's a fighting game."

In practice the numerical count is not an actuality. You can begin the Dozens after two or three insults or exchanges, and if you are a real "punk" (low person on the totem pole), the Dozens are thrown at you without any provocation. For example, if a group of youngsters are walking past a movie house and a monster movie is being advertised and the kid in the group who is the lowest in the pecking order ventures to say, "Hey, did you see Frankenstein and the Monster?" one of the group might retort, "Oh, was that Frankenstein? I thought that was your mother." In a situation with no established punk, the exchange might go like this:

(*In a school yard*)

Tom: Hey Billy, that gym teacher pushed you around like a dog.

Billy: Pushed who! Man, I pushed him back too.

Tom: Man, you lie, you ain't pushed nobody.

Billy: Who you calling a lie? You can't see straight anyway.

Tom: Yeah, well I can see well enough to know that you're wearing your sister's drawers.

Billy: Your sister ain't got no drawers.

Tom: Your mother wears cement drawers.

At that point Billy is compelled to prove his manhood. The Dozens has become institutionalized as a verbal ritual to show who is the toughest, mentally more than physically. There are times in some neighborhoods when simply using the expression "your mama" following a comment will trigger an exchange of blows.

The Dozens can be compared to the term "ranking" in the sense that they both involve the game of one-upmanship and are both designed to instigate combat. But the unique feature about the Dozens is that the mother is sacred and you fight for her honor. You prove you're a "man" in this society. If you don't prove it, "you are a punk." Anyone can dump on you. This exercise in verbal and physical sparring is usually engaged in by males, but many girls at ages ten to twelve get into some good hair-pulling hassles over the Dozens. They also do a lot of signifying and instigating. You can hear them saying, "Hey, did you hear what Mabel said about your mother?" And without waiting for an answer, "Well, she said something bad about your mother." Among adults, out of respect for one another and for mothers, the game loses its game element. But it does not die a natural death. Mother is too sacred to be joked about or used for bait in a light vein. The Dozens is employed by adults, but on a different level of understanding. Adults are well aware of the role that the Dozens play in the street life of children, and mothers somehow seem to accept their role in this game without much questioning.

The forms of celebration of the role of motherhood, as portrayed by the Dozens and Mother's Day, should not be interpreted as meaning that all is love, honor, respect, and appreciation for the Black mother. These celebrations exemplify the ritualization of motherhood as precious. It is a practice that has its roots in African tradition and is a part of Black culture. As such it plays an influential conceptual role in an analysis of behavior on the part of Blacks.

The Black mother, however, is also a woman, and herein lies the great contradiction. The "honored" mother is the same second-class citizen who is often regarded and treated as an object to be used, bruised, and abused for years and who is considered to be used up after thirty, forty, or forty-five years. The societal attitude toward Mother is one of both idealization and degradation. The mother's role in the family is symbolic of contradictions and contrasts.

She simultaneously embodies love, nurturance, and accommodation and has the power to withhold love, nurturance, and accommodation. Thus, in the eyes of her children, she can cause conflict and resolve conflict. She defies classification, as:

She works inside and outside of the home.

She is breadwinner, bread giver, and bread withholder.

She both bakes bread and slips you some "bread" when things get rough.

She lives vicariously through her husband, lives without a husband, browbeats her husband, and is beaten by her husband.

She rewards and encourages her children and is ignored and bored by her children.

She schemes with her children against "Pops," and collaborates with them against "the man."

She teaches her children when and whom to hustle, preaches cleanliness and the golden rule, and liberally sprinkles intermittent spankings and beatings.

She fusses at her children and is cussed by them (*sotto voce* and out loud).

She visits them in correctional institutions and at prestigious colleges.

The multifaceted roles that Black mothers play as they visit one child in prison and another at college, and all in the same week, symbolize the continuous nurturing and caring roles that are often neglected by scholars in Black studies and women's studies. Of course, not all mothers possess or display the described characteristics and attributes. Some Black mothers overprotect their children and some don't seem to give a damn. Some work and others stay at home. Some take drugs and others take pleasure in other women's husbands. Some work two jobs and others sit, looking out of windows, thinking and hoping. The burdens and joys the mothers share may vary, but what they all share in common is being viewed as women and consequently as inferior and subordinate to male dominance. This attitude is part and parcel of a heinous American institutionalized value. The interfacing of this type of sexism—this societal view of women—with the uniqueness of the culturally defined role of Black mothers forms the backdrop for the ensuing discussion of the interactions of the Black mother and daughter.

Mother/Daughter Data Analysis

The respect that Black daughters have for their mothers, which was addressed in the preceding section, is statistically affirmed from the data obtained from my questionnaires. Responding to the question, "What about your mother do you respect the most?" a decisive 94.5 percent expressed respect for their mothers in terms of strength, honesty, ability to overcome difficulties, and ability to survive. Only 1.8 percent of the Black women surveyed stated that there was nothing about their mothers that they respected. The remaining 4.2 percent of the responses were not scorable—e.g., no response, the mother was absent during the woman's childhood, or the woman presented a question or statement about the question itself.

The high incidence of respect that daughters show for their mothers, as reported in the survey, should certainly not be interpreted as meaning that all is love and understanding between Black mothers and daughters. Nor should the high incidence of respect be interpreted as a reflection of an absence of conflicts, antagonisms, hostilities, or even fear. Surely, these all exist. But the responses show that daughters did not get "hung up" or "fixated" on the interpersonal problems encountered with mothers to the extent that the problems became primary or intense focal points in the relationships. In spite of the existing problems, the daughters still respect "Momma." And the reason for this, as indicated in the responses, seems to be located in the Black daughters' familiarity with the circumstances within which their mothers existed and raised their children and an empathy caused by understanding these situations. The psychological, mental, and physical hardships that Black women have had to endure as a result of racist and economic oppression have not changed substantially from one generation to the next. Mothers and daughters in many situations share similar problems.

The interpersonal problems and conflicts are transcended to accommodate the cooperative effort needed to solve the common problems they face as Black women in today's America. It was and still is necessary for Black mothers and daughters to collaborate in their fight against powerful societal conditions that continue to force fathers out of work and out of the home; that push brothers and boyfriends into prisons and/or onto drugs; that make it necessary to raise babies without economic support from the father; that make it difficult to scrape together college tuitions and fees or to buy a new piece of furniture on the installment plan. There are, of course, numerous Black families that do not face such dire conditions. Middle- and upper-class Blacks experience fewer economic difficulties, but they do not escape the more insidious discriminatory practices of racism. This collaboration is reflected in the ways in which Black mothers teach their daughters highly adaptive mechanisms designed to promote physical and mental survival. "Black females are socialized by adult figures in early life to become strong, independent women who, because of precarious circumstances growing out of poverty and racism, might have to eventually become heads of their own households. Black mothers teach their female offspring to perform adult tasks, such as household chores, when they are still in their preadolescent years."[6]

Female children as young as five years old assume adult-like behaviors on an emotional level as well as performing physical duties. It is not unusual for a Black female youngster to respond to her mother on an emotional level with a maturity and understanding that belies her youthful age. In homes with a working mother or an overworked mother, the child becomes consciously aware of the mother's endless housekeeping activities, her moods, and the care and concern extended to the daughter. This child observes her mother making plans to stretch food and money; remembering birthdays and making a cake; rubbing a chest with camphor salve, or cooling a fever with witch hazel; and when obviously tired, performing one more task like washing clothes or ironing before retiring. The daughter experiences an empathy with and a sensitivity to the many roles her mother is performing and insightfully reacts with deep feelings and perceptions. These feelings become evident in caring behavior.

Examples: It may be well past time for the daughter to have a new pair of shoes when the mother finally says, "Tomorrow we are going to buy you that new pair of shoes." At the shoe store the child will know that the price is more critical than the style and will try not to show her disappointment in not getting the preferred but much more expensive pair. When the mother says to the child as she tries on the shoes, "Do you like them?" the youngster replies affirmatively, knowing that her mother is doing the best she can. The child also knows that when she returns home her siblings may joke about her "plain" shoes. Humor plays a curious and strategic role in surviving. These same family members who joked at the shoes will defend her with rocks and bones (fists) if the wrong outsider makes a negative remark about those shoes.

On other occasions the child will recognize that the mother is not feeling well and will ask, "Mama, you're not feeling good today?" She or he will then volunteer to play quietly and to help the mother with her tasks.

Black daughters learn at an early age that their mothers are not personally responsible for not being able, through their individual efforts, to make basic changes in their lives or the lives of their children. This recognition enables daughters in later life to be more appreciative, understanding, and forgiving of their mothers when they are unable to fulfill and meet the daughter's expectations and needs for material and emotional comforts. (This is not to say that the emotional comforts were not missed nor that there was an absence of consequences.) This reality must be interpreted and evaluated in light of the culture of Black families within a society that has denied Black parents the opportunity to offer their children a protected status comparable to what White parents can offer their offspring. A look at some of the open-ended responses to the question regarding respect for the mother clearly shows that hardships were recognized and that the daughters appreciated their mothers' ability to endure and survive these hardships in their lives.

QUESTION: What about your mother do you respect the most?

RESPONSES: "The way she loved all nine of her children and kept us all together; also, how she kept herself together. I think my mother is the most beautiful person in the world and I will respect and love her until the day I die." (18-year-old secretary—mother, 50)

"She works a job she hates so I can have this fine education." (20-year-old student—mother, 50)

"Ambition, perseverance and the refusal to take shit from anyone (with the exception of my father)." (20-year-old student—mother, 50)

"Her beautiful creativity, her love for people. She doesn't know how to make money, but so what?" (21-year-old student—mother, 48)

"Everything, she is a wonderful lady." (22-year-old unskilled worker—mother, 40)

"I respect my mother's ability and strength as a woman. (My mother reared eight children without the ample support she should have gotten from my father and only a strong woman can do such.)" (23-year-old student—mother, 43)

"The fact that she raised the six of us by herself and we never went hungry and she never went crazy." (23-year-old student—mother, 52)

"Her courage to continue working with the bullshit that society gave her. The bullshit my father gave her. Her courage to raise all seven of her children. Just for her being herself." (27-year-old administrative assistant—mother, 57)

"That she is my mother. With all her faults, she is still my mother." (33-year-old housewife/student—mother, 53)

"Her ability to be a mother to any and everyone." (36-year-old counselor—mother, 72)

"Her ability to manage money and making ends meet on her low wages." (38-year-old nurse—mother, 80)

"Her knowledge and strength of character." (47-year-old teaching assistant—mother, 65)

"Her honesty, housekeeping, and her love." (50-year-old clerk—mother, over 70)

"Thriftiness. Keen mind in spite of limited education. Ability to endure despite hardships. Ability to hold her own and extended family 'together.' Secret philanthropy to downtrodden. Always able to 'rescue' with the saved almighty dollar, although it was grudgingly given—the dependable banker." (56-year-old secondary school administrator—mother, died at age 69)

"Her diligence, frugality, and the ability to make wonder from nothing." (62-year-old teaching superintendent of nurses—mother, deceased)

"She was always there." (63-year-old housewife—no age listed for mother)

More than one-third of the women included honesty in their descriptions of what it is/was that they respected most in their mothers. If we interpret honesty as being a tendency to "tell it like it is"; to not deny or protect their daughters from the real world as it exists for Black women; as a sharing of life's expectancy for Black women; or as a tendency to openly express anger—i.e., yell, cuss, fuss, strike, give cutting looks (looks that could stop a Mack truck cold)—we can see that there would exist less tendency for double messages being given to the daughter from the mother. This would in turn result in less ambivalent feelings of the daughter toward the mother.

As previously mentioned, the respect that the daughters had for their mothers did not mean that there was an absence of tensions, anger, or fear on the part of the daughters. When we look at the responses to the question: "In what ways did you (do you) fear your mother?" and compare these responses with the responses to the question on respect, we can see how respect for the mother is related to "fear" of the mother. The fear that is expressed here should not be confused with a psychological, traumatic, phobic fear. It is a fear that is peculiar to many Blacks and working-class Whites. It is linked to respect. When discussing or explaining this fear, there is a note of proudness and respect. The person who instilled the fear is admired, not despised or hated.

FEAR: "When my mother gave me a certain look, fear would run all through me in seconds."

RESPECT: "Her attitude toward others, especially the people that have done something against us." (18-year-old student—mother, 42)

FEAR: "She had a quick temper. She hit us often. She was strict."

RESPECT: "How much she really loved us and did for us when we were children. She was always around when we needed her." (20-year-old, no occupation stated—mother, died at age 45)

FEAR: "My mother has a terrible temper, and she's also vengeful. If I made her mad she would remember it for a long time. I wanted her to love me."

RESPECT: "Her strength. She is a strong woman. She is trustworthy, hardworking and thrifty. She has worked very hard for the things she has attained. She is also beautiful." (20-year-old student—mother, 46)

FEAR: "When I came in late she would hit me with her shoe. Other than that, she is a beautiful woman."

RESPECT: "She did not smoke and was very nice to everyone. She was a warmhearted woman." (20-year-old, no occupation stated—mother, 53)

FEAR: "At a young age, I feared her beating my behind."

RESPECT: "Her determination in bringing us up." (20-year-old student—mother, 57)

FEAR: "Her mouth."

RESPECT: "Her determination and success in raising me without a husband." (21-year-old student—mother, 41)

FEAR: "If she says that what she says goes in her house, I know I better respect her wishes."

RESPECT: "Her sense of humor, perseverance, determination. Her belief in the conviction that you never say you 'can't' do something. You try first. Her outspokenness, her ability to make friends wherever she goes (without even trying)." (21-year-old student—mother, 52)

FEAR: "Her naggin's. Putdowns."

RESPECT: "Her perseverance, sacrifice, and insistence on the best for her children." (30-year-old educator—mother, died at age 56)

FEAR: "She was a strict disciplinarian and didn't mind using the strap."

RESPECT: "She is very open and we can express opinions about everything. She is dependable and shows a lot of concern for her entire family." (32-year-old counselor—mother, 62)

FEAR: "She had an overly righteous and fearful temper. She cussed incessantly but used TV cuss words, unlike me. I feared her physical strength, which seemed overwhelming."

RESPECT: "She had a respect for and an ability to work like twenty men. She was generous to a fault and was reliable and if not always understanding, she was genuinely appreciative of kindness shown to her; she was able to be relatively optimistic in the face of shoveling through tons of bullshit; she could laugh; she was very open in her pride of me." (33-year-old free-lance writer)

FEAR: "She was a strict disciplinarian and we had to adhere to her rules no matter what our friends were able to do or my father said."

RESPECT: "The way she maintained her dignity. She never felt anyone was better than she or her family. She gave us a good set of values and our sense of worth." (54-year-old budget officer—mother, deceased, would be 82)

FEAR: "That one day she might lose control and take out sixteen years of aggression on me that I might have caused."

RESPECT: "Her dedication to make sure her children get what they want and deserve and what she didn't have." (16-year-old student—mother, 40)

FEAR: "Because she used to beat the hell out of me and tried to kill me three times."

RESPECT: "Her honesty and the way she feels about me." (39-year-old hairdresser—mother, 57)

In addition to the responses that reflected fear of physical punishment, there were a number of responses that reflected fear of being manipulated and disapproved of. These responses occurred in only about ten cases.

FEAR: "My mother is always aware of what's happening for me. So I feel like I am constantly exposed, which in turn has created a tense relationship between us."

RESPECT: "Her strength to endure and provide for her children." (19-year-old student—mother, 40)

FEAR: "Don't want to disappoint her. I feel guilty if I let her down."

RESPECT: "Her love and desire for her children to succeed. Tremendous encouragement and support." (19-year-old student—mother, 56)

FEAR: "I don't want her to think I'm going to 'fuck up.' At the same time I fear letting that idea obsess me—with wanting to please her most."

RESPECT: "Her high standards she set for herself and her family. Her hard work (not to be cliché) and how she demanded and received respect from bosses, banks, etc. When she divorced my father and had to make a way for herself." (21-year-old student—mother, 44)

FEAR: "I really fear her when she is angry with me or when she is displeased with something I have done. When I haven't lived up to her expectations—this is a real issue for me."

RESPECT: "That she was able to bring my sister and myself up in a ghetto area where she felt isolated being Cape Verdean not knowing Blacks, she fit in. But also we did not stay in the ghetto, she got us out of that." (21-year-old student—mother, 50)

FEAR: "Mother knows all my weak points. Can manipulate me anytime or place she wishes."

RESPECT: "As a child, her knowledge about 'everything.' As an adult, her ability to always 'take care of self.'" (24-year-old secretary—mother, 50)

FEAR: "Disapproval and different opinions on major issues. Disliked strict authority throughout adolescence."

RESPECT: "Endurance, strength, capacity to love. Fearless attitude. Supportive to all family members." (30-year-old secretary—raised by grandmother)

FEAR: "Her disapproval was a fearful, hurting experience. Verbal disapproval was bad, but nonverbal worse."

RESPECT: "Her ability to dispense love, sympathy, and wisdom whenever and wherever needed. Not imposing her own sorrows and needs on others. The strength to put aside herself in order to give to others." (55-year-old woman, unemployed—mother, 77)

The coupling of the "fear" and "respect" responses reveals the mothers as being tough and tender. The daughters seemed to accept the "tough" behaviors as a necessary part of both the mother's personality and of the socialization process. Raising Black children, often as many as eight or nine, with the mother having the prime responsibilities, requires a unique set of characteristics, many of which seem incompatible. The mothers were resilient, devoted, and self-sacrificing; caring, hardworking, and taskmasters; loving, shrewd, honest, and aggressive; showed great wisdom and had tons of pride. They performed the functions of providing the socio-emotional support; they kept the family together in a relatively contented fashion, and at the same time they "cracked the whip." Bringing home the bacon and cracking the whip are basically incompatible with providing the emotional support needed to keep a group together in relative harmony and cooperation.

Historically males perform the tasks of engaging in transactions with the external environment (their workplaces) and bringing home the bacon, while females perform the tasks of providing for the internal socio-emotional needs of the family and individuals. The Black working mothers perform both tasks, fulfill both roles. The daughters point this phenomenon out when they say, "She hit us often, she was strict [cracking the whip] . . . but she really loved us and did for us . . . She was always around when we needed her [providing emotional support]." "When I came in late she would hit me with her shoe, other than that . . . She is a beautiful woman—a warmhearted woman." Now how many people can hit you with a shoe and still be regarded as beautiful and warmhearted? Another example of the dual roles played by mothers: "She was a strict authoritarian," but was respected for her ". . . endurance, strength, capacity to love, and supportiveness to all family members."

These comments are indicative of the fact that the mothers' aggressive and harsh behaviors were acknowledged and appreciated in light of their being carried out in the context of caring for the daughters (and other family members) and trying to instill the need to be prepared and to be able to cope within a society where choices for Black women are frequently between the dregs of the keg or the chaff from the wheat. There is a necessary quality of toughmindedness that goes with being a strict disciplinarian and this quality is frequently interpreted in Black women as tough, cold, harsh, and evil. The daughters were able to view their mothers' behaviors more analytically and place it in a more positive light. This is not to say that the daughters did not recognize shortcomings in their mothers' behavior, such as the absence of physical and verbal shows of affection. One-fifth of the daughters responded that what they "respected in their mothers the least" was the lack of demonstrative affection.

The reasons for the lack of shows of affection are multiple. Frequently there is little energy left after expending the physical energy needed to support the family financially (working on a job) and the psychic energy constantly expended protecting the family members from the emotional hardships of the society. Demonstrative affection ends up being a low priority item. Another explanation for the lack of overt affection is that daughters have been conditioned by their mothers and in many ways behave similarly—like mother, like daughter. We hear the expression "A chip off the old block" and of course it refers to fathers and sons, but it readily applies to females as well.

The fact that when the mother did not show much affection overtly, neither does the daughter is a cycle that must be broken in order for the Black female to experience more self-fulfillment and be freer in her emotional relationships with adults. Respondents were asked the question, "If, when, or as a mother (of a daughter), in what ways would you raise your child that are different from the way your mother raised you?" Interestingly enough, 44.7 percent said that they would be more open and accessible to their daughters and show more affection—so there is a positive trend.

Responses to the question, "What about your mother do you respect the least?" were as follows (they are listed by category):

24%   Nothing—i.e., there is nothing about their mothers that they have no respect for.

21.2% Lack of demonstrative show of affection/appreciation.

16.3% Too domineering.

12.5% Too submissive.

9.6%   Their mothers' attitude toward the "significant other" man in her life.

5.8%   Incompetence.

4.8%   Overprotective.

5.8%   Other. This category included no response, nonscorable responses, and comments such as "She favored my brother," "Her addiction to gambling—horse betting," and "Her conservativeness."

The younger respondents were more likely to find their mothers "too domineering" and those in the twenty-five to thirty-five age range found their mothers "too submissive."

A closer look at the ways in which the daughters least respected their mothers revealed one significant trend when age, occupation, and regional variables were considered. The age and occupational variables showed a scattering of responses throughout all the categories. It was the regional variation that showed a significant trend. The Caribbean women (those women whose parent[s] were from the West Indies and who were born either there or in the United States) less than any other group responded that their mothers were too submissive. Also, more women from this group than from any other showed lack of respect for their mothers' attitude toward the "significant other" male. They expressed a dislike for the fact that their mothers allowed these men to "hang around." The more marked double standard for men and women that exists in the Caribbean, as compared to the United States, would account in part for this response from the Caribbean women who now live in the United States. The women from the rural South scored lowest in this category.

The women from the urban North were least likely to indicate that their mothers were too dominant. This group saw their mothers as being submissive and lacking in affection. Northern urban life is especially hard on Black family life. There is less of the traditional family structure that has been pertinent to Black family life and less incidence of a domineering mother. The southern urban women were the least likely to say that their mothers were not affectionate. They were most likely to say that there was "nothing" that they respected least about their mothers. The daughters from the urban South were least critical of their mothers and saw them as warm and loving to a greater extent than women from other regions.

The warm affection found in the relationships of mothers and daughters from the South corresponds with the findings reported in an *Ebony* magazine article in January 1979. The article, entitled "Northern Black Women, Southern Black Women—How Different Are They?" was based on a survey conducted among 25 persons— male and female, southern and northern. They were asked their impressions of northern Black women and southern Black women.

The article begins by saying that the northern Black woman ". . . is well known for her sophistication and manners, her interest in art and culture and her taste in clothing." It must be assumed that reference is being made to the middle- and upper-class Black northern women, because the inner-city welfare mother existing on an income below the poverty level certainly is not known by that description.

The article goes on to describe the northern Black woman as cold, callous, and skeptical. "Men say she is standoffish and harder to get to know and other women view her as unfriendly." On the other hand, the southern Black woman has ". . . charm and grace and friendliness . . . likely to overwhelm you."

The response from the 25 subjects contained statements verifying the impression that southern women were more open, warm, and easy to get along with. Northern women, on the other hand, were considered to be more calculating and less open. The data showed that southern women, rural and urban, did express the greatest amount of affection and warmth in the mother/daughter relationship.

In responding to our questionnaire, the daughters whose mothers were blue-collar workers and teachers felt that their mothers were too submissive. The daughters of women who were unskilled workers felt that their mothers did not show enough affection; such feelings were less evident among daughters of mothers who were higher up on the economic scale.

Other trends in the data disclosed were: the daughters whose mothers were professional found them to be "too domineering." Black professional females *have* to be assertive to attain their professional goals and this quality may be what the daughters are reacting to and labeling as domineering.

The data analysis, in addition to revealing information about the daughters' attitudes toward mothers, disclosed important messages that the mothers gave to their daughters. The daughters' interpretations of their mothers' behaviors are an indication of the content and intensity of the messages that mothers gave to daughters.

Literature and formal and informal discussion on Black families often stresses the importance of and gives explanations for the ways in which Black mothers raise and socialize their sons. A major reason given for why the mothers stress survival skills in raising their sons is to protect them from White society, which has historically targeted Black men for brutalization, incarceration, lynching, scapegoating, and dehumanization. Since it is the male who will be dealing with the external world more so than the female (due to institutionalized sexism as well as the influence of Black culture), Black males are taught specific survival skills. Males in general have more freedom to move away from the home, the block, the community for social and occupational/employment reasons. They have to be taught "safe" ways of dealing with the White community.

"See but don't see; be aware of what is going on around you, but don't leer, especially at White women; know, but don't tell all," are some of the lessons that must be learned by Black youth as part of their repertoire of survival skills. Black mothers know very well the consequences of being Black in America. As indicated in *Urban Research Review*, Spring 1979, the Black child, the Black family, and the Black community have historically been subject to negative labels and stereotypes, which symbolize their powerlessness and the victimized status they hold in the society. The relationship between the larger White society and the Black community is a reflection of this unequal power relationship, a relationship in which members of the Black community have learned to play roles that enable them to survive yet maintain their dignity, self-respect, and culture. Since Black males are designated as the ones who will interact with the larger White society to a greater extent than the females, they have had to develop highly adaptive mechanisms designed to ensure physical and mental survival in the broader American society. It has been no easy task and the statistics on Black male deaths, incarceration, school dropouts, drug addiction, alcoholism, suicide, homicide, and intermittent desertion of family and children attests to the hardships involved in trying to survive. It can be readily seen why Black males have to be carefully taught what is and isn't "allowed" for survival.

What is not so well researched and discussed is the parallel phenomenon of teaching survival skills to Black females. What was startlingly evident, as revealed in the mother/daughter questionnaire, was the teaching of survival skills to females for their survival *in* and for the survival *of* the Black community. Intra-group survival skills were given more importance and credence than survival skills for dealing with the White society at large. There is a tremendous amount of teaching transmitted by Black mothers to their daughters that enables them to survive, exist, succeed, and be important to and for the Black communities throughout America. Black daughters are actually "taught" to hold the Black community together. These attitudes become internalized and are transmitted to future generations. The skills and behaviors and values that the mothers instill are those that are necessary for that purpose; these skills and behaviors are in fact being practiced in Black communities and families today. The courage, strength, concern, care, mothering, perseverance, and sacrifices that were mentioned by the daughters as characteristics that they respected in their mothers are learned in due time—"adopted" —by the daughters. One way that Black mothers teach their daughters about life is through oft-repeated comments such as: "Be independent and as financially independent as you possibly can"; "Get an education"; "Have self-respect or no one else will respect you"; "Don't trust any man"; "It takes two to make a marriage successful." The daughters heed their mothers' teachings, as is shown in their responses to the question, "The best way to 'get ahead' (be successful in terms of security, home, job) is to: (write in your response)." The daughters' answers fell into the following categories:

44.8% "Your own efforts."

21.8% "Education plus your own efforts."

20.9% "Education."

6.4% A rejection of traditional aspirations.

5.5% Divergence from the Protestant ethic. A desire to get ahead, but not through working.

3.6% Other.

87.5 percent of the daughters felt that the best way to get ahead was through their own efforts, or through education, or using both in combination.

The vast majority of Black women are working women who are not on welfare. In addition, many of those who are on welfare work in spite of the unrealistic welfare regulations. A look at the pattern of labor force participation shows that Black women, regardless of a metropolitan or non-metropolitan residence, show a similar pattern to males (Black and White). The rate of participation increases steadily into the prime working ages (35 to 44) and declines thereafter. This pattern among Black women probably reflects a greater economic need for employment, a larger proportion of single-parent, female-headed households, and the availability of familial assistance for childcare.[7] The expected pattern of labor force participation is high among young women, declines during early adulthood (when marriage and childbearing are most common), and increases again after age 34 when most children have reached school age. When we look at the types of occupations participated in by Black women the reality of the situation is that, compared to White women, Black women are locked into blue-collar jobs. The blue-collar service occupations include private household, hotel, and motel cleaning and laundering workers, beauticians and barbers, shoemakers, and dressmakers. More Black women than Black men are found employed in households, as cleaning women, as laundry workers, and as beauticians and dressmakers. These occupations are not known for their ability to bring one in contact with varied levels of society.

The Black community has profited from the work ethic and independence of Black women. Historically, education has been the most popular professional field among Black women. Nursing and social work were also high on the ladder of prestigious professional occupations for Black women. These professions were initially encouraged because segregation laws and later gerrymandering tactics assured the country of segregated Black areas. Black students and patients had to be served, so Black schools and hospitals had to be staffed. The nurturing and caring continued.

Being a domestic was the most popular nonprofessional work among Black females prior to World War II, at which time factory jobs opened up to Black women (in defense plants). But caring for the household and children of others is still very much a domestic affair as opposed to a foreign exposure. Being a domestic in the White House gets you a wide exposure to very fancy and very expensive pots and pans and cutlery, linens, wines, and poor little doves' breasts under unnecessarily imported glass—but it doesn't get you to faraway places or even to Wall Street.

The education that enhances the independence of the Black woman both aids her marriage and often results in fracturing it. While her job helps to provide financial support for her family and her independent spirit helps her through periods when there is an absence of emotional support from husband or children, these same factors unfortunately may serve to threaten the husband.

One might speculate that younger women would respond differently than older women in relation to family dynamics, but this is not the case. Many of these younger women contribute to the support of their mothers, brothers, or sisters, and frequently the younger women who are unmarried provide the main support for their children.

In discussing the transmission of messages from mother to daughter, it is important to mention that mannerisms of the mother are also a part of the message. These mannerisms are learned through latent learning or "vibration" learning, i.e., a person absorbing (learning) skills and information without being given a formal verbal lesson and without even being consciously aware that learning is taking place. The constant exposure to a mother's mannerisms or behaviors —be it cooking or sulking or braiding hair—can result in a lesson being learned. The meanings and interpretations associated with these mannerisms and behaviors are composed of a style and nonverbal language transmitted from mother to daughter in very subtle yet complex manners. These behaviors include: the glance, the smirk, the shifting of a posture, nuances and gestures, as well as cooking secrets, housekeeping tricks, acting satisfied when you're not and vice versa (depending on *his* mood), and keeping baby healthy and happy without the aid of a "how to" book. All of these are part of the culture and learning process of the Black female.

This does not mean that all Black women have the same mannerisms or that other cultures—Appalachian poor Whites, midwestern Bible Belt believers, California counterculturists, Scarsdale uppityuppers—do not have comparable behaviors that have been passed on. The uniqueness for Black women lies in the style and interpretation of these behaviors that have their genesis in a Black culture. These behaviors have helped Black women survive and keep home and community together to the extent that they are today. They are personal survival skills and mechanisms. For example, sometimes you laugh to keep from crying and other times you laugh to keep from dying. Humor and laughter are very important survival skills of Black women. A Black woman learns to say "baby" with at least nine different intonations or inflections and each one carries a different message. It can intone camaraderie, patience, affection, love, sarcasm, compassion, empathy, derogation, or flirtation. Black women learn—from female to female—to take complaints, criticisms, and contrariness from many sources. When asked, "Why do you take so much shit?" or "Why do you stand for that?" how often do they say, "It's so you and others can survive?" They are also asked, "Why do you always act so evil?" or "How come you're so moody or sometimesy?" When one doesn't have space or a room of one's own, a free or quiet fifteen minutes is very precious; when this is interrupted, the intruder may not be received with the usual openness. The ways of dealing with trying situations that are passed from Black mother to daughter are an extremely important part of the Black mother/daughter relationship. Much of this transmission of ways to cope takes place through latent learning.

The effects of the socialization of Black females, which relegates them to internal affairs, was illustrated during the Civil Rights Movement of the Sixties. During this time, Black women were very active on a local level and assumed positions of leadership within this sphere. However, when the situation called for face-to-face encounters with White society, it was the men in the groups who were called upon. It was literally a man-to-man confrontation or discussion. Now and again a female might be included, but the general pattern was one that put men in the forefront when activities outside the community were concerned. It should be mentioned that during the active period of the Civil Rights Movement, it was a conscious and willing decision on the part of women as well as men to send the men forth. This phenomenon of Black male leadership was also common on the college campuses. Rarely was there a female president or head of any of the numerous Black student organizations that were popularly called by such titles as the Afro-American Society or the Black Student's Alliance. These organizations were formed to develop Black consciousness, to encourage a feeling of solidarity among Black students, and to represent a legitimate power base for confronting college administrations with their concerns as Black students. Female students consistently played strategic roles in the organization, but the males dominated the top of the lists of officers.

The most prominent and popular Black leaders during the Sixties were men: Martin Luther King, Malcolm X, Stokely Carmichael, Ralph Brown, Floyd McKissick, Bayard Rustin, James Forman, James Farmer, and Eldridge Cleaver. Comparatively speaking, even strategic Black women leaders of that time—Fannie Lou Hamer, Gloria Richardson, Daisy Bates, Rosa Parks, Ella Baker, and Lorraine Hansberry, who was as much a political progressive as she was a playwright—never obtained the popularity or status given to the Black male leaders.

The supportive roles that women played in the movement paralleled the roles of many mothers in the family. They offered emotional and spiritual comfort and support to members of organizations and groups; they performed duties of a secretarial nature, and grass-roots campaigning. They offered nurturance in the form of procuring, preparing, and serving victuals and they provided the leadership with ideas, strategies, and tactics. The point being made is that men were the ones chosen to deal with the external society and women performed much of the groundwork in preparation for the efforts of these men. (Even when Black women started complaining about their roles in the Civil Rights Movement organizations, their complaints were directed mainly at their roles *within* the groups themselves.)

Black women have become so conditioned and accustomed to operating within the confines of the Black community that when global issues arise that concern them directly, there is still a residual reluctance to interact with the larger world even on issues critical to

their well-being. The attitudes of Black women toward the current
feminist movement exemplify this phenomenon. Part of the Black
women's reticence and reluctance to become active in the feminist
movement can be traced to the fact that they have not been
sufficiently prepared or programmed to deal with the outside world, a
world in which they have a large stake, and yet hardly any say. The
greater American society systematically and historically has ignored
Black women's condition.

On the occasions when Black women interact directly with the
larger White society, the welfare of the Black family and community
are held as priorities. The case of rape in American society is an example. When a Black woman reports a crime of rape by a Black man
(and more than 90 percent of rapes are in*tra*-racial), it often results
in a worsened situation for the Black community. The unfair and
brutal treatment and sentences given Black men deter many a Black
woman from reporting the crime. Reported cases are usually handled
by the police with indifference or rudely or facetiously dismissed. As
such, Black women frequently allow the problem to remain within
the Black community. When Blacks refer to an issue or incident as a
"family affair," it stems from their nonreliance on society to deal with
them justly and adequately. (The term "family affair," when used by
White police, social workers, or law enforcement officials more often
stems from racist and sexist attitudes, fear, ignorance, and laziness.)

In the arena of politics (government), the Black male vs. female
count is again indicative of Black women sticking closer to home and
remaining at a distance from national affairs. The Honorable Shirley
Chisholm is an exception. Patricia Roberts Harris, Secretary of the
Department of Health and Human Services, is representative of
the token Black women in public office. The outspoken, unbossed
woman, White or Black, does not last long in top government positions; this is confirmed by the abrupt departures of Bella Abzug,
Midge Costanza, and Dr. Carolyn Payton, the Black former Peace
Corps director. Lillian Roberts, although not a government official,
is another exception. She is the associate director of the nation's
largest municipal union, the 108,000-member District Council 37 of
the American Federation of State, County, and Municipal Employees.

A young high-school-age Black woman who is destined to move
out in the larger world and experience an international education is
Karen Stevenson, the first Black female Rhodes Scholar. She owes

her success to her mother, a divorcée who moved from Texas to Washington, D.C., with her two daughters in the early Sixties.

Upon examination, both Lillian Roberts' and Mrs. Stevenson's lives show that they were not spared any of the typical conditions faced by Black women in America. Both were divorcées, the extended family played a prominent role in their lives, and hard work, education, and being independent figured predominantly in their lives.

The discussion of Black women's involvement with and influence on Black communities does not mean that Black men have not participated in key roles and issues in Black family life and the community. Black men are recognized for their leadership qualities on both local and national levels. Black men, too, work hard—very hard —many of them holding down two jobs, and they represent a reservoir of support for the Black American population against the cold vindictiveness of too many Whites. However, this article is about Black women—an analysis of their roles in this society—and certainly the brothers want their beautiful sisters to receive some long overdue positive recognition.

The final theme of this discussion of the implications of the socialization processes among Black mothers and daughters concerns that ever-enticing institution of marriage. Black women follow a formula which ensures their centrality in the Black world. A breakdown of the formula reads: Black *society* (A) needs a Black *community* (B) which requires Black *families* (C) which involves *parents* (D) which implies *marriage* (E) which means *woman* (F) becomes legal partner to *man* (G). Women have been faithfully following this formula for generations, with variations on (E). Meanwhile (G), man, has been relying on (C), neglecting his role in (D) and in and out of (E).

The majority of Black mothers see men as: abusive, no good, and unreliable; but the same mothers also assume and accept as a given that their daughters will marry these men. These two facts are seemingly incompatible. Logically a person would steer away from a nogood, unreliable person. In a very graphic and dramatic fashion, this "logic" is defied in the mothers' messages to their daughters.

The question was asked: "What stands out in your mind most clearly with regard to what your mother told you about men?" The categorical results were:

1) Abusive comments about men; warnings of the potential of being abused by them: 43.9%
2) Men are unreliable, undependable; ways to avoid dependency on them: 33.1%
3) A few good ones: 5.5%
4) Other: 17.5%

Examples of the first category, "Abusive comments about men" (43.9%):

"They're dogs. Always in heat, move from one woman to another without a thought in their minds." (age 19)

"Every man has some dog in him." (age 20)

"Never allow yourself to be used." (age 20)

"He who lies with dogs shall rise with fleas." (age 20)

"They are all no good and they are only after you for what you have to offer them sexually." (age 21)

"Men are no good." (age 21)

"My mother told me that men 'won't buy the cow if they can get the milk for free.' I guess that says more about my mother than about men." (age 22)

"All men are degenerate animals." (age 26)

"That they were no good and you should always be ten steps ahead of them." (age 27)

"Most men are dogs." (age 28)

"That all men are the same and they will try to use you if they can." (age 29)

"All men are dogs." (age 30)

"She used to say that all men are dogs, and that 'You can't depend on them. You have to rely on self.'" (age 33)

"That they were no good. They love to leave you alone." (age 39)

"They are no good." (age 41)

"That they are no good." (age 47)

"All men are dogs." (age 48)

Examples of the second category, "Ways to avoid depending on unreliable men" (33.1%):

"Never become totally dependent on them." (age 19)

"Not to trust them." (age 20)

"Never depend totally upon a man." (age 20)

"They get you into trouble." (age 21)

"That they were undependable." (age 26)

"Not to put all your faith in them." (age 30)

"Do not rely upon them." (age 34)

"Don't be totally dependent upon them." (age 34)

"Do not trust any man. Not even your brothers." (age 35)

"She said never depend on a man to support you." (age 35)

"Don't trust them too far." (age 38)

"Don't trust them." (age 39)

"That you couldn't rely on them to satisfy your needs or fulfill their responsibility." (age 48)

"Always be sure you could take care of yourself and without the husband's knowledge, have money on the side for yourself. Really to be sort of independent and keep your own identity." (age 54)

"They are not to be trusted." (age 54)

"Be very careful of them. You can't trust them. Most of them will use you and not really care if they hurt you. Save yourself for the man you marry." (age 55)

"Don't trust them." (age 74)

Examples of the third category, "A few good ones" (5.5%):

"A good one is hard to find and my grandfather was one in a million, we both thought so." (age 40)

"Although many of them like to chase women, drink, and gamble,

you can find a man to respect you by the way you carry yourself."
(age 42)

"Try to find a good one." (age 45)

"Some are good, honest, and loving." (age 50)

Examples of the fourth category, "Other" (17.5%): (This category
contained a variety of responses unsuitable for the three preceding
categories.)

"There aren't too many in a class of their own with ideas of their
own." (age 16)

"Don't just lay up with any and everybody. Don't go off with strange
men." (age 16)

"Black men are not willing to admit they're weak." (age 21)

"Three-way tie. 1) Sidney Poitier is handsome. 2) It's just as easy
to marry a rich man as a poor man. 3) Don't depend on any man
to support you—get your own show together." (age 21)

"That they are very different from women in thinking, and a woman
has to take the bitter with the sweet." (age 21)

"Men are just tall little boys. Meaning, they are happy when their
stomach is full and they have some 'mommy' to look after them."
(age 21)

"Don't give yourself to anybody unless you love them enough to
have their babies and to settle with them the rest of your life."
(age 21)

"The best way to keep a man is to let him go out and fool around
with his woman. As long as he brings the paycheck home to you
and don't get another woman pregnant let him have his fling."
(age 22)

"Not to get pregnant until I was able to handle the responsibility of
raising a child." (age 23)

"That Black men needed to be listened to and supported. That
Black men and women need to begin to deal with issues that
create tension due to the hostile environment." (age 25)

"That relationships are not about competition, but about cooperat-
ing and pulling together." (age 26)

"No man is perfect so find one that you can relate to most easiest and help him to feel confident in himself." (age 27)

"Black men are often negated in society and Black women need to understand this and not buy into negating her man further. She was always very supportive of my father." (age 27)

"You can't tell them everything; they can't handle it." (age 31)

"The fact that I might be too supportive and show him too much concern, and that I would be taken advantage of in the affair." (age 32)

"If you want to leave one be sure to always take your children with you." (age 32)

"All men have their faults, like women, and you'll never find a perfect man. Try to find one who'll love you and your children more than anyone else." (age 33)

"That one day a very special man would show up and I would know him immediately (I did)." (age 39)

"They were immature and incapable of seeing women as equals." (age 46)

This question was followed by: "What stands out most clearly in your mind as to what your mother told you about marriage?"

Category 1:   Responses with an explicit or an underlying assumption favoring marriage. This category was subdivided into four groupings:

1)	Not to marry at too early an age	17.6%
2)	Encouraged marriage without qualifications	9.6%
3)	Marry but maintain independence	5.6%
4)	Don't have sex before marriage	3.7%

These four groupings accounted for the 36.5% of the responses that fell into the first category.

Category 2:	It takes mutual effort to make a marriage work.	30.6%
Category 3:	Discouraged marriage.	10.2%
Category 4:	Other.	22.7%

The style and choice of words used by the mothers in encouraging their daughters to marry reads like a "Philosopher's Almanac on Marriage." The sayings are witty, philosophical, folksy, on target, religious, and moralistic. Samples of responses from each category follow:

Examples of encouragement (36.5%):

"Don't marry at an early age." (age 16)

"Everyone in the *world* should get married and have children. Marriage is fulfillment." (age 19)

"Marriage is needed for the raising of children." (age 20)

"Always maintain your personal financial stash—don't give up everything." (age 21)

"It's important to be married in order to have children." (age 21)

"Be sure, don't rush, you've time." (age 21)

"Get married as opposed to living together because she feels that the woman had the most to lose in the long run if the living-in arrangement fails." (age 21)

"Marriage is an *important* step in life. It shouldn't be rushed; but it is a natural *must*." (age 21)

"Look before you leap." (age 21)

"My mother is divorced, so she never really gave me much info/advice about marriage. She sort of wishes I wouldn't marry a poor man though, and she is also worried about me entering into an interracial marriage." (age 21)

"Wait until you are ready, the men these days are not worth it." (age 22)

"Don't rush it—there is plenty of time." (age 22)

"Make sure you have two irons in the fire because you will never know when the man's going to walk out on you." (age 22)

"Look out for #1. Make sure your husband works with you and not for himself. Also share the responsibility of the children (if any) and sharing in housework, paying bills, etc." (age 22)

"We never really sat down and discussed marriage. However, she did give (through actions) advice:
  1) Keep a separate (unknown to husband) bank account.
  2) Look pretty at all times." (age 24)

"It should be forever or close to it." (age 28)

"Marriage is secondary to happiness. Live life and experience many things prior to marriage." (age 32)

"Do it." (age 34)

"Do what your husband wants you to do." (age 42)

"There were many hard times for her and my Dad, but overall they had found a lot of happiness. She could only wish the same balance for me." (age 42)

"You must stand by and stick to the man you marry. So don't marry in haste and repent in leisure." (age 55)

Examples of mutual effort (30.6%):

"Marriage requires both work and open communication by both partners." (age 21)

"That it isn't always wine and roses, it takes a lot of giving and taking. Only the strong survive." (age 21)

"Work to make it last, understand that it is a two-way road—you have to give as well as take." (age 22)

"That in marriage you always have to give up something." (age 22)

"You must put in your best to get the best in return." (age 23)

"It is beautiful—however it takes two people to make a marriage. Also one of the most important factors is *trust* between the two parties." (age 25)

"It takes two people to make a marriage work. Both partners have to make it work." (age 26)

"Learn how to deal with the 'ups' and 'downs' of life and let neither of them control you." (age 27)

"It's a two-way street." (age 38)

"It takes two to argue, love, and make a successful marriage. You cannot 'like' someone all the time even though you love them." (age 39)

"It's like a job. Both will have to work hard at it." (age 50)

Examples of discouraging marriage (10.2%):

"Don't." (age 20)

"My mother told me not to get married." (age 32)

"Avoid it." (age 34)

"Don't do it." (age 75)

Examples of other responses (22.7%):

"Don't get married until you get your career, and don't marry a man you don't love." (age 19)

"First marriage, marry a man for love; second marriage, marry for love of money." (age 20)

"It is not the assurance of happiness." (age 20)

"Don't marry because of a baby because you could be miserable the rest of your life. Don't have a trial marriage, the test will go on until the man gets tired of you and wants to test someone else. 'Why buy the cow if you can get the milk free.'" (age 21)

"Don't get hooked if you can take care of yourself, and if you do, he'd *better* have something to offer." (age 21)

"I mentioned it. She told me she didn't expect me to have a traditional type of monogamous hook-up. She expected me to be assertive with my ideas about the oppressive nature of 'marriage.' We couldn't really agree or need to agree about what marriage should be." (age 21)

"That the road to 'success,' if it lay outside the 'traditional' roles of Blacks and of females, would be a bumpy one for me as a Black woman, but I should not let that hamper me—just realize it and strive on." (age 21)

"Nothing." (age 21)

"Have your own money and keep a separate bank account." (age 21)

"It's a woman that makes the marriage work! And it's *true!*" (age 23)

"It's a rigid institution (imprisonment)." (age 23)

"It's hard work to keep a marriage together—both partners have to work at making it work—but it's well worth it. If she had to do it over again she would and she'd still marry Dad." (age 27)

"My mother's conservative nature prevented her from really rapping to me about the nature of men, marriage, life, etc." (age 29)

"She said to put it off as long as possible. It is probably better to remain single." (age 31)

"Put a pillow under my behind and take a towel to bed with me. (I wonder if she meant a crying towel?)" (age 33)

"It's bad to have sex if you're not legally married." (age 34)

"That I should not have gotten married to that no-good man." (age 38)

"No matter how angry you are with your husband always have his meals cooked." (age 39)

"Make sure what you want and it's for love or it will be unbearable and even then it will have its ups and downs." (age 40)

"It's a hard/necessary evil for mankind." (age 46)

"At best marriage is difficult. But if you love your husband, it makes marriage endurable. Therefore, love is the most important thing." (age 48)

"You make your bed and you have to lie in it." (age 48)

"Marriage was to offer some kind of security and protection—sort of to legalize sex and keep you from going with numerous men." (age 54)

"Nothing." (age 63)

There are several noteworthy findings revealed in the data concerning messages about men and marriage. The age variable made no difference whatsoever in the types of messages about men. Similar attitudes were expressed by women ages 16 to 75. The younger daughters (16 to 22) more often than any other age group were advised "not to marry too early." This leads to conclusions that mothers in the age 40 to 46 range gave more realistic and less romantic messages while advocating marriage. Mothers of daughters 31–35 encouraged marriage more than those in any other group. (Perhaps they were getting worried about their daughters' chances for marriage becoming slimmer and slimmer.)

When we look at the region variable we find some differences. The southern mothers accounted for the largest number of respondents in the first category (abusive or potentially abusive men). Mothers from the urban North were highest in the "men are unreliable" category. There were no noticeable distinctions among the respondents in the "be independent" category.

Looking at the class variable, the mother who was a blue-collar worker was not likely to say that men are abusive; discouraged marriage; and was least likely to say that marriage was a mutual effort. On the other hand, the professional women (including *all* of the teachers) were the least likely to discourage their daughters from marrying. Only one of the respondents mentioned marriage as a way to get ahead or be successful.

67.1 percent of mothers gave explicit or implicit messages favoring marriage, while 77.1 percent gave negative messages about men. The overwhelming majority of Black women link their existence as wife and mother with their adult intimacy with Black men. There is an acute awareness and sensitivity on the part of Black women to the problems associated with and encountered in the traditional monogamous marriage or in other marital living arrangements. The sensitively coded messages and advice given to the daughters reflect this knowledge; the daughters are given ample warning of the inevitable problems that lie in waiting. The seemingly incompatible messages about men and marriage are in actuality honest assessments of and realistic responses to an oppressive and restrictive society.

The following story, which is representative of a certain stratum of Black women, should be enlightening. Some years ago at a wedding reception, an unusually unenthusiastic, very attractive, once-jilted bridesmaid made the comment: "When the minister said, 'Do you take this man for better or for worse?' and Janice said, 'yes'—well, I just *know* that deep in her heart Janice *knew* it was for worse. She just *had* to know."

The bridesmaid was familiar with the problems that Janice and the groom, Jim, had been having and knew that it would be unrealistic to suppose that these problems would not continue. An analysis of the "better" and "worse" required an examination of Janice's present situation in society as a Black woman.

Even against this background of realistic appraisal, the ideologies of romantic love set the scene for marriage American style. Racism and classism enter the scene, subtly but definitely limiting and shaping the choices. Economic, moral, and status pressures converge upon the now vulnerable victim and jab away.

Within this setting, Janice (along with all the other Janices) contemplates: "Jim has a job, not too bad—works for a company, a small company that repairs heating units and air conditioners. He's qualified to do better, but racism keeps him out of the union. If he can't keep me in the clothes and things that I am used to, oh well, I have a good, steady job and can always buy my own things, and I'll keep *my own, private* bank account—sort of a nest egg. He may run around a little, but what man doesn't?

"He seldom gets angry with me—doesn't discuss many things— hardly anything, come to think of it, but he never hit me. And when I'm out with him he shows me a lot of respect. He's a good dancer and real good in bed. He spends a lot of time watching sports on TV or playing cards with his friends, but he's not a real heavy gambler.

"At age 28 I can't say that I'm *rushing into marriage.* I just hope his first wife doesn't hassle him too much for that damn child support. What else is out there for me? Single life is just not for me. I want children—a family! And it's for sure I'm not going to consider low-life, pervert white boys! Jim is way above any of those power-hungry, sex-starved-because-the-white-women-so-cute-they-can't-get-down, antiseptic, hypocritical vultures! No way, none of that, for me —ever!

"So, like Mom said, Jim may be *irresponsible, chase other women* a little, but it *takes two to make a marriage work,* and *requires trust and open communication and some give and take.* All in all, he's a better-than-average risk."

Janice's case is representative of a daughter who is marching to the beat of the messages given to her by Mom and at the same time feeling the effects of how racial oppression forces Black men into precarious economic and social conditions. The outstanding messages that mothers gave to daughters, as indicated in the survey, were incorporated into the thoughts attributed to Janice regarding her marriage to Jim. (Notice the italicized words.) Janice had been prepared to cope with the realities that have existed in the lives of Black women for generation upon generation.

Other Black women have wedding ceremonies and "happily ever after" experiences that differ from Janice's. Some Black women have gala extravaganza weddings; their husbands may be groomed for financial success, having attended a college and having the right contacts. At the other end of the spectrum we have the fifteen-minute justice-of-the-peace ritual with one member of the wedding temporarily unemployed and the other scuffling and barely making it with odds-and-ends jobs. There are also endless numbers of marriages, formerly called shotgun marriages, necessitated by impending parenthood. Marriage represents various goals for the women, some short-range, but all their goals are products of their personal and societal realities.

In summation, what are the realities for Black women and what is the changing nature of these realities? To begin, the Black woman's socialization processes have determined: (1) her defining herself, her existence, in relationship to Black men (2) while simultaneously seeing herself as an independent being. This duality may seem incongruous, but only if "womanhood" in Black mothers and daughters is compared to White patterns of "womanhood," marriage, and relationships with men. In *To Define Black Womanhood*, Jualynne Dodson cites Hortense Powdermaker's investigation of Black women's motives for choosing a mate, which adds some historical continuity to the discussion: "The white pattern regards love and economic interest as mutually incompatible. This disassociation is not in force for Negro women . . . possibly it is never so strong with women who are self-supporting."[8]

The mothers' advice to daughters to be independent was concretized in two ways. One, they were told to "get an education" and this in turn helped them to become economically independent. Secondly, the daughters experienced seeing their mothers have a life outside of the home (working). (Working outside of the home does not conflict with the previously stated facts about Black females' socialization being more directed to the internal than the external world. Sexism plays a major role in keeping Black working women in kinds of employment that do not include involvement in decision-making and strategy development that shape the society.) At the same time, Black daughters, while growing up, see males in the home being shown concern and granted privileges. The male is a definite part of their lives, whether they are in the home 90 percent of the time, 50 percent or 20 percent.

A second reality is that the world of the Black woman is fraught with oppressive conditions. The racism, sexism, and classism that she faces daily compel her to seek solutions, to cope, to do for self, to use her wit, her intellect, her charm, and to gather support from other women as she strategizes for survival.

The contemporary Black woman is faced with the challenge of having to adapt to a reality that makes it exceedingly difficult for her to break ties with the previously mentioned well-established socialization behaviors. The acute shortage of Black males (which will be discussed at length in the following chapter) necessitates new strategies for the Black woman. The development of a new Black woman's consciousness is also affecting the modes and styles of the contemporary Black woman. This consciousness is being reflected in the writings of Black feminists, the emergence of various Black women's organizations and groups that have a stated purpose of trying to assess and deal with problems faced by today's Black woman, and in the messages that the generation of mothers in their early forties are giving to their daughters about delaying marriage. The challenge for Black mothers is not to cease to socialize their daughters to be independent and to have concern for Black males, but to enable their daughters to live an emotionally and sexually fulfilled life and to maintain good mental health in the process. The challenge to the daughters is to develop new strides in keeping with the present reality without unwittingly or recklessly abandoning the basic human values of caring and nurturing, which are needed for the cohesiveness of Black culture and the maintenance of Black families. This is no small task given the complexity of our current society and given the political and social disposition of the contemporary Black male—but if anyone can succeed at this task, it will be Black mothers and daughters in concert.

Addendum: Comments on Questionnaires Administered to White Women

In the process of administering the questionnaires, some White women were included. Due to the small number of respondents, it was not possible to conduct a comparative study between the White subjects and the Black ones. However, it was possible to recognize some distinct trends within the White sample population that, upon inspection, appeared to be significantly different than the responses from the Black sample population.

In response to the question on respect for mothers, in general the comments from the White women were much briefer. As for the content, there was a definite accent on the mother's personal traits. Characteristics that the daughters admired in their mothers—for example, "her creativity and talents," "her evenness," "her intellect and organization"—were listed simply as traits that were possessed by the individual; they were not described as being extended for the benefit of others. These comments, compared to Black subjects' responses, show that the same characteristics were mentioned, but they were not mentioned in terms of the mother using these characteristics for the benefit of the daughter and other children or people. Contrasting examples of responses from Black daughters are: "her creativity and talents in keeping her family together in spite of the difficulties she had to face"; "her intelligence and organization in managing a household without the support she should have had from her husband."

The comments on men from the White mothers were descriptively less graphic and were more specific in terms of advising their daughters what to look for in men. The Black mothers were far more direct and overall gave more negative comments. Messages about marriage also showed some observable differences. There was more romanticism in the messages from the White mothers. "Marry for love" was a popular response. The ways in which the White daughters said they feared their mothers disclosed an area that was rarely, if ever, mentioned by the Black daughters. The response was, "I fear I might be like her. I want to be independent of her."

An interesting observation concerning the responses of the White women was that the class variable appeared to make a significant difference in responses about men and marriage. The working-class women (mothers) gave responses that were more similar to the Black mothers' responses.

Within the White subject groups, with regard to the respect question, the response from lesbians was distinct from the non-lesbians' answers. The respect the lesbians had for their mothers tended to be based on her having "endured" intolerable situations or having put up with a lot of oppressive conditions. In other words, they respected her not for her initiative or for admirable traits, but for surviving despite the victimization she suffered as a woman. Among the other responses, there was no significant difference between the lesbian and non-lesbian women.

As was mentioned initially, the sample of White women in the study was small, so these comments have to be viewed as speculative. The trends mentioned, however, were unmistakably present.

NOTES

1. Adrienne Rich, *Of Woman Born*. New York: W. W. Norton, 1976, p. 253.

2. Carolyn M. Rodgers, "IT IS DEEP," *how i got ovah*. New York: Doubleday & Company, 1969, p. 11.

3. Sara Lawrence Lightfoot, *Worlds Apart*. New York: Basic Books, 1978, p. 158.

4. Joyce Ladner, "Labeling Black Children: Some Mental Health Implications," *Urban Research Review*, Howard University Institute for Urban Affairs and Research Publication, Vol. 5, No. 3, Spring 1979, p. 3.

5. John Henrik Clarke, *Black Women*, unpublished collection of articles.

6. Ladner, op. cit., p. 5.

7. David L. Brown and Jeanne M. O'Leary, *Labor Force Activity of Women in Metropolitan and Nonmetropolitan America*, United States Department of Agriculture, Economics, Statistics, and Cooperatives Service, Rural Development Research Report No. 15, Washington, D.C., September 1979, p. 12.

8. Jualynne Dodson, "To Define Black Womanhood: A Study of Black Female Graduate Students," an occasional paper, The Institute of the Black World, Atlanta, Georgia, p. 8.

IV

Mothers, Daughters, and Feminism

". . . Intransigent in [our] own fierce survival[s]"
—Robin Morgan

The process of working with Gloria on this book over several years has been endlessly revealing as it has highlighted acutely for us the different histories and cultures that sustain our consciousness in specifically racial terms. So many things I assumed and had never thought to actually articulate had eventually to be spelled out to her and thus to myself. The collaboration exposed each of us to arguments, perspectives, and the struggles of women of our different constituencies. The stakes involved have been slowly coming clear to each of us: the gradual development of an understanding of what is not generally evident in the dialogue of Black women and White women. Each of us needs to engage in such an explosive dislocation of the taken-for-granted vision that each of us, and the political arena we relate to, have been shaped by, if the most basic understandings are to become clear.

The understanding of mother-daughter relationships has emerged as pivotal to the understanding of each other's history and the political incentives those histories have generated. My momentum in writing about it here comes from two simultaneous sources. First, I am aware of the need to engage with Black women in the discussion of all the different levels of the formative ground from which White feminist struggle emerges. This involves keeping in mind three specific attitudes/ideas that Black women often articulate: that "women's libbers" are dissatisfied housewives who should recognize their privileged position as such, and know when they've got it good; their disbelief and even contempt when White women, in the privileges racism concedes to them, talk of powerlessness, lack of confidence, loss of identity; the odd contrast of the Black woman's respect and admiration for her mother, and what she stands for, with the curious refrain among White women of *fear of becoming* like their mothers. I want to talk here about the family and its terms of existence in the heritage that White women of today are passing on, and about the painful irreconcilables of that heritage which are enacted between mothers and daughters in today's society. This necessitates questioning what the terms of family existence have been, what it has meant/means in the heritage of White women "to become a mother" and what it has meant/means "to become a daughter" to a mother in a society that has structured systematic male dominance and female oppression into its economic, legal, cultural, and psychological organization.

The second, simultaneous stimulus in doing this is my personal need to bring together my own political journey in the women's movement through the questions and explorations White feminists are engaging in now—my own need to confront the political implications of new perceptions and challenges over the last few years. I could not have begun to think about these without the demanding words and ideas spoken and published over the last five years by Nancy Chodorow, Tillie Olsen, Jane Flax, Margaret Cerullo, Nina Payne, Adrienne Rich, Robin Morgan, Ann Oakley and other feminists who in their various ways have opened up radically new and important ways of understanding the institution of motherhood and the social construction of gender—the real germs of the experience of motherhood in contrast to the images projected around it.

> *the daughters and the mothers*
> *in the kingdom of the son*
>
> Adrienne Rich
> "Sibling Mysteries"

Black experience bears powerful witness to the fact that family, community, and kinship networks are vital arenas of political survival and cultural resistance. In White women's histories the family has also been a key site of political formation.[1] The terms of the marriage contract, the relations of parenting, the relationship of family membership to productivity, to access to economic survival, and to terms of employment, have all defined specifically the context in which a woman becomes wife, is expected to become mother, and into which a daughter is born.

On the one hand the glib images of the "norm" of the housewife/mother belies the reality that women as mothers usually have to work outside the home. Adrienne Rich notes that in 1973 "the United States Census reported more than six million children under the age of six whose mothers worked full time outside the home"[2] and that in the 1970s there were over twenty-six million children with wage-earning mothers, and eight million children in female-headed households.[3] Nancy Chodorow quotes from 1975 statistics, that "as of 1974, about 46% of mothers with children under eighteen were in the labor force—over half of the mothers with school age children and over a third of those with children under six."[4]

The ideologies of ideal motherhood evolved most powerfully from the nineteenth century onward and were reinforced by psychological theories of "natural maternal instinct" and correct performance of motherhood, which were spelled out forcefully from the 1920s onward. These attitudes greatly affected men's and women's thinking. However, they did not confront the material situation that women faced on becoming pregnant, but glossed over it. It was not true that most White women stopped working outside the home and glided gracefully into the luxurious role of housewife and mother. Certain of the upper- and middle-class women who had never been expected to be anything *but* wives and mothers, of course, did. But for significant numbers of women, pregnancy has meant facing the *impossibility* of combining full-time work with caring for children, or doing so against tremendous odds and at great cost—as shown in the vivid account of the mother in Tillie Olsen's "I Stand Here Ironing."[5] The social reality women have had to face is that motherhood and paid employment are objectively incompatible in a world that puts the isolated nuclear family (the American dream unit) against the capitalist organization of work in Western industrial society.

In a survey published in 1979 by Ann Oakley in Britain, where similar family structures and economic organization underlie daily life, 33% of the new mothers interviewed returned to work, but of these only 4% returned to full-time work and 29% worked occasionally and/or on a part-time basis.[6] She observed that: "The paid work mothers do is generally lower in status, less skilled, less remembered and more likely to be part-time than that undertaken by women in general."[7] For example, 1969–71 data from England showed that 61% of employed women with children under five years old earned less than five pounds (then approximately $12) a week.[8] Of the new mothers who were *not* employed outside the home after the birth of their children, 61% had reason to regret not being able to work, and 80% described themselves as feeling very tied down by the problems of baby care.[9]

This is all worth quoting to emphasize that the images of family and motherhood and "housewife" which are projected around assumptions of White women's lives conceal a complex and difficult reality that has to be looked at more closely if the heritage of the "model" nuclear family and the women it contains and produces are to be understood.

The mother/daughter relationships which White women live— and which have produced the feminists' struggles for women's liberation—have evolved within, or out of, a family situation within patriarchal systems.[10] Both mother and daughter exist within a tightly woven fabric of family: biological connections which are socially constructed from specific histories of social organization of both gender and economics. In the widest sense, the settling of the United States and the very processes of immigration involved a splintering of community which both broke the kinship and support networks women had in different, smaller-scale European communities, and reinforced the family as an isolated, self-contained nuclear unit. The pioneer momentum and the ideologies of "making it" were sustained across centuries in the demands of industrialization, and urged a process of mobility of the husband/wife unit, and physical distancing of daughters from mothers and siblings.[11]

While the nineteenth century saw a proliferation in the dominant culture's ideologies of love and romance at the same time as codes of sexual repression and restraint were argued and popularized, the family was nonetheless constituted within the grid of a social system based on institutionalized inequalities—from slavery to the economic exploitation of wage labor to a legal and economic system which systematically created an order legitimating male dominance and female dependence. In fact, the notion of the correctness of the male-dominated family sanctified a daily reality shaped by laws that denied women citizenship rights, property rights, and medical rights over their own bodies, and even deprived them of rights to control their sexuality in marriage and to have custody rights over their own children. Capitalist economic organization in conjunction with the Protestant work ethic made *paid labor* the valued commodity; social status and power (however limited) were conferred via *money*. Meanwhile, the family was to become a privatized domain where women, financially and socially dependent on men, were to care for home and children. Women working for pay were, and are, paid less than men, producing and reinforcing their dependence on men at the most basic economic level.

American society in reality never made family survival a priority. The priorities were private and corporate interests, not the daily-life needs of people surviving on the wages for their labor. Industrial production and technological development produced outer space exploration and a multi-billion-dollar nuclear armament industry and military complex in a society where millions have little or no access to adequate health care and the infant mortality rate is still shockingly high. The institutional framework and the organization of daily life into polarized areas of paid labor versus family nurturance and survival, along with ideas of competition, possessiveness, and individualism, placed "the family" in the crossfire of exploitation, authority, and power. Images and notions of femininity (embodying fragility, dependency, obedience, and passivity) versus masculinity (embodying strength, authority, autonomy, and activity) flowered in and around the daily reality of most women's lives, which both confirmed and contradicted them.

The objective material conditions of women's lives and the economic and cultural options available to them systematically situated women in positions of inferiority and powerless dependency in relation to the men they chose or were forced to live with. Isolation within marriage, inferior economic and legal status, and cultural images and norms which praised femininity while disempowering women, limiting and devaluing their sphere of activity, are the *material* conditions in which White women's mothers were daughters and became women. The marriage contract was never, and is still not, an imagining of equal partnership. It institutionalized, at one level among many, a gender-based division of powers and responsibilities where women were always—immediately or ultimately—oppressed, excluded, and dependent. White feminism has been the struggle against the injustice of the institutional and cultural codes which have used gender to rationalize inequality. "Becoming aware of gender in a patriarchal system means recognizing that men and women are not valued equally, that in fact, men are socially more esteemed than women."[12]

"Denying, removing, isolating"

It is true that others of my women friends live quiet and happy married lives, or would claim to do so. I watch them curl up and wither gently, and without drama, like cabbages in early March which have managed to survive the rigors of winter only to succumb to the passage of time . . . Down among the women, if you are very careful and shut your eyes and ears, and keep your knees together nearly always, you can live really quite happily . . . Down among the women . . . where men seduce, make pregnant, betray, desert, where laws are harsh and mysterious, and where the woman goes helpless.

—Fay Weldon[13]

The patriarchal conditions, divisions, rules, and images of marriage and of "the family" are the context in which our mothers encountered, through their own pregnancies, the confines and regulations of the institution of motherhood.[14] Motherhood has been projected in idealized and idyllic images. With greater and greater frequency from the nineteenth century onward, happiness and harmony, fulfillment of "natural maternal instincts," and the performance of daily nurturant activities have been depicted in the dominant White culture as rewards for acting out the "natural" and proper destiny of women. Although during the last fifty years women have been having fewer children, the role of a mother, now totally divorced from other social and economic activities, has become more and more highly charged as a significant emotional activity. Feminists in the last decade have begun to explore and question the history of the "institution" of motherhood—that is, the cultural, legal and economic practices that have determined how and why motherhood was and is enacted and imagined in the dominant White culture.

Adrienne Rich, in *Of Woman Born*, has challengingly explored the myths, limits, rules, and realities which have ensured the "regulation of women's reproductive power by men" in the cultures and traditions of Western and industrialized societies.[15] Alongside the dreams and idylls, and the "normality" of terms of "alliance" with men, she began to render visible the invisibilities, the unnaturalness and violence of patriarchal systems where women are devalued and disempowered *as mothers*. Nancy Chodorow and Jane Flax have stressed the political necessity of understanding the psychological development of women mothered by women in the isolated nuclear and patriarchal family in contemporary capitalist society. Nancy Chodorow's work examines in depth "how sexual asymmetry and inequality are constituted, reproduced, and change.[16] She explores the "ways that family structure and process, in particular the asymmetrical organization of parenting, affect unconscious psychic structure and process."[17]

Ann Oakley has contributed historical and theoretical attempts to come to grips with the *institution* of motherhood (as opposed to the idealized cult of motherhood or the indictment of motherhood itself as being intrinsically oppressive to women), with its traditions and inner mechanisms. She writes a vivid account and analysis of the actual conditions of motherhood as experienced by a British group of White middle- and working-class first-time mothers in the 1970s.[18] In contrast to the unrealistic images of motherhood which, five months after birth, more than 80 percent of the women confessed to having believed in while pregnant, Oakley charts in the women's own accounts key features of the institution of motherhood that the *experience* of motherhood underlined: the experience of intense isolation caused by their situation in a "normal" nuclear-family marriage far from kin; the absence of opportunities to participate in a community; the resulting exclusive responsibility for the child, in the absence of any context of shared or social childcare; the loss of any sense of autonomy because of being excluded from the economic and social world of paid employment; greater sexual division of work and roles in their marriage; the experience of losing status and identity; exhaustion from interrupted sleep and extra hours of domestic work; loss of personal freedom. These experiences were parallel to the rewards and pleasures of loving and caring for their children. Oakley's analysis shows how sexual discrimination is systematically institutionalized around motherhood and argues that motherhood is a crucial transition into and confrontation with the "full significance of the way femininity is socially constructed in our culture."[19]

In a different discourse—this time a powerfully written fictional text—Tillie Olsen, in her short story "Tell Me a Riddle," bears strong testimony to the overwhelming reality that the experience of motherhood involves. Written through the consciousness of a dying grandmother, who as a first-generation immigrant lived the years of the 1920s–1940s as wife and mother, the account of her passionate struggle to nurture her family into survival is given in antagonistic and resentful tension toward her husband. The distance between the life *she* led as mother and *he* as absent, "unseeing" father, out in the working and social world, is the poignant context for her flood of memories of what it was to mother. She remembers being on the go eighteen hours a day, without any help, having no time for what she wanted to do; years of being unable to go out; endless nursing, tiredness, being alone with the babies, gradually abandoning her interests; the humiliation of having to ask for money, of having to cope with poverty—"old humiliations and terrors"—while trying to meet the *needing* of the children. She recalls mending, renewing, repetitive cleaning—that "endless defeating battle"—making do, being left behind with a feeling of vacuity as her children moved off. The passions and pleasures of mothering opened up a world of "drowning into needing and being needed," where her existence depended on this alone and her identity was submerged into it. In the isolated nuclear family, the experience of motherhood was for her one of "denying; removing; isolating" and wondering "how was it that soft reaching tendrils also became blows that knocked."

Ann Oakley has analyzed childbirth itself and women's transition into motherhood. Her findings that women systematically experience loss of control, are encouraged to be passive, undergo taken-for-granted dramatic restrictions on their economic and social activity, and experience loss of status with an ongoing sense of devaluation are summed up in the following theoretical language:

Childbirth happens in a medical, social and economic context that has the capacity to shape the contours of a woman's reactions to it. There is a crucial dialectic between the way childbirth happens in modern industrialized cultures and the way mothers are supposed to be—married, at home, economically disadvantaged and dependent, and blessed with a maternal instinct that enables them to rear children without learning how to. The interplay between the ideology and practice of childbearing on the one hand and motherhood on the other, catches women in the dilemma of chasing personal human satisfaction across the psychological wasteland of alienated reproduction and captive motherhood.[20]

Ann Oakley shows how the passage into motherhood in a patriarchal, capitalist context concretely and symbolically initiates women into a process of demobilization of their social, leisure, relational, and political energies—what Tillie Olsen calls in *Silences* "powerlessness, division, exhaustion, and narrowness."[21]

Isolated from kin and community in the highly mobile society of today, lacking exposure to the experience of childcare, bereft of any systematic collaboration or help given the strict sexual division of labor which catapults the man into the productive-earning or state-supported world from which the woman is excluded or in which she is devalued, our mothers found their own more or less viable ways of navigating the feminine confines available to them as mothers. Ann Oakley found that regardless of their class background, the women she interviewed recurrently expressed a sense of enforced loss of control and increased dependency as they became mothers. This repeatedly activated in them a feeling of being disabled, of losing their self-worth, and made lack of self-esteem surface frighteningly. Both at conscious and unconscious levels the women expressed an acute sense of themselves as weak. Their repeated statements of lack of confidence in themselves stressed that "the 'achievement' of becoming a mother represents primarily and essentially a loss of identity."[22] So Tillie Olsen writes of "this inexplicable draining self-doubt, loss of aspiration, of confidence,"[23] which White women have recurrently expressed across the years. What is confirmed and reenacted through entering motherhood is "the leeching of belief, of will, the damaging of capacity"[24] intrinsic to the traditional confines of White womanhood. "What was needed to confirm and unify has been meager and occasional, accidental. The compound of what actively denies, divides, irritates, has been powerful—and continuous, institutionalized."[25] As Adrienne Rich summarizes it, "The most notable fact that culture imprints on women is the sense of our limits."[26] Or, in Ann Oakley's words:

. . . For it seems likely that what has not been sufficiently appreciated is the chronicity of low self-esteem in the psychology of women, the fact that a low estimation of self stems not from the possession of a different genital organization or from a disturbed pattern of family relations, but from the simple impoverishment of being female in a male world and experiencing a life-long syndrome of personal and institutional subordination.[27]

And the woman becomes mother to a daughter

Given the ambivalences that White women have about their condition of being women in this "life-long syndrome of personal and institutional subordination," producing a daughter is of itself riddled with ambivalence and contradictory responses. The heritage of our mother-daughter interaction is simultaneously many things: a celebration of similarity and continuity; a process of overidentification with its risks of overimplicating each other in one's needs and dreams; a reliving for the mother of her reactions and ambivalences concerning her own mother, whose life also embodied all the unresolved contradictions patriarchal society produced in her; anger, frustration, and irritability connected to the experience of powerlessness, which is projected onto the baby girl.[28] What has been at stake in the mother's strategy to survive the processes of sexual oppression and limitation is unconsciously and consciously projected in all its ambiguity onto the daughter. The mother's isolation urges her to cling to her girl child and discourage her from acquiring an autonomous sense of herself—the message is "Be like me, be with me, depend on me, stay with me, prolong me." At the same time the mother does not want her daughter to be confined and disabled by the patriarchal system in ways *she* has been—so the message is "Do not be like me, be strong, be active in the nonfeminine sphere, don't get pulled down."[29] The daughter represents the possibility for the mother to live out the dreams that were thwarted in her own process of surviving the premises and constructs of male domination. The divisions between which the mother has had to choose produce conflicting messages. On the one hand, the daughter is told to go, do, be different. The mother, whose reality has been contained within complex patriarchal limits, nonetheless acts as if the daughter can live ahistorically, *beyond* the patriarchal boundaries. Robin Morgan's poetry records the mother's idealistic and misleading message:

> There is nothing you cannot be, she said crossly,
> if you want to be it enough.[30]

Or again, the daughter in Fay Weldon's novel comments about her mother: "She gave me dreams I couldn't hope to keep up with in later life."[31]

Yet this encouragement to go beyond the confines of the mother's existence is undercut by "the fearful subliminal message: 'Don't go too far.'"[32] While the tradition of our mothers is not to transmit a conscious history of the limits of being a woman in a male-dominated, male-privileged society, their urging us into achievements —into differences possible only outside the *institution* of mother-hood—is undercut by half-sensed messages of compromise which have implicit in them their need to keep us with them. "To be a woman means to make compromises, to fail, to give up one's dreams, to settle for less than one wishes."[33] Only within the patriarchal definitions that evaluate females as inadequate in the productive world are we allowed to become mothers ourselves. Our mothers unconsciously, and yet cunningly, weave us into the contradictory patterns of womanhood. Robin Morgan's poetry speaks of this:

> And I was her miracle, her lever, her weapon,
> the shuttle of her loom
> I didn't mind that until later . . .
> . . . She seemed to sit at the center of my life,
> secreting my future, dividing herself
> into two half-bodies, one of which was meant for me.[34]

The creative processes, productive experience, passions and rewards of motherhood—ever at odds with the contours of a patriarchal society— are often pleasurable and alluring, in spite of the traumatically high costs patriarchy writes into White womanhood through motherhood. Within the patriarchal organization of gender in the White dominant culture, as women enter the prescribed roles around reproduction and have their sexuality organized in the "normative" isolated nuclear family context, "by mothering their daughters, women induce in other women the desire to be mothers and the relational capacities and psychic structures that match this goal."[35]

And the daughter becomes daughter to a mother

My worst fantasy is that I will end up to be like my mother.[36]

> . . . a ragged truce, an affirmation in me
> that your strength, your pushiness your sharp love,
> your embroidery of lies—all, all were survival tools[37]

As once our mothers were, we as White feminist women are born as daughters into our dominant culture's heritage of the ambivalence lived out in our mothers' lives. We are daughters born of mothers whose lives, viabilities, choices, and self-definitions were woven into a particular fabric of patriarchal values and laws. We are produced as daughters, from our earliest childhood, within the terms of our mothers' ambiguity. Our need for nurturance and for caring relationships, which our mothers represent, is pitted against our need to become autonomous, working, achieving persons, valid in our own right. Because we are women, the patriarchal society will sabotage in material, cultural, ideological, and economic ways our struggle toward autonomy as women. But our mothers, too—because of their need for our alliance in their already sabotaged paths through male dominance, and because of our need not to reject the caring nurturant world they represent—are likely to sabotage us as well. The roles and choices our mothers offer—because as mothers they have passed through and *are of* the institution of motherhood—embody aspects of "regression, passivity, dependence and lack of orientation to reality,"[38] which we have political imperatives to struggle against. And yet our mothers' struggles are ours too, we are "active responders and appropriators"[39] in relation to the realities they have lived and embody. The dilemma of the daughters is that in our blood is the conflict *and* resolution of our mothers' journey.

For reasons outlined in the earlier section on the Women's Liberation Movement, feminist awareness of the nature of the conflict and of the stakes involved in the offered resolutions has become more obvious and acute over the last fifteen years. The contradictory pressures society has brought to bear on women, and the intolerableness of possibilities along with old impossibilities have, since the 1960s, motivated whole new realms of resistance, rebellion, and crises of "rejection" of the mothers by the daughters. Key areas of sexual-political struggle have emerged in the feminist efforts to resist and restructure the negative features of womanhood which we have inherited through the ambivalence of our mothers. The feminist imperative emerges at the collective, active level—consciousness-raising, fighting for specific rights, working to end specific discrimination and to change specific structures at the political and analytical level. Women are learning to understand more fully the processes of female subordination and male dominance, in order to engage in the most necessary struggles at as many levels as possible, including the personal level, with reference to our personal political histories as daughters:

This above all, to refuse to be a victim. Unless I can do that I can do nothing. I have to recant, give up the old belief that I am powerless.[40]

The political momentum to sexual political struggle comes therefore not just in terms of consciously perceived injustices, but also in struggles to transform the unconsciously structured features of the oppressed—the psychology of inferiority which, unless dislocated, undermines the conscious, specific struggles by demobilizing the political energies in our woman-lives.

Our struggle with our mothers is pivotal in this process. Of course, it is not a matter of mother or daughter winning at the cost of the other. The significance is in the *process* of struggle with the conflicts that the mother-daughter relationship inevitably necessitates in a patriarchal society:

> She sang me to sleep
> made sure I had her dreams
> and then protested
> when I awoke
> from her nightmare[41]

The heritage of White women from the dominant White culture necessitates the political understanding of the conditions and social relations in which the dreams of the mother are shaped and polarized, so that the daughter may know how to begin to dislocate the mechanical nightmare processes of sexual oppression in her own life.

Judith Kegan Gardiner has commented interestingly on how—in contrast to nineteenth-century women writers who, in the course of resolving the lives of their characters, "better" or prolong the terms of their mothers' lives—twentieth-century women writers frequently have the mothers die in their fiction of the "disease of nurturance gone sour." The daughters in the novels manifest rage at the sex-role socialization, sexual repression and loss of self-boundaries that their connection with their mothers has produced in them.[42] Agnes Smedley's novel *Daughter of Earth* is fascinating in its account of the daughter's resistance to love and tenderness, and her horror at sexuality, which are structured out of her earliest realizations that the "inevitable" path, via love and sex, to motherhood involves loss of pride, loss of control, and "pain, suffering, defeat, the repetition of my mother's life for another generation."

The fear of becoming our mothers, our refusal to emulate them, is neither a lack of respect nor a personal vendetta. It is a fear of the specific conditions of motherhood and womanhood, which necessitate our oppression. It is a rejection of the nonviable patriarchal separation of nurturance and autonomy, caring and achievement, loving and power. The fear stems from our knowledge that, through our relationship with our mothers, we are cyclically part of those conditions, as Adrienne Rich evokes:

When I think of the conditions under which my mother became a mother, the impossible expectations . . . my anger dissolves into grief and anger *for* her and then dissolves back into anger at her . . .[43]

> . . . Remind me
> how her touch melted childgrief
> how she floated great and tender in our dark
> or stood guard over us
> against our willing
>
> and how we thought she loved
> the strange male body first
> that took, that took, whose taking seemed a law
>
> and how she sent us weeping
> into that law
> how we remet her in our childbirth visions . . .
> . . . and crawled and panted toward her.[44]

Consequences of Conflict

> It has been difficult too,
> to know the lies of our complicity
> from the lies we believed.[45]

Recognizing the historical and psychological constraints on the mother/daughter heritage does not make it less painful to live out the consequences of the conflicts involved. The conscious attempts we make to decode the political complexities of what is at stake in our most personal experiences of the social construction of the "woman" in us are only the beginning. Meanwhile the lived realities of mother/daughter conflict continue within our societal context. For the daughter, there is the quandary of learning to understand the mother's seeming collaboration with impossible contradictions and the nature of the paralysis involved. It is easy to oversimplify and to blame or accuse. There is a feeling of having been lied to, of having been given conscious projections of cohesion and normality over underground currents of ambiguity and irreconcilability. There is resulting anger on both sides. The choices seem to be either collusion, acceptance, complicity, and continuation *or* conflict and fear. Either option carries with it mutual accusations of failure. Our mothers' anger is evoked by their daughters' failure to enter into the kind of "womanhood" that will produce terms of feminine self-definition similar to those they survived on. In other cases, daughters, by adopting these self-images, evoke anger by failing to embody the dreams of achievement that are first projected onto her potential for rising above the conditions common to most women, and later onto the man invented to definitively concretize her success. The mother's anger or distress is either at her daughter's failure to reproduce a mirror-image of her own irreconcilable aspirations (i.e., the daughter's attempts to subvert the patriarchal options) or at her failure to resolve (i.e., individually transcend) the options that patriarchal society makes irresolvable.

The anger of the daughter is aroused by the impossibility of the sensed expectations, the lack of viable options, and the fear of being controlled, manipulated, and suffocated by the mother's overinvestment in her. The daughter staggers under the weight of her mother's energies and dreams, which are frustrated by the material limits of the mother's own experience and then projected onto the daughter. There is also the daughter's anger at her own dependency on her mother, her own overinvestment in her mother as having been the pivotal figure in the daughter's own learned self-image as woman, her realization that her psychic self is structured *through* her mother. Robin Morgan evokes this overwhelming centrality of the mother on the horizon of the daughter's identity:

> What is intolerable here
> is the voice of a three year old child in me
> who cries that with this death the world is ending.[46]

There is a first-level anger at the mother for seemingly not having struggled enough, not having demanded and refused more. This anger is painfully linked, in the absence of consciously articulated messages about oppression of women, with the daughter's realization that her imagining of her mother as someone who was *limitless* clashes with a reality of someone who seems to have "chosen" limits. What we have to come to terms with is that our mothers did not freely choose limits, but lived *within* certain economic, cultural, and institutional limits, and *in spite of* them.

The key feminist interventions in these destructive processes of anger, failure, and guilt are the imperative to learn about our mothers out of the historical amorphousness of "White" childhood, to understand the conjuncture of oppressive practices in our heritage, and to reevaluate the complex contradictions and compromises in our own lives as women of this heritage. Our incentive is to understand how we are constructed and produced and situated as women in the dominant male-defined culture within a capitalist setting. We have to find constructive ways of coming to terms with our shared and systematic exposure to multifaceted experiences of dependence and powerlessness.

Our starting point is an unviable choice between acceptance and rejection. To simply accept our mothers' situations is to prolong the surface and undercurrent contradictions. To simply admire and reproduce their compromised roles within male-dominated society is to engage in the politically ineffective passing on of ways of accommodating the dilemma. Our love for our mothers binds us to them and helps us to recognize the immensity of the pressure they underwent —the confines of the choices, means, or options they faced. Nonetheless, our imperative has to be to name the injustices from which these pressures came, to point toward the socially and historically shaped *causes* of the limited possibilities to which our mothers creatively accommodated themselves. As we begin to understand the stakes involved in the ways our mothers strategized our lives, we begin to refuse the confines of those options. We reject the *terms* which demanded those strategies. The effort to structure our lives on different terms cannot, of course, have fully positive results unless the economic structure, the institutions, and the ideological processes of the actual dominant culture are *all* transformed.

The fragmentation of the Women's Liberation Movement into myriads of national, local community, and personal struggles is a necessary and inevitable process. The media portrayal of the feminist movement as a man-hating crusade against the *family* has in fact been a caricature of a much more complex process of feminists refusing to accept the *terms* of human coexistence, which have inherent in them women's subordination, restriction, and devaluation. As educational opportunities and the changing job market have rapidly diversified many women's experience and sense of their capacities over the last fifty years or so, many daughters of this process have gone too far to be able to resume a quiet reproduction of the mothers' dilemma. The fear of becoming our mothers grows out of a struggle between the love ties which urge us to join them and our consciousness of inequality and oppression, which the women's movement has activated and enabled in us. There is a sadness in the political separation this necessitates, but there is also a relief in that feminism brings with it incentives for new kinds of mutual respect and recognition of differences at play between mothers and daughters. It is the tradition of the mothers which produces the consciously articulated struggle of the daughters, albeit in conflict, anger, and pain. In the words of feminist poets:

> . . . Meanwhile, she is afraid to read my poems, that best of me
> I offer her—afraid she will not understand them
> or afraid she will.
> She waits alone with still more Yahrzeit candles each Yom Kippur,
> alone, and I intransigent in my own fierce survival
> knowing at last her way is not my way.
> —Robin Morgan[47]

> This was the silence I wanted to break in you
> I had questions but you would not answer
> I had questions but you could not use them.
> —Adrienne Rich[48]

> [I] . . . sought a birthright elsewhere,
> beyond the oasis of your curse,
> even beyond that last mirage, your blessing.
> Mother, in ways neither of us can ever understand,
> I have come home.
> —Robin Morgan[49]

The women's movement erupted at two key levels. First came the naming of and rebelling against obvious sexual injustices and abuses in the public practices of American society—informed and inspired by other political struggles against capitalism and racism. Secondly, the personal-political dilemma of the White feminist daughters was experienced at a time when the contradictory aspirations in the dominant culture conflicted more acutely than ever with the real possibilities for women's lives. The daughters' dilemma was and is the personal journey across or around the institution of motherhood— both in our own and in our mothers' lives. Public political practices were seen to meet the personal experience in new and politically urgent ways.

In the absence of supportive, collaborative kinship networks, the site for nurturance—women mothering in isolation in the nuclear family—becomes a site of danger, disempowering, and devaluing. Our struggle is to learn to create more viable networks for relationships between women in a culture which has decimated them. It is to learn (whether we become mothers or not) to live motherhood as daughters of our mothers—not in spite of them individually, but in spite of the institutions that surround motherhood with ambivalence and violence. At stake are not only our personal problems, but the nature of our political imagination—and the possibility or impossibility of a wealth of new strategies. The Women's Liberation Movement's imperative has to be to break set with the *institution* of motherhood that defined the possibilities of our mothers' lives. The answer is not simply to "obey the patriarchal stricture"[50] by opting for nurturance via motherhood *or* achievement via autonomy and non-nurturance, in male-defined terms. The goal is to create new contexts that do not require a conflict-fraught dichotomy between nurturance and autonomy. The means of approaching this goal are specific political struggles over sexual discrimination, oppression, injustice, and violence, as well as over the interpretation of the sexual division of powers institutionalized in capitalist, patriarchal culture. It is these struggles, engaged in at different levels throughout the movement, that are enabling significantly new kinds of relationships between women, and demand of men fundamentally new terms of collaboration and relationship at every political level.

The political significance is that in the painful choices *away* from the worlds of our mothers, we are learning to understand the terms of those worlds, and to reject the isolation and powerlessness which risk rendering us, as women, politically ineffective. The risk is also that unless we engage in this separation, we will passively collude and participate in the oppressive practices that capitalism, and its patriarchal and racist spine and nerves, depend on to proceed. Our imperative is to break the immobilizing patterns whereby women are prevented, excluded, and paralyzed into a resigned repetition of collusion. Our demand must also be that the "men of our mothers" learn to participate, too, in dislocating the economic, ideological, institutional and personal/sexual practices that perpetuate oppression. The need to create a positive context for nurturance beyond the dominant culture's capitalist and patriarchal structures motivates us to struggle against the offered options. Neither repression of nurturance (choosing male-styled achievement in the male-dominated work world—an option accessible to the non-mother or to upper-class women), nor normative balance of powers in a heterosexual marriage or relationship (necessitating abdication of autonomy, along with inevitable inequalities in sexual divisions of labor and images of gender), nor a simple stepping out of the larger society into women-centered communities is, in isolation, a viable solution. Feminists are and will be involved in all of these practices: working for economic independence and survival and to break the codes which exclude women from certain forms of work; living with or in relationships with men and trying to negotiate new terms for this in the public and private worlds; mothering children—their own and other women's; affirming women-centered existences and relationships and women-generated culture and care systems. But each and all of these practices is loaded with tension and struggle. No feminist, whatever her choices or possibilities, is immune to any of that tension.

Being daughters of our mothers, we have the heritage of nurturance and caring on our side. Despite the ambiguities that flourished around and within them, they managed to breed certain powers in us. The love of our mothers has urged and is urging us into the necessary transformations in ourselves, always beyond the imagining of our mothers, yet motivated by them. The needed transformations involve eliminating the structured isolation and competitive individualism which the separate nuclear family unit breeds. In the patriarchal, capitalist society, isolation and individualism have meant going it alone, self-centered achievement, material success in spite of others and in spite of the social conditions of others' lives, the suburban and high-rise capitalist fantasy of being the *exception* who makes it to the top. The feminist struggle is to create, out of aloneness, new forms of family and chosen kinship connections which can, along with the endless series of concrete political fights and demands, generate solidarity, a shared determination to fight oppressive conditions. It was the image of such solidarity that prompted us to adopt the word "sisterhood."

I return to where I began—the images of "privileged" housewives, the curious articulation of powerlessness and lack of confidence among racially-privileged White women, the fear of becoming like our mothers. I have tried to suggest the significance of certain historical trends, certain psychological patterns, and certain paths to resistance and struggle from which women shaped in the dominant culture and dominant family structure of White experience have been, and are, articulating their thoughts, ideas, activities and lives. We have the will to make conscious these images, to explore and problematize the terms surrounding the dilemmas, the importance of certain choices and struggles. The gender-defined divisions, the institutionalizing of oppressive gender-specific roles, and both the gentle and violent discriminations and abuses which emerge from these sexual codes are the "givens" from which feminists struggle to shape more positive, liberating "deviancies."

Black women know that their struggle is to avoid being drawn into the dominant culture—to end their victimization by the exploitation and oppression which capitalism in its patriarchal form embodies. Their struggle is not to "be like" Whites (I hear your very political laughter of dismissal as I write that). The struggle against oppression is to disrupt and dislocate the very terms on which that oppression feeds, not to change bits of it or to be absorbed into it or to coexist with it. The White women's movement, recurrently threatened by cooptation or fragmentation, is jarringly exploring its own *materially based* paths into the very necessary choices White women are learning to make.

> If I cling to circumstances I could feel
> not responsible. Only she who says
> She did not choose, is the loser in the end.
> —Adrienne Rich[51]

NOTES

1. It is a huge generalization to talk about "the family" in *White* experience, given the range of ethnic groupings and cultural traditions, plus the very real conditions of *class*, which the White experience incorporates. However, the impact of industrialization over the years, the processes of suburbanization and the building of high-rise apartment houses as big business monopolized city and town centers, as well as the social relations which capitalism necessitates, invests in, and exploits, have produced many similarities in the standardized features of the nuclear family among Whites of different classes and of varying ethnic origin.

2. Adrienne Rich, *Of Woman Born: Motherhood As Experience and Institution.* New York: Bantam Books, 1977, p. 35.

3. Adrienne Rich, "Motherhood in Bondage," in *On Lies, Secrets and Silences*. New York: W. W. Norton & Co., 1979, p. 196.

4. Nancy Chodorow, *The Reproduction of Mothering. Psychoanalysis and the Sociology of Gender*. Berkeley: University of California Press, 1979, p. 216.

5. Tillie Olsen, *Tell Me a Riddle*. New York: Dell, 1976.

6. Ann Oakley, *Women Confined: Towards a Sociology of Childbirth*. Oxford, U.K.: Martin Robertson, 1980, p. 130.

7. Ibid., p. 201.

8. Ibid., p. 186.

9. Ibid., p. 130.

10. I am in no way arguing that every individual mother-daughter relationship is the same within these larger contexts. I am merely summarizing some of the wider factors within which the family, marriage, and motherhood are constituted. Although within these each family, mother, and daughter has specific journeys which take specific shapes, they still have to occur within the famework of the limits and possibilities that the larger social, cultural, and economic factors establish.

11. Carroll Smith-Rosenberg, "The Female World of Love and Ritual: Relationships Between Women in Nineteenth Century America," *Signs: Journal of Women in Culture and Society*. Chicago: University of Chicago Press, Vol. 1, No. 1; Agnes Smedley's novel *Daughter of Earth*, Old Westbury, N.Y., The Feminist Press, 1973; Tillie Olsen's novel *Yonnondio*, New York, Dell, 1975, and her short story "Tell Me a Riddle," in the book with the same title, as well as Adrienne Rich's poem "From an Old House in America," in *Poems Selected and New, 1950–74*, New York, W. W. Norton, 1975, all suggest poignantly the effects of isolation on women across American history.

12. Jane Flax, "The Conflict Between Nurturance and Autonomy in Mother-Daughter Relationships and Within Feminism," *Feminist Studies*, Vol. II, No. 2, p. 173.

13. Fay Weldon, *Down Among the Women*, Harmondsworth, U.K., Penguin Books, 1974.

14. Although nearly one-fifth of all pregnancies do not occur within marriage, although over 44 percent of poor families are headed by women and one in three marriages ends in divorce, marriage and the nuclear family are the ideological and economic contexts in which the social images of motherhood are projected. The pressures that women face to define themselves centrally in terms of these institutions are present no matter how women choose or are obliged to live their lives.

15. Adrienne Rich, *Of Woman Born*, p. 24.

16. Nancy Chodorow, op. cit., p. 6.

17. Ibid., p. 49.

18. Ann Oakley, *Becoming a Mother* and *Women Confined*, Oxford, U.K., Martin Robertson, 1980.

19. Ann Oakley, *Women Confined*, op. cit., pp. 184, 187.

20. Ibid., p. 178.

21. Tillie Olsen, *Silences*, New York, Delacorte Press, 1979, p. 213.

22. Ann Oakley, op. cit., p. 178.

23. Tillie Olsen, *Silences*, p. 194.

24. Ibid., p. 195.

25. Ibid., p. 196.

26. Adrienne Rich, *Of Woman Born*, op. cit., p. 250.

27. Ann Oakley, op. cit., p. 265.

28. See Nancy Chodorow, op. cit., especially pp. 100–103; Jane Flax, op. cit., pp. 174 ff.; Adrienne Rich, *Of Woman Born*, op. cit., pp. 245 ff., for detailed discussions of intricate psychological and cultural patterns of these processes.

29. As expressed by Jane Flax in a workshop on "Mothers and Daughters" at the University of Massachusetts during International Women's Week, March 1978, and in her article, op. cit., p. 179.

30. Robin Morgan, "Network of the Imaginary Mother," *Lady of the Beasts*, New York, Random House, 1976, p. 63.

31. Fay Weldon, op. cit., p. 22.

32. Adrienne Rich, *Of Woman Born*, op. cit., p. 251.

33. Jane Flax, op. cit., p. 181.

34. Robin Morgan, "Network of the Imaginary Mother," *Lady of the Beasts*, op. cit., pp. 63 and 66.

35. Ann Oakley, op. cit., p. 290.

36. Flax, op. cit., p. 171.

37. Robin Morgan, "Matrilineal Descent," *Monster*, New York, Random House, 1972, p. 39.

38. Nancy Chodorow, "Family Structure and Feminine Personality," in *Woman, Culture and Society*, ed. Rosaldo and Lamphere, Stanford, Stanford University Press, 1974, p. 65.

39. Nancy Chodorow, speaking on Freud and feminism at Smith College, Northampton, Massachusetts, March 1979.

40. Margaret Atwood, *Surfacing*, London, Virago, 1979, p. 191.

41. Michelene Wandor, "Lullaby," *Cutlasses & Earrings*, London, Playbooks, 1977, p. 49.

42. Jean Kegan Gardiner, "A Wake for Mother: The Maternal Deathbed Fiction," *Feminist Studies*, Vol. II, No. 2.

43. Adrienne Rich, *Of Woman Born*, op. cit., p. 225.

44. Adrienne Rich, *On Lies, Secrets and Silences*, op. cit., p. 189.

45. Adrienne Rich, "Sibling Mysteries," *Dream of a Common Language*, New York, W. W. Norton, 1978, p. 48.

46. Robin Morgan, "Network of the Imaginary Mother," *Lady of the Beasts*, op. cit., p. 65. She is writing about her mother dying.

47. Ibid., p. 66.

48. Adrienne Rich, "Cartographies of Silence," *Dream of a Common Language*, op. cit., p. 18.

49. Robin Morgan, "Matrilineal Descent," *Monster*, op. cit., p. 39.

50. Tillie Olsen, in a talk on "Caring, Mothering and Nurturing" given at Amherst College, Amherst, Massachusetts, Spring 1978.

51. Adrienne Rich, "Twenty-one Love Poems," (XV), *Dream of a Common Language*, p. 33.

SECTION THREE

Sexuality and Sexual Attitudes

V

The Media and Blacks—Selling It Like It Isn't

Spotted skin is for leopards, not pussycats like you. Try Ultra Bleach & Skin Tone Cream.

Pad-a-Panti. Adds instant curves to your figure.

Clinches Away Inches. Order #494; price, $7.99.

Clairol Keeps America Beautiful.

Gentlemen Prefer Hanes.

These ads may appear to be trivial or clever or obnoxious to the reader, but they play a vital role in the economic and political machinery of American values. Advertisements are as essential to American society as life is to death. Billions are spent in order to sell products which gross additional billions in return. But ads sell a lot more than products: advertisements sell attitudes, values, goals, and fears. They "sell" a self- and world-concept designed to maintain and ensure the perpetuation of sexual, racial, and economic inequality, which are all necessary to the existence of a patriarchal, capitalistic economic system.

How is this done? "Advertisements depict for us not necessarily how we actually behave as men and women, but how we *think* men and women should behave. This depiction serves the social purpose of convincing us that this is how men and women *are*, or want to be in relation to each other. They orient men and women to the idea of men and women acting together in concert with each other in the larger part or scene or arrangement that is our social life."[1] The designers of advertisements strategically produce powerfully manipulative ads which psychologically prepare us for the selling of a product. These ads create and shape our values and fears in such a way that we come to believe that these imposed values/fears/attitudes/goals are our own, as if we ourselves had chosen them. And from there it simply becomes a matter of manipulating these imposed attitudes/fears/etc. The aim is to be able to flash the product before the viewer's eyes in such a way as to not only sell the product but to sell a bill of goods as to how one *should* behave, feel, and think. In other words, what is being sold beyond the obvious product is the American way of life, a way of life that inevitably continues to ensure the success of the multi-billion-dollar advertising business and a capitalist way of life that depends economically and socially on the maintenance of sexism, racism, and economic oppression.

One feature of this chapter is an examination of leading magazines read by White women and leading magazines read by Black women (hereafter referred to as White magazines and Black magazines). Within this context, this chapter will dissect and delineate the ways in which the media, via magazine ads, define female sex roles, sexuality, and "beauty" in such a way as to ensure the continuation of the economy based on the profit motive and a systematic exploitation of a stylized culture of sexuality. The threefold purpose of the magazine ad survey was: 1) to determine how female sex roles are presented and portrayed; 2) to discover the recurrent themes as to how women are valued; and 3) to understand how organized, systematic power is distributed between men and women.

To gather information about Black and White magazines, five groups of women (each group consisted of three college students, two Black and one White) went to stores that sold the largest and most varied commercial magazines. They asked the proprietors which magazines were the leading sellers. Based upon this information, the following magazines were reported to be the most popular among White women: *Cosmopolitan, Seventeen, Harper's Bazaar, Glamour, Mademoiselle,* and *Viva.* Those magazines most popular among Black readers were: *Ebony, Essence, Jet, Black * Tress, Right On,* and *Black Star.*

The ads in these magazines were analyzed from several different perspectives. The scenes were analyzed on the basis of sexual objectification of females, and this was considered in relation to consumerism as a vehicle for acquiring a self-image. The human beings in the scenes were analyzed for the concepts of masculinity, femininity, power, and powerlessness as portrayed by the poses and postures and wording that accompanied the ads. In addition, frequency counts for the types of ads were made and classified on the basis of the product, i.e., women's beauty aids, men's products, drugs (alcohol, cigarettes), jobs, household products, services, commodities (records, tapes, etc.). The largest number of ads were the "beauty ads" category. Beauty ads refer to products whose claim is to make women more attractive, appealing, desirable, and "beautiful"—primarily for men. These products include perfume, clothes, facial cosmetics, and products designed to improve hair, hands, and body shape (the latter referring to bust developers, waist slimmers, thigh trimmers, weight reducers, etc.). The following summary was made of the percentage of beauty ads in ten of the magazines:

Magazine	Price	Total Number of Pages	Total Number of Ads	Total Number of Beauty Ads	% of Beauty Ads
Cosmopolitan	$1.50	364	270	164	60.9%
Seventeen	1.00	144	204	130	63.7
Harper's Bazaar	1.25	218	179	142	79.3
Mademoiselle	1.50	155	125	84	67.2
Viva	1.50	115	61	33	54.1

Magazine	Price	Total Number of Pages	Total Number of Ads	Total Number of Beauty Ads	% of Beauty Ads
Essence	$1.00	157	123	55	44.6%
Ebony	1.25	170	169	119	70.4
Jet	.75	66	10	1	10.0
Black * Tress	1.00	97	42	34	80.9
Right On	1.00	66	16	2	12.5

Cosmopolitan, Harper's Bazaar, Mademoiselle, Viva, and *Seventeen* were all considered by the student analysts to be women's trend-setting magazines. *Cosmopolitan* was rated as "the chic-est commercial magazine for women" and *Seventeen* was judged to be a teenage fashion-oriented version of *Cosmopolitan*. *Harper's Bazaar* was described as "an elitist, classy fashion magazine aspiring to attract the upper class," and *Mademoiselle* as "the Seven Sisters Special" (the Seven Sisters refers to the Ivy League sister schools). *Viva* received the comment, "They try harder," indicating second best.

Among the magazines most popular with Black women readers, three—*Jet*, *Right On*, and *Ebony*—cannot be considered magazines geared exclusively to Black women. They are leading publications among America's entire Black population. *Ebony*, a monthly magazine, is designed to take the pulse of the Black world. It covers entertainment; Black history; careers of Black stars, celebrities, and scholars; sports; trends; lifestyles; careers; literature; and has special departments including fashions, foods, and letters to the editor. *Jet* is a weekly publication; its feature articles on Black society and Black gossip keep its readers in touch with the ambience of Black culture. Both *Jet* and *Ebony* serve a vital function to the Black community, since the White press cannot be counted upon to include noteworthy accounts of grassroots Black life. *Jet* and *Ebony* are included in the survey of leading Black women's magazines, but it is important to keep in mind that they are directed to and read by both men and women within the Black community. (The issue of *Jet* that was analyzed contained ten ads: three for cigarettes, two for liquor, and one each for perfume, a religious wall plaque, Preparation H, mayonnaise, and Join the Air Force!) This is the typical number of ads per issue.

Right On consists of brief synopses of movies, TV shows, and concerts, plus items on popular personalities, featuring photos. It also includes fashions, record reviews and "newsy gossip." *Black Star* is more popular among teenagers than among adults, and is truly a magazine about Black celebrities, including up-and-coming as well as fading stars. Most of the ads (there were eight) were for subscriptions to the magazine itself, and six of the ads featured a male model posing in the latest in male fashion. *Black * Tress* is primarily concerned with hairstyles for women.

A breakdown of the ad survey for *Cosmopolitan* and *Essence* exemplifies how all the magazine ads were classified:

Cosmopolitan (364 pages—price $1.50)

TOTAL ADS: 270

BEAUTY AIDS: 181 (68%)
Bust 3
Skin 9
Weight 11
Exercise 1
Blemishes/Acne 4
Perfume 22
Clothes 26
Underclothes 9
Jewelry 19
Eye Makeup 11
Fingernails 13
Lip Products 8
Eyeglasses/Contact lenses 3
Hair 16
Cheek Blush 4
Tampons 2
Napkins 2
Douche 1

MISCELLANEOUS PRODUCTS AND
  SERVICES
Records 3
Tapes 3
Stereos 3
Magazines 2
Books 11
Movies 3
Cars 3

HOUSEHOLD PRODUCTS
Decorating 3
Washing 3
Food 3

Recipe Holder 1
Satin Sheets 1

DRUGS
Alcohol 20
Cigarettes 10
Contraceptive Foam 2
Contraceptive Cream 1
Pregnancy Test Kit 1
Vitamins 2

MEN'S PRODUCTS (Men's Beauty
  Aids)
Aftershave 2
Cologne 1
Soap 1
Shirts 1
Hair toner 1

SERVICES
Kelly Girl 4
Air Travel 1
Love and Poor Child 2
Hotel 1
Dance Lessons 1

JOBS
Medical/Dental Assistant 4
Window Display Artist 1
Travel Agent 3
Writing 3
Police 1
Stained Glass Artist 1
Bookkeeper 1
Animal Care 1

Essence Magazine (157 pages—price $1.00)

TOTAL ADS: 123

BEAUTY AIDS: 56 (44.7%)
Hair Dye 1
Tampons 2
Lip Products 3
Hair Conditioner 12
Clothes 13
Cosmetic Kit 4
Skin Lotion 3
Hair Products 1
Nails 1
Wigs 4
Geritol 1
Bath Items 1
Douche 1
Hair-styling Dryer 2
Jewelry 1
Bust Developer 1
Beauty Aids For:
    Weight Loss 1
    Sagging Buttocks 1
    Crash Diet 1
    Waist Slimmer 1

DRUGS
Alcohol 13
Cigarettes 5
Hair Vitamins 1

MEN'S PRODUCTS
        0

MISCELLANEOUS PRODUCTS AND
    SERVICES
Records 3

Sweepstakes 1
United Negro College Fund 1
Soul Train 1
Rosicrucians 1
Trips 1
Watches 1
Gulf 1
United Airlines 1
Las Vegas 1
McDonald's 1

HOUSEHOLD PRODUCTS
Kitchen Utensils 3
Dog Food 1
Furniture 7
Food 11
Baby Needs 2

SERVICES
Borrow by Mail 1
U.S. Savings Bonds 1
National Black Network 1
Xerox 1
Mail-order Photo Developer 1
Magazines 1
Insurance 1
E. F. Hutton 1
Bell System 1
American Express 1

JOBS
Army Reserve 1
Speed Writing 1
Hair Presser 1

The following critique is based on the underlying recognition that institutionalized sexism operates in advertising in such a way as to maintain the image of women as dependent sex objects who are inferior and subordinate to men.

The most salient aspect of the ads was the selling of a value-biased image of women. The summation of that image is: women as "sexy"; women as subordinate to men; women as seductresses; women as isolated from other women; women as competitors with other women for men; women as alluring beauties; women as dependent.

Page after page, the message remains the same: To be a woman you must conform to particular images. *Look* like this image and BE A WOMAN (Ultra Sheen Hair Products). *Smell* this way and BE A WOMAN (Noir Perfume). *Sit* this way and BE A WOMAN (Hanes Panti-Hose). *Smile* this way and BE A WOMAN (Kissing Slicks, a lip gloss). *Have* young-looking skin and BE A WOMAN (Moisture Wear). These ads say that women must be delicate and shy, yet wily and confident. Their skin and hair must be smooth and silky and always clean. Their lips must be soft and wet and alluring. Their smell must be inviting and linger on "long after she has left the room." (All natural smells must be powdered/sprayed/douched/perfumed away.) Women's attire must be the height of fashion, with impeccably matched accessories.

An image is something that one endeavors to achieve for oneself, something that one must work for (for better or worse) and only approximates the real person. The female media image, as summed up by one of the surveyors, requires women to be simultaneously sensuous, slim, sexy, soft, smooth, shiny, subtle, and seductive! A plethora of aids are needed for women to achieve this image, which conveys an underlying message that the "cosmetically unenhanced" woman must be dull, unattractive, unclean, smelly, and misshapen. Will the *real* woman please stand!

The question must be raised as to why women "buy" this media image of themselves—why so many women want to fulfill this particular image—and use billions of dollars of beauty products annually, plus countless hours, in an effort to "attain" this image. More than 48 million dollars is spent annually on eye makeup alone. Beauty aids do not help women to maintain their health, nor do they help them economically; in fact, they are an economic drain. So where does the value lie? The value of these aids can be traced to a capitalist economy which endeavors to promote consumerism for its economic self-interest by keeping women in a constant state of self-doubt and self-denigration. Thus, they are led to constantly aspire to reach an impossible standard of beauty and sexuality by spending. The selling of the image of woman as a sex object is big business and results in women competing against one another in a futile race to achieve this illusionary image.

Ultimately, we must begin to question women's motivation for achieving personal satisfaction from their appearance and behavior. In other words, what are the rewards and benefits that can be gained? For the vast majority of women, the motivation for buying this image comes from several sources: a conspicuous consumption culture; a conditioned mentality that says women *must* look a certain way; a socially constructed competitive urge to be equal to or better than other women in appearance; the desire to be appealing to and approved by men, by achieving and emulating "essences" of "natural"(?) femininity. The women thus become male-identified, in the sense that they dress and behave on the basis of male definitions and expectations of what it is to be a woman.

Why the emphasis on pleasing men? One reason stems from the fact that in our society the institution of marriage has been glorified, magnified, and identified as *the* ultimate goal for women. Despite the statistics on divorce, despite the reality of the oppressive nature of marriage, despite gross inequalities in marriage laws and contracts, the combination of normative heterosexuality, a gross build-up of romantic love, and propaganda about the joys of marriage and motherhood serves to keep America's female population aspiring to attain that ultimate goal of marriage. Herein is meant to lie fulfillment, meaning, and status.

In addition to the images of women that are portrayed in the ads, values about the "nature" of woman are also transmitted to the public. Although conveyed in more subtle ways, the impact of these messages is as strong as the more blatant images. The ads that displayed women as part of the scenes were examined on the basis of the postures of the women, their facial expressions, and their relationship to other figures in the scenes. It was observed that women were presented with men in such a way as to convey a sense of powerlessness or subservience, while the men were posed in a manner that depicted power. The message is clear. Look, Jane, look. See the man. He is standing erect, feet and legs spread wide apart, fists balled up at his sides and confidence written all over his face. He is in a pose protecting the female, with his arm around her waist or shoulders or ass, directing her, showing her the way, helping her. He is clearly the leader, the one the woman depends upon for guidance, strength, direction. If the picture representation does not sufficiently depict the woman as dependent, coy, trivial, seductive, or unintelligent, the words in the caption will complete the job.

Women in scenes with other women were relatively isolated from one another and maintained very little eye contact when in groups. The "woman on the go" was alone in the scene or, when presented with other figures, was rarely depicted in competition with men. Always, the image was one of a very attractive and alluring female according to the standards of beauty set by a White-dominated patriarchal society.

In comparing the Black magazines with the White ones, the major difference in the presentation of men was one of degree rather than diversity. The Black women featured poses and clothing and styles and makeup similar to the White women, the major difference being that Black women must "become White" before they can do all the things the White women do (i.e., *be* the image). By altering their physical state to appear with lightened skin and silky hair, Black women, too, can compete and thereby gain status and security by being with (having) a man. White and Black women were equally seductive in their poses in the ads.

The concept of beauty for women is based on White male values —the values of those who are empowered to make the rules. Therefore, standards of beauty for both White *and* Black women are set by White males. It is highly questionable to downright ridiculous for any woman to measure her physical features against a contrived set of standards designed to please the male imagination and desires. It is even more *ludicrous, since it is striving for the impossible* and since sound reasoning would deter trying to reach this goal, for Black women with non-Western features and coloring to aspire to White men's standards. You cannot give a group of people the ingredients for a delicious spice cake and then enter the spice cake in a contest for a luscious lemon cream pie. The best they can produce will be but a caricature—not a winner. White males created the values; White women strive for the image; and Black women have to strive even harder. Black women run the spectrum in skin color, facial features, and hair textures. Those women having "White" or European features certainly have nothing to apologize for. It is the adulation, glorification, and exploitation of those features that is demeaning.

Once the political wheels of the cosmetic industry were in gear, consumers (in a fashion similar to other oppressed peoples) became the instruments of their own oppression. Hence, we have women entering the cosmetics and fashion industry and promoting beauty shows and operating charm schools. The use of jewels, paint, makeup and other adornments have cultural significance in many non-European cultures. The use of cosmetics in and of themselves is not being totally condemned. Braids, curls, Afros, face powder, and lip rouge can and do enhance the well-being of Black women, but the extremes and expense to which women go are detrimental to the development of their self-esteem. It is interesting to note that the first female millionaire in the United States was a Black woman who made her millions in the beauty industry. Her name was Madame C. J. Walker—and what is to her credit? The hot iron, or straightening comb, was the Walker Method, which consisted of a shampoo, a pomade "hair grower," vigorous brushing, and the application of heated iron combs to the hair. It was used by millions of Black women in order to get their hair "pressed" or "straightened" or "done"—all in an effort to become more like the White image, with the consequence of becoming more unlike themselves.

During the Sixties, the phrase "Black is beautiful" became popularized. The original intent and meaning behind the phrase was that there was something beautiful in being Black. To be Black meant not simply a particular shade, but to have pride in one's ancestry, one's race, one's history. It meant developing a world view of humanity based on equality and marked by an absence of personal greed or the desire to exploit others. But very soon "Black is beautiful" came to stand for something very different—something very similar to the dominant White society's interpretation of beauty. The biased, self-serving, White-male-defined standards of beauty were imposed on Black life within the context of "Black is beautiful." A story run by *Cosmopolitan* magazine, "Health and Make-up Tips to Make the Black Woman Even More Beautiful," illustrates the mockery that was made of the original political statement. The original statement also embodied an attack on the racism of the dominant White society. This society, to protect notions of racial superiority and defend institutions embodying White power, had caricatured Black people with images of ignorance, low intelligence, and ugliness. "Black is beautiful" underwrote the inhumanity and dominance of the White society with the indictment, "White is ugly."

The late Lorraine Hansberry definitely had a handle on the true meaning of "Black is beautiful." As Julian Mayfield, in an article on the playwright, commented, "In 1959, when Hansberry told Mike

Wallace in a TV interview, 'What we want now is a recognition of the beauty of things African, the beauty of things Black,' the slogan 'Black is beautiful' had not even been raised.'"[2]

The beauty of things Black clearly does not apply to a "Miss America" with Black skin. For a Black woman to be beautiful does not mean that she has skin and hair and features that closely resemble the White woman. The beauty of Blackness is historical and should be defined by Blacks along lines that are germane to their African heritage and genealogy and their Afro-American culture—*not* on the basis of the distribution of genes, tissue, and pigment. Being beautiful must include an element that stirs the inner sense, that touches the soul and mind. If you see a person and that person's physical looks make you feel sensually aroused, then it should be said that the person's looks are, or the person is, *titillating*—not beautiful. That is to say that the person hasn't as yet earned the distinction of being beautiful. To be beautiful isn't simply a physical state. It has to be active in the sense that it arouses more than a sexual response—that it is inspirational and enhances the mental well-being of others—and it cannot be defined with finality.

Beautiful Black women should include personalities such as Lorraine Hansberry, who was beautiful until her death, through sickness and pain. She was beautiful in her art and her politics. She stirred others, she was inspirational, she was unselfish. Beautiful is Bernice Reagan, who at five feet (plus or minus an inch or two) produces a powerful combination of art and politics in her songs and music. Beautiful also was Mahalia Jackson, in her simplicity, devotion to her people, and soulful commitment to the church. She did not use the church in order to become filthy rich or to maintain a male harem. Beautiful also are Miriam Makeba, and Lena Horne in their words and songs and deeds. And beautiful are the countless Black grandmothers with aged features, rheumatic bones, and distant memories, who raise the spirits and lighten the burdens of others with their encouraging, comforting words and selfless deeds. The beauty was in the heritage of communal struggle and cultural collaboration —both to survive and to challenge oppression. The beauty in the ads of today is defined by individualistic, competitive values which promote the woman as dehumanized property for one individualistic man.

The way in which the image of the Black male was projected in the ads (and this is true of Black male superstars) was very different from the way the Black females were presented. The males were not presented as copies of White males. Black males in the ads looked like your ordinary, everyday Black male, sufficiently handsome without White features or White hair texture. Sidney Poitier, Jim Brown, Muhammad Ali, Harry Belafonte, Sammy Davis, Jr., are presented in the media as Black men with little attempt to alter their physical appearance to make them resemble White men. Their Negroid features and Afro hairdos are cultivated, not altered. There is no attempt to make or create a Black John Travolta or a Black Jon Voight or a Black Robert Redford. In contrast, Black female stars such as the late Dorothy Dandridge, Lena Horne, Pam Grier, Jayne Kennedy, and Diana Ross represent the female media image. Some speculations can be made as to the reasons for this occurrence. The American society may consider Black males a sexual threat to White males, and therefore no attempt is made to equalize them in appearance. To do so might make Black males more attractive to White women. Along this same line of racist thought, the thinking could be to let the Black man appear to be less "sophisticated" by appearing "less White." Keep him in his place as a *Black* man. On an economic basis, it could be reasoned that male beauty products can be sold for a large enough profit without claims being made that they will alter the physical characteristics of the Black man. Also, as the media concede images of "sexual power" to White women while in fact reinforcing their social and political oppression, so the conceding of "sexual power" to Black men in the media undercuts the realities of unemployment, imprisonment, and menial jobs available to Black men in social reality.

The sexual objectification of the Black male, however, is a phenomenon that is not allowed to flourish freely *inter*racially. Mainstream media do not encourage Black males to become sex objects for the White public. Of course, Black males are viewed as sex objects among some White women, but the media do not promote this truism. Black *women*, on the other hand, have a history of being ruthlessly forced into situations that make it extremely difficult to avoid being sexually objectified. The media capitalizes on this history by propagandizing an image of woman which disguises the Black woman so that she is "any woman" and therefore can be sexually objectified. The media's influence on making the Black woman "look White" psychologically helps to remove some of the taint of the held-over image from slavery of the Black woman as sexually promiscuous or as a whore—but the media leave just enough daring in the images of Black women's poses and dress to keep alive a spark of her having something extra-spicy to entice and titillate males. Given the desexualizing of White women that White male culture has emphasized over the last centuries, and the racist imaginings of Black women being intrinsically *nothing but* sexual, the very presence of Black women shrouded in sexual suggestiveness is loaded in particularly racist ways.

Immunity to ads is quite a task for any woman. Readers are addressed in a manner that makes them immediately compare themselves with the women in the photos. This causes them to assess themselves in terms of the products to be consumed. The perfectly crafted faces and figures are praised as being attainable if one purchases these products. In this way the characteristics of the products become the characteristics of the image and this becomes the characteristic of the consumer. And woman, you have been hooked!

The ads are fraught with contradictions and paradoxes. They rely heavily on language to combine dichotomized feminine stereotypes. "You're beautiful and believable. You're restless and romantic." The ads attempt to merge the ideal of innocence with a passionate erotic antithesis, the sex object. Images, language, and logic in advertising construct an imposed value by attempting to define consumer interests. Ads will tell you to increase the bust while the models, the images that women are supposed to "be," are bustless. Models are super-slim while American women have an obesity problem. The contradictions and illogic are features of advertising by which the consumer has become virtually stupefied.

Beauty magazines and cosmetic ads are not generally purported to be political organs or for that matter political in any real sense; their content is often trivialized, and their effects on the consciousness of millions of women are easily ignored. This is a dangerous practice, because many complex meanings are coded in their use of language and imagery. That so many women passively and uncritically accept their messages in no way lessens the significance of the coercive measures used to communicate the messages. In fact, given that more than 50 million women purchase a woman's magazine every month (i.e., nearly three-quarters of the entire adult female population) and that TV with its relentless barrage of commercials reaches 95 percent of the homes in the United States, the political importance of understanding the forms of women's oppression that advertising sustains cannot be denied.

This section on media would not be complete without some comments on Black images on prime time television. It should be kept in mind that this is not an inexhaustible critique on the subject of Black images on TV. However, there are several critical arguments that deserve mentioning.

Television is a major factor in the lives of children and also a major socializing agency. Under the guise of fictional entertainment, television programs purport to reflect the world of which we are a part; in so doing, some aspects of social and political issues and attitudes are shown. However, television reflects selectively and also transforms images of reality to the viewer, so that, while being entertained, the viewer is also viewing very definite messages about American life in general.

American television programming and programs are dominated by White males. There is little question that television presents a set of well-defined stereotypes to viewers with respect to gender, ethnic characteristics, race and occupational roles. The images of Blacks in television continue to depict subservience and comedy. The long-standing racist idea about Blacks being either incapable of great success or unable to handle it is expressed in series after series. The difficult struggles Blacks face in striving for some modicum of decent standards of living are made light of under the guise of humor. Now, humor by Blacks and for Blacks is an exchange that is fully appreciated, understood, and consumed by the Black community, but on television, honest ethnic joking becomes something else. The media tend to validate and reinforce the stereotype as a true representation of a race. Julia, the title character in a former TV serial, was a widowed Black nurse with a son. Julia and her son were the only Black characters on the show, except for occasional interaction with other Blacks. Julia was supposedly working-class, but lived the life of an upwardly mobile middle-class woman, exhibiting the tastes of the very affluent. The quality of her lifestyle—her wardrobe, in particular —in no way reflected the status of the working-class Black woman. The leading women in series like *Good Times, The Jeffersons,* and *That's My Mama* were all portrayed with humor as the medium, and thereby carried the message that Blacks are jokers. Flip Wilson's portrayal of Geraldine was noteworthy in that Flip Wilson, as a male in White America, would not be able to be in complete control of every situation. White America is too insecure to face a Black man who commands and demands respect, but it was acceptable that, with Geraldine, as she felt, so she spoke.

The millions of Black women who spend hours watching not only Black TV characters, but the soap operas, are inundated daily with fictional people, involved in unrealistic (for the viewer) conditions and finding stereotypical solutions, only to reengage in still another dramatically unreasonable situation. Women, Black and White, spend hours munching and crunching chips and cookies, growing wider and heavier and living out these soap operas as though they were truly their own lives.

Outcries from the Black community against the images of Blacks portrayed on TV go virtually ignored. When they are not ignored, they still are not acted upon. Unfortunately, there doesn't seem to be much in the way of change for Blacks and the TV medium. The way things are now is too profitable.

NOTES

1. Vivian Gornick, "Introduction," in *Gender Advertisements*, Erving Goffman, Harper/Colophon Books, 1979, p. *vii*.

2. Julian Mayfield, "Lorraine Hansberry: A Woman for All Seasons," *Freedomways*, Vol. 19, No. 4, 1979, p. 263.

VI

Sexual Subjects of Media

> If . . .
> . . . someone has courage to enter the fire
> the young man will be restored to life.
>
> If, the girl whispers,
> I do not go into the fire
> I will not be able to live with my soul.
>
> —Adrienne Rich[1]

By exploring more closely the invitations and suggestions that media images of women offer, it is possible to begin to understand important connections in the political system that White, male-dominant capitalist society sustains. We want to stress here the relationship of capitalist corporations to ideas of "free choice," profit, and male dominance. There are significant connections between the images of motherhood, love, and femininity and parallel images of violence, pornography, and rape on which the media industry prospers. Processes which exploit, dehumanize, and affirm models of dominance and subordination are intrinsic to the systematic perpetuation of racism and imperialist exploitation in the Third World. These systems of oppression are intricately interwoven and are symptomatically present in the media's construction and organization of sexuality.

If more than $20 billion a year is spent on advertising in the
United States, if TVs are in 95% of the homes in this country, if
Playboy magazine alone estimated that in 1977–78 it sold six and a
half million copies and reached at least twenty million readers,[2] if
pornography is estimated to be a $4-million-a-year industry, the
monstrous media empire has to have a significant presence in the
lives of all Black women and men and White women and men. We
have to recognize the significant political, economic, and ideological
roles that advertising plays in this society and in the shaping of each
of our lives. For there to be mass consumption, the corporate interests which control and own the means of production need not only
to make their products known, but to create needs which seduce us
into buying things as if they are essential. The very existence of mass
media—television and radio programs, magazines, films—depends on
the income from advertising. "It could almost be argued that the articles in magazines and programs on television are simply a device to
keep the advertisements and commercials from bumping loudly together."[3] Yet, as the ads direct our vision toward objects to buy, they
also, in the images they use, enmesh us in a whole system of power
distribution, suggesting desirable patterns of dominance and oppression which are most immediately and significantly present in the
gender roles that the advertisements blatantly and subtly suggest.
The images used are fragments of daily life, which we readily recognize. They are relentlessly reconstructed in repetitive patterns of
power in the advertisements themselves. They invent and represent
stylized "universally" experienced pictures, which divert, distract,
and absorb our attention. Yet they operate in a censored space—their
emphasis on adventure, nostalgia, extravagance and fantasy depends
on the systematic absence of aspects of daily life which are selectively
excluded, just as other aspects are selectively always present. In particular, the process and work of producing the commodities, the
daily consequences of work conditions, unemployment, poverty, and
exploitation (on which the controlling corporations depend) are always absent. We see advertising in a state of "suspended disbelief,"
which eases us into "believing" and actively recognizing and con-
firming the behaviors and content it systematically presents us
with. Women do certain things and not others, evoke certain attitudes and not others. The first condition of advertising is that it fragments social reality, desensitizes us to the complexities of daily reali-

ties, selects elements of daily life and fictionalizes these in ways that produce political meanings about "normal" social relations. So certain things—like the happy nuclear family, the ardent housewife, the beautiful marriage—are repeated, while the realities of high divorce rates, child assault, wife beating, and rape are consistently absent.

Advertisements are aimed at us individually. Each of us must buy for the profits to be made. And each of us is invited, as a sexual person, to enter the images of "selling." As we are offered a "free choice" between competing products, we are offered a free choice of emotional and sexual relations which we "individually" respond to. As buyers (or nonbuyers), as sexual beings (or potential ones), we are, the advertisements suggest, "discriminating people—united by unique tastes."[4] The free individual purchases and acts out of individual choice—if, of course, money, class, race, and gender put you in a position where you can enjoy these privileges of choice. "Freedom is in fact part of the most basic ideology, the very sub-structure of advertising."[5] We are invited, of our free will, to participate in free choices. Or are we?

Just as our lives are limited by class, race, and gender, so the options in the advertising images themselves are closed systems. We enter images which have been constructed based on carefully defined assumptions and systematic symbolic suggestions. There are systematic criteria, for example, for selecting certain types of shows for TV—and that is that a certain percentage of media time in them has to be dedicated to the exposure of "T&A."[6] While we consciously interpret (and even dismiss) the overt "message," our active reading of the ad in itself involves us in unconsciously agreed-on "positions," unchosen involvement in images of power and domination. We see not *real* men or women, mothers or dates, but models posing and acting out approved (but very selected) typifications of normality, in costumes "constructed from commodities."[7] Many things take place as we observe and digest and interpret the images. We create meaning for the product advertised, and we take meaning from it. We invent ourselves by the terms the ad sets up, and we invent ourselves *into* the images it is controlling.[8] Both products and images are chosen by us only *after* the corporations and their media machinery have chosen to produce them. So the choices we are pressured to "live up to"—both as buyers or as sexual, gendered subjects—are not really choices at all.

> Each sister wearing masks of Revlonclairolplaytex
> to survive.
> Each sister faking orgasm under the System's very
> concrete bulk
>
> at night
> to survive.
>
> Our smiles and glances
> the ways we walk, sit, laugh, the games we must play
> with men . . . among ourselves—these are the ways we
> pass.
>
> —Robin Morgan[9]

It is only on returning from a socialist country that you realize how all-pervasive advertising, broadcasting, and mass-distributed
commercial magazines are in this culture. By seeing and registering
advertisements regularly, as a key feature of our capitalist culture, we
are continually being drawn to take up positions in relationship to
the images, attitudes, and suggestions that the ads contain. The sexual politics of the advertisements are symptomatic of the political organization of power on many interconnecting levels.

Men are the central reference point in the aura that advertisements evoke. The images of advertisements are organized around
a male presence which is either explicitly depicted *in* the advertisement—engulfing and absorbing the female attention, suggesting
direction, decision, control of the situation—or implicitly "outside"
the ad, looking on, receiving the expressions the women in the ad
turn toward the observing world from which we *all* participate in the
offered images. The images involve polarizing of attitudes and poten-
tials in terms of *gender* in all of us. These are suggested as if they are
natural, and we are expected to respond to them naturally, from our
socially experienced patterns of gender behavior in the "natural"
family units of which reality (so the ads tell us) is comprised. The
omnipresence of the *male* subject defines women's presence in terms
of men *all the time* in this "natural" world of images. Sheila Rowbotham vividly evokes the dilemma for women created by the media's relentless portrayal of male attention being at the center of
whatever female stance is portrayed:

I was experiencing the situation . . . through men's eyes. I was being
asked to desire myself . . . Catching myself observing myself desiring
one of my selves I remained poised for an instant in two halves . . . I

knew the gestures she made to excite them from inside. I knew how to drop into the stereotypes we learn as female sexuality . . . I could see through their eyes but I could feel with her body. I was man-woman. I had thus contributed towards making an object of myself and other women.[10]

The questions we need to be asking all the time are: What does the constructed male presence in and around the composition of the "woman in the ad" ask of the female presence? What do the images of feminine women demand from the psychological and social presence of the masculinity they imply? What ideologies are implicitly underlying the sexual images we take for granted, and what power relations do they ritualize? What needs do they meet and shape in each of our minds, as we mindlessly traverse this world of ads, magazines, films, and television?

In the magazine world directed at women and in the public world of TV commercials (as opposed to the underground and male-segregated worlds of pornography and prostitution), certain images and roles of women are central to the consumer culture of femininity. The images are in fact highly idealized and have carefully written into them useful imaginings of failure. If Black women encounter the impossibility of reaching or realizing the White standards of beauty the images demand, White women are in fact only a hairbreadth nearer to fulfilling a self-image in relation to them. The women invented in the ads project unattainable "qualities" outside the grasp of the vast majority of women. However, the images suggest a never-ending quest (through the buying of products, of course, and the finding of a man who could enable those purchases) to "live up to" the fabricated ideals they portray. They are images of "what I am not" as well as "what I might be" if. . . . Anxiety and insecurity, as consequences of these carefully constructed, artificially composed images in the context of the chaotic, daily realities of actual women's lives and work, serve the impulsive consumerism necessary for capitalism to thrive on its home front. These unreal, synthetic images of women nonetheless haunt the "normal" landscape of any woman's life in that they are organized around themes of love, romance, femininity leaning toward male support, marriage, motherhood, and family. The attitudes and situations that these embody in the advertising images are very important and symptomatic of the power relations they evoke, produce, and reinforce.

If we think of the normal characteristics that "feminine sexuality" suggests in advertisements, the list emerges as follows: fragile, coy, yielding, assertive only to suggest the arousal of overpowering responses; "sleek, docile, decorative and inert";[11] "eroticism cathected to conquest and surrender";[12] a sexual potential which is never specific but vague, evocative, alluded to, never direct; ingratiating, appeasing, and appealing; infantilized, defenseless, and vulnerable; dreamlike, inactive, leaning; isolated from other women in the all-pervading, special male presence, or competing through sexuality itself with them; luxuriating in an atmosphere or among material objects provided by men; passive anticipation and suggestive availability.[13]

Without turning to the male-orientated pornographic literature of sexuality, where else in the dominant culture do we have *any* other images of women as sexual beings? Where do images of sexuality come from in White culture, since the family traditionally inhibits and represses ideas of sexuality, and the dominant cultural portrayal of women puts their sexuality *in opposition* to the other roles of wife and mother. Romance and love bridge the gap between these elusively suggested images of women never present as active sexual subjects but recurrently implicated in codes of sexual submission, and the confined roles associated with "*my* woman," as depicted in wifedom and motherhood. The love motif is presented in advertisements (and in romantic fiction) as being shrouded in breathtaking glamour, immeasurable uniqueness, spontaneity, dreamlike disbelief in front of an irresistible and overwhelming reality. Males are represented as the source of specially conceded gentleness out of potential ruggedness, promises, fulfillment, and anticipated resolution. The resolution which is proposed and inferred for women is, of course, the socially anticipated marriage contract, the state of wifedom and the institution of motherhood. And yet, if we linger further with the images the media consistently produce around these roles, other images, which subtly support the subordinate portrayal of feminine sexuality, emerge. Wife and mother: personal loyalty against the world; competition with other families' images of happiness and success (whiter than, tastier than, more accommodating than . . .); willingness to service others, to support others unconditionally; availability to the needs of others, selflessness, self-sacrifice; a domain of safety and niceness in the home (which is beautiful, ordered, elegant, middle-class); no need for a sexual identity—the ambivalences of femininity being "resolved" by the appropriation of her life by the man;

rewards for faithful service; mediation of others' demands and conflicts; all in all, a state of fulfilling dependency centered around an
abandoning of self and a harmonious notion of love and caring.

Although these images of women are alleged to project a natural
story of timeless, universal femininity, they are, of course, very
specific cultural constructions of femininity and womanhood. Moreover, they are very specific to the White, male-dominated cultural
projection, although *in the advertising world Black women are being
depicted along very similar lines.* The portrayal of women's destiny
in these terms in fact legitimizes male dominance. Within the ideological labyrinths of romance, nostalgic tenderness, and subdued titil-
lation (which are resolved, flattened out into the domestic scenes of
hygiene, food, and child servicing) the apparent contradictions in the
images actually embody a coherent landscape for violence. The passivity, inertia, idealized stasis, and systematic lack of autonomous sexual energy in the "nature" of feminine sexuality as we see it explicitly structured across the media, produce endless permutations of
women as a site *to be acted on* by the omnipresent male whose masculinity invents itself in terms of these passivities the woman offers.
The highly personalized context of love is ritualistically acted out by
anonymous models who (or which) project idealized features of
unreal, artificially perfected bodies celebrating conquest and surrender. Although the family image of "motherhood" (on the White,
nuclear, patriarchal model) is incompatible with the sexual images of
the invented feminine sexuality,[14] there is a consistency of dependency and subservience which carries over into the notion of wife and
mother.

The wife/mother image in the media celebrates confinement in
the home, being provided for by the man, being enclosed in the
safety and security his presence embodies. The woman is seen glory-
ing in the "benign control"—"a loving protector is standing by in
the wings, allowing not so much for dependency, as a copping out of,
or relief from the 'realities.' "[15] As the emphasized *availability* of the
sexual, feminine female construct calls for the active intervention of
the dominant, possessive male, so the *nonavailability* of the wife and
mother, as sexual agent, concludes the similar terms of that dominance and possession. Somehow both images transmit the *absence* of
woman as subject and, in place of her as active, autonomous agent,
produce a stylized feminine presence which posits a male, active, determining presence.

Women are consistently shown finding pleasure (and even "freedom") in a patriarchal "dominion of submission, sacrifice and acceptance."[16] The alluring, natural images, which have sufficiently recognizable features of our already gendered psychic and social reality, suggest the inevitability and ritualized enjoyment of sexual subordination and ideologically dispersed rituals of bondage. The woman the media produces and reproduces is never an autonomous individual, actively engaging in nurturance or in achievement, but a mass-produced object ritualizing selected, one-dimensional aspects of these. She is not "entitled to ideas, opinions, preferences of her own," but is "only a shadow."[17] These fetishized constructs of femininity and masculinity propagated by the media embody the fundamental power relations of *institutionalized* heterosexuality based on the sexual oppression of women and sexual dominance by men.

So in the gendered images of the media, contradictions, struggles, exhaustion, anxieties, frustrations, and failures of the daily social relations between men and women and involved with reproduction are eliminated, marginalized, and smothered in overdetermined romantic ideologies. Yet the personalized isolation, celebrated passivity, mechanical deference to male power, psychological and economic dependency on male benignness and protection—*and* the complementary male sense of self necessitated and capitalized on by these images—lay solid ground for the diverse forms of sexual violence which we find elsewhere in parallel areas of the media industry in direct and explicit terms. This violence is lived out psychologically, emotionally, and physically in the lives of most women.

While evocative sexual passivity, love, domestic harmony, and the endless intricacies of fashion and beauty flood women's consciousness on one level of the social construction of femininity, another world of war stories, sports, mechanics, horror, science fiction, and pornography trace the paths of complementary media productions of "masculinity." The media realm of men stresses control and knowledge—access not only to property, but to the technology around it and to the concentrated, muscular, active presence needed to set machinery in motion—productive, political, or sexual. The images of abandoned, cornered, helpless, to-be-swept-away, willingly inhibited and self-sacrificing women evoke taken-for-granted "recognition" of "active subordination,"[18] which in turn legitimizes and requests active domination. The terms of sadomasochism are all on stage. When it is possible to describe the dominant image of marriage as one of "practical and emotional *bondage*"[19] where women "attach a sort of pride to the voluntary surrender of their own will,"[20] it is only one step to recognizing the way that the capitalist, male-dominated cultural production of masculine/feminine depends on a "psychology orientated to prostitution and misuse."[21]

Women as *captives*—both in media images and in the institution-alizing of their personal lives—are key to the advertising industry. Once the models of control and subordination are prevalent, the margins for acting them out are variable. Assault, battering, rape, prostitution, and pornography are legitimized and necessitated by the polarities of masculine and feminine which the male-dominated capitalist economy develops to sustain its profits and hierarchies. While indeed more than $48 million is spent annually on *eye makeup*, $455 million was spent in one year by an average weekly audience of 2.5 million people to see hard-core pornographic films.[22]

When people become symbols they need not be treated as human beings . . . looking away from people or social phenomena (and their material circumstances) to their supposed abstract "significance" can be at worst an excuse for human and social atrocities, at best, a turning of reality into apparent unreality, almost unlivable while social dreams and myths seem so real.[23]

The struggles of the White Women's Liberation Movement embody a "rebellion against the established typifications of womanhood,"[24] which the dominant White culture produces and elaborates. The initial oversimplified angers in front of the blatant sexist objectifications of women's bodies by a simple male enemy is moving in all kinds of directions to understand the material conditions of both reproduction and production which produce, reproduce, and perpetuate systematized sexual oppression in the dominant White culture. "All of us as women 'achieve' our subjectivity in relation to a definition of women"[25] which is implicit in histories of family structure and psychology, sexual division of labor, gendered division of power, and the institutionalized organization of sexuality itself. As Black women are, via the media, drawn into the terms of the dominant White male culture, the feminist struggles can highlight the implications of those terms. As Black women specify their own histories of oppression and the construction of *woman* out of their culture and history, White women can learn to identify the specific terms of their sexual heritage and the forms of oppression it embodies.

A culture which has in its White, male-dominated, *class-defined* history institutionalized female subservience has the widest implications for White feminists and for Black liberation. This culture has evolved ideologies of dependency supported by chemical industries, drug industries, gadget technology, instant technical or consumer solutions, and media images which psychologically reinforce specifically "useful" forms of alienation, what appear to be "ahistorical" hierarchies of power, and legitimized patterns of subordination. By the early 1970s, the United States media were already broadcasting in 35 languages in 123 countries. The media's corporate interests function not only at home but abroad, where imperialist strategies in population control, economic strangleholds on primary resources, and political manipulation of economies and governments feed the United States' economic, political, and ideological power.

As the draft looms imminent, the provocative, sarcastic slogan against army conscription (satirizing a TV and magazine advertising campaign actually used by the U.S. Army) can be paralleled with the "normally" alluring sexual images of cocktail advertisements. Evoking the actual army advertisement, which promised excitement, travel, training, and social life, the anti-conscription slogan stressed what was left out:

JOIN THE ARMY. TRAVEL TO EXCITING, EXOTIC PLACES. LEARN EXCITING SKILLS. MEET EXCITING AND EXOTIC PEOPLE. AND KILL THEM.[26]

In this way, underlining the social relations sustained in conjunction with the alluring images of, say, a cocktail ad, we could write:

DRINK THIS COCKTAIL. TRAVEL TO EXCITING, EXOTIC PLACES. LIVE THE GOOD LIFE. ENJOY EROTIC ENCOUNTERS. MEET EXCITING AND EXOTIC WOMEN. AND OWN/USE/RAPE THEM.

The elaboration of passive, dehumanized female subjects and the kind of active, forceful, controlling male subjects they evoke is not only an axis for legitimating sexual exploitation and oppression. It also implicitly legitimates the notion of the national, "free" American subject, defending all-American values, asked to consent to and be active in (or passive in) the exploitation of Third World countries or the taken-for-granted terms of racism at home. There are structural echoes between the female sexual "object"—either exotic, mysterious, and inviting conquest, or subdued, tamed, legitimized under male authority and control—and the racial "object" invoking

White superiority, dominance, and civilized "normality." Racism produces media images of the exotic, erotic, and mysterious Black subject; these images provoke the need for conquest, containment, and repression by the White subject. Other images—of the tamed, ridiculed, coopted, "harmless" Black subject—confirm the hold that White authority and precedence have on a potentially dangerous reality, which could disrupt the "normal" terms of social power.

The media images present positions in power and powerlessness which, while harmonizing or eliminating the conflict that capitalist class relations actually entail, ensnare gender and race in a complex web of power relations, wherein "classless" White men, and the White women they appropriate, assume positions of dominance and authority.

NOTES

1. Adrienne Rich, "Leaflets," *Poems Selected and New, 1950–74*, p. 118.

2. Andrea Cammarata, "Pornography and Sexual Consciousness," Hampshire College, 1978 (unpublished paper).

3. Alice Embree, "Media Images/Madison Avenue Brainwashing—The Facts," *Sisterhood Is Powerful*, ed. Robin Morgan, p. 195 ff.

4. Judith Williamson, *Decoding Advertisements*, London, Marion Boyars, 1979, p. 49.

5. Ibid., p. 42.

6. Tits and Ass. This was discussed on the CBS network program "60 Minutes," 1979.

7. Janet Winship, "A Woman's World: Woman—an Ideology of Femininity," in *Women Take Issue: Aspects of Women's Subordination*, ed. Women's Collective of Birmingham Centre for Cultural Studies, London, Hutchinson, 1978.

8. Judith Williamson, op. cit., p. 41.

9. Robin Morgan, "Letter to a Sister Underground," *Monster*.

10. Sheila Rowbotham, *Woman's Consciousness, Man's World*, p. 41.

11. Marge Piercy, "Hello up There," *To Be of Use*, New York, Doubleday, 1973, p. 30.

12. Vivian Gornick & Barbara Moran, eds., *Woman in Sexist Society: Studies in Power and Powerlessness*, New York, New American Library, 1972, p. *xxii*.

13. See in general the illustration of these and other characteristics in Erving Goffman, *Gender Advertisements*, New York, Harper & Row, 1979.

14. See Ann Oakley: ". . . as though the structure of the male psyche requires a separation between sexual partners and mothers, an identity between the two posing an obscure threat to the male's fragile rejection of the feminine element—his own childhood identification with the mother as the childrearing person," in *Women Confined*, p. 286; see also detailed discussion of this in Nancy Chodorow, *The Reproduction of Mothering*.

15. Erving Goffman, op. cit., p. 5.

16. Gornick and Moran, op. cit., p. *xxii*.

17. Jessie Bernard, "The Paradox of the Happy Marriage," *Woman in Sexist Society*, p. 154.

18. Janet Winship, op. cit., pp. 134–35 and 140.

19. Margaret Adams, "The Compassion Trap," *Woman in Sexist Society*, p. 557.

20. Jessie Bernard, op. cit., p. 153.

21. Margaret Adams, op. cit., p. 562.

22. Kathleen Barry, *Female Sexual Slavery*, Englewood Cliffs, N.J., Prentice-Hall, 1979, p. 84.

23. Judith Williamson, op. cit., p. 169.

24. Ann Oakley, op. cit., p. 207.

25. Janet Winship, op. cit., p. 134.

26. Political slogan frequently used by pacifist organizations in London in the 1970s.

VII

Styling, Profiling, and Pretending: The Games Before the Fall

SLAVE RITUAL

when I asked him about
    it
he said he had to do
    that.
had to
    knock her down, slap her,
beat her up, chastise her . . .
how else
would she know
he loved her?

she understood
it wasn't nothing serious
nothing, "personal"
    she'd get up knowing
she was going down again
she never would hold the floor
and wait out the count,
somehow
that would have been unfair,
not part
    of it . . .

she never even imagined
    packing her bags and
leaving him.
what you leave a good man fuh?
he paid the rent, went to work everyday
bought groceries,
occasionally,
why, where would she go?
and to who? who would
love her better? any "differently"
she knew he would never
kill her
she seldom had a bruise,
that showed . . .
just a knock here & now
a slap there and then
to ease the pain of
    BEING
together . . .

once, I knocked on their door
and asked if I could help
They BOTH became angry at me
"Go home stupid! Don't you have any of your own business
    to mind?"
Sometimes when my neighbors are not
    fighting
they talk to me
They Say,
THEY LOVE EACH OTHER.

              —Carolyn M. Rodgers[1]

The Afro-American culture with all its unique features of caring, sharing, kinship networks, upward mobility aspirations, and color caste complexes interacts with and reacts to a racially and economically oppressive environment. This "double consciousness" (Afro-American culture and Western society), these two warring souls in every Black female and male body, become further compounded and complex as women's consciousness comes to the fore. In any discussion about Blacks—and Black female and male relationships are no exception—we must never lose sight of these actualities. However, these facts must not be allowed to become excuses for any and all apolitical, irresponsible behaviors on the part of Black women or men, such as Black fratricide or poverty pimping. Nor must Black women and men unwittingly enter the game of blaming the victim. Put in other words, Black men must not put a heavy blame trip on Black women, and Black women must not put a heavy, accusatory putdown on Black men. What is needed is an honest—a putting-aside-pride-and-frail-ego honest—assessment of the reality of the conditions that surround and exist for and between Black females and males. Knowing and facing one's reality is a first step, a necessary first step in any struggle. "Our reality, like all other realities, has positive aspects and negative aspects, has strengths and weaknesses . . . Man is part of reality. Reality exists independent of man's will . . . those who lead the struggle must never confuse what they have in their head with reality."[2]

It is a political reality that Black people in America are victims of institutional racism and economic oppression. To put it simply, Blacks who imagine they have escaped these oppressions have been psychologically duped. They have bought into the media's massive and successful efforts to promote and popularize the mistaken belief that inequality and racism are social ills of the past. The media cite evidence of Black professionals in the high-income brackets, token Federal appointees, and local politicians to accommodate the belief that the system is no longer racist. The problem of racism was supposedly solved in the Sixties; therefore, Blacks who don't make it have no one to blame but themselves. This, of course, is not true. The record from the Seventies clearly shows that conditions for Blacks have worsened. (See table on page 15.)

In this chapter we are concerned with the realities of the sexual relationships between Black women and Black men, emphasizing Black women's sexual attitudes and behaviors. In so doing we must keep in mind that there is no monolithic group of Black women or Black men. Their conditions and situations vary according to income levels, careers, regions, age, education, and early life experiences. We are interested in the underlying commonalities that exist despite societal forces and circumstantial differences which have had substantial effects on the lives of Black women (and men).

Initially, there are several undeniable facts about Black women's lives that must be recognized and acknowledged. Their lives have been characterized by: (1) high achievement and outstanding accomplishments by a few; (2) an unending cycle of poverty for the vast majority; (3) always defining themselves and their womanhood in terms of their connection with Black men; (4) strong feelings of autonomy and independence.

In her book *Of Woman Born*, Adrienne Rich wrote, "What we bring to childbirth is nothing less than our entire socialization as women."[3] Similarly, a Black woman's sexuality is nothing less than her entire socialization as a Black female. The sexual socialization of the Black female is largely determined by her early childhood and adolescent upbringing, the influences of family, school, and religion intertwined with the roles played by culture and society. Of course, her socioeconomic class, religion, geographical region, and sense of self-esteem influence the child-raising practices to which she is subjected, as well as the ways in which resisting or succumbing to the cultural and societal pressures are enacted. These considerations remind us once again that Black female sexuality cannot be viewed through "monolithic lenses."

An analysis of the role of socialization in the Black woman's sexuality is necessarily complex. The early life experience of the female is a good starting point in examining the configuration of Black female sexuality. The "puritanical" upbringing of Black women is said to be a key cause for the problems that Black females experience as they approach womanhood. This puritanical upbringing is said to be responsible for the attitudes among young girls that sex is dirty, that it is not a subject for polite conversation, that masturbation is unnatural, and that sex will get you in trouble.

This explanation must be juxtaposed to the realities of families that view the role of sex in a more celebratory fashion. In these homes there are various messages that say sex is desirable, sex is satisfying, sex is "good," and everyone gets involved, sooner or later. The popular songs that are heard and sung in homes and on the streets, the jokes and innuendoes, the signifying and sounding in conversations, are all fraught with sexual tones. In overcrowded dwellings it is impossible to keep sexual relations a secret. In homes at the lower socioeconomic levels, attitudes toward having babies—a most direct connection to the sex act—are an indication of the family's and community's feelings about sexual relations. Carol Stack, in her book *All Our Kin*, points out that:

Unlike many other societies, Black women in The Flats feel few if any restrictions about childbearing. Unmarried Black women, young and old, are eligible to bear children, and frequently women bearing their first child are quite young.

A girl who gives birth as a teen-ager frequently does not raise and nurture her first born child. While she may share the same room and household with her baby, her mother, her mother's sister, or her older sister will care for the child and become the child's "mamma." People show pride in all their kin, and particularly new babies born into their kinship network. Mothers encourage sons to have babies, and even more important, men coax their "old ladies" to have their babies.[4]

Puritanical attitudes exist in many homes, but in many other homes the attitude is definitely not puritanical. What is common and true in most homes is that regardless of whether or not sex is an open or discreet issue, Black women do not receive necessary and accurate information about sexual matters. Young Black girls pick up a lot of misinformation from the streets and from their female and male peer groups. Beauty parlors long have been a stronghold for the dissemination of facts about men and about women's involvements with men. Young ears always have strained to pick up some information about sexual matters. The adult women's talk would sometimes be guarded so that the young female would not get the full picture, and other times the adult's intent was to deliberately give messages to the young sisters. Comments about mistreatment from men, the sweetness of men, two-timing men and faithful women are topics that typically elicit animated conversations.

The following scenario illustrates how one young female receives messages about men and sex. An older woman enters the beauty shop, and her response to the welcoming greetings of the beautician is an unenthusiastic, half-hearted, semi-articulated utterance. Another customer and good friend says, "Hmm, what's the matter with you? Didn't you get any last night?" Or she might say, "Girl, you acting like you just lost your ole man. What's happening?" Men and sex are viewed as necessities for feeling good and/or causes for feeling bad. Either way, the female is a reflection of the male. The ambivalence seen throughout male/female relationships is again apparent.

The important roles of music and dance in Black culture have historically been influential in the sexual socialization of young Black females. Traditionally music—spirituals, gospel, blues, and jazz—has figured prominently in the lives of Black folks. The blues dealt with the real stuff: there's no escaping from the hard, bitter, day-to-day struggles.

Female blues singers were unique in recording Black women's history and struggles via song. The topics and words in their songs, combined with their personalized and expressive deliveries, created an idiom that has helped Black women remember the past and live the present. The sexual content of these songs reflects themes and delivers messages about: the nature of and ways to deal with two-timing men; men mistreating women; cheating women; women longing for their men and willing to pay any price to be with their men; men who can't quite measure up sexually; the hardships associated with being a poor Black woman; and the glorification of sex. The titles of the following songs reflect these themes: "Mean Mistreater Blues" by Memphis Minnie; "All Fed Up" and "Ain't No Fool" by Big Mama Thornton; "Yellow Dog Blues" by Lizzie Miles; "Tricks Ain't Walkin' No More" by Bessie Jackson; and "Empty Bed Blues" by Bessie Smith.

Bessie Smith, the legendary Bessie Smith, the Empress of the Blues, made a historical contribution to the sexual lives of Black women. Michele Russell made this point succinctly:

Bessie Smith redefined our time. In a deliberate inversion of the Puritanism of the Protestant ethic, she articulated, as clearly as anyone before or since, how fundamental sexuality was to survival. Where work was often the death of us, sex brought us back to life. It was better than food, and sometimes a necessary substitute.

For Bessie Smith, Black women in American culture were no longer to be regarded only as sexual objects. She made us sexual subjects, the first step in taking control. She transformed our collective shame at being rape victims, treated like dogs or worse, the meat dogs eat, by emphasizing the value of our allure. In so doing, she humanized sexuality for Black women.[5]

Bessie Smith's songs about house rent parties and buffet flats gave graphic accounts of entertainment and sex as a part of economic, spiritual, and emotional survival. The musical talents of Black women blues singers were as outstanding as were the social commentaries in their songs. House rent parties and buffet flats were common in Black urban areas and offered pleasures that were not restricted to sex, such as card playing, eating, drinking, and gambling, but sex was certainly a dominant part of the scene. In a 1971 interview with Chris Albertson, Ruby Smith (Bessie's niece by marriage, who traveled with her) described a buffet flat located in Detroit:

RUBY SMITH: . . . faggots dressed like women there it wasn't against the law, you know—that Detroit was a *real* open town for *everybody* in that town. Bessie and us all, went to a party. Some woman there had a buffet flat.

Bessie Smith paid tribute to this establishment in her recording "Soft Pedal Blues":

> There's a lady in our neighborhood who runs a
>   buffet flat,
> and when she gives a party she knows just where
>   she's at,
> She gave a dance last Friday night, it was to last
>   till one,
> But when the time was almost up, the fun had
>   just begun.

ALBERTSON: What's a buffet flat?

RUBY SMITH: A buffet flat is nothing but faggots and, and, uh, bull dykers and—open house—everything goes on in that house . . .

ALBERTSON: A gay place?

RUBY SMITH: A *very* gay place.

ALBERTSON: Strictly for faggots and bull dykes?

RUBY SMITH: —Everything! Everything that was in the life, everybody that's in the life. . . . Buffet means everything—everything goes on. They had a faggot there that was so great people used to come there just to watch him make love to another man. That's right, he was real great, he'd give him a tongue bath and everything. People used to pay good just to see him come there and see him do his act . . .[6]

A graphic reflection of the urban phenomenon of the poor, the house rent party, is heard in Bessie Smith's rendition of "Gimme a Pigfoot (and a Bottle of Beer)." Her candor is amazing as she sings of "reefers and a gang of gin, lay me cause I'm in my sin," and "Check all your razors and your guns, we gonna be wrestling when the wagon comes." Fats Waller, in his recording of "The Joint is Jumping," makes similar references. A police whistle sounds as an indication that the joint (house, not marijuana) is being raided. References are made to "sissies switching around," and he warns people, "Don't give your right names!" At parties and performances Bessie Jackson (Lucille Bogan) sang "Bulldyke Woman's Blues" and Al Miller and his Swing Stompers did "Ain't That a Mess" (a song about all kinds of incestual relations in one family). These songs were sung without compunction. But it must be remembered that this was before the current women's liberation and gay activist movements, and they were recorded in a milieu that regarded homosexuality as a simple fact of life (during the Twenties and Thirties).

Women blues singers from the past to the present—Ida Cox, Mamie Smith, Ma Rainey, Bessie Smith, Bessie Jackson, Billie Holiday, Dinah Washington, early recordings of Lena Horne, Esther Phillips, Aretha Franklin, Nina Simone—were heard in the homes of Blacks. Hence young females have listened to and identified with the women in the songs for generations. The younger females observed that the behavior of adult females frequently paralleled the behavior of the women described in the songs. The idea and image of men and sex being integral to and necessary for life became firmly embedded and eventually internalized in their minds. The similarity in the sentiments expressed in the songs remains relatively unchanged from generation to generation. View the following lyrics.

People have different blues and think they're mighty sad/But blues about a man is the worst I ever had . . .

—Ma Rainey (1920s)

The blues ain't nothin' but a woman crying for her man/When she wants some lovin'. I'm sure all you women will understand . . .

—Dinah Washington (1950s)

Don't send me no doctor to fill me up with all those pills/Got me a man named Dr. Feelgood/Takes care of all my pains and my ills . . .

—Aretha Franklin (1960s)

Among the Black youth of today, house rent parties are not even a memory, but the youth of today still party. They eat, drink, smoke, and dance. The Mess Around and Black Bottom (dances) have been replaced with the Grind (1950s), the Funky Chicken (1960s), and the Freak, the Rock, and the Dog (1970s). Generation upon generation apply different names to the sexual gyrations, with the implicative term "dry fuck" remaining unchanged.

Music—live entertainment, radio, and records—continues to provide the rhythms for the latest dance steps while lyrics continue to pour out sentiments about the material conditions of life for Black people and the personal problems and crises that exist between men and women. However, the messages and meanings in the songs are no longer so astute in portraying social conditions within a political context. Commercial recording industries, with their number one goal being profit at any cost, did not allow music by, for, and about Blacks to retain its authenticity. Companies were established to record Black music. That music, one of the few areas where Blacks presented their own definitions, was violated and exploited.

Classic blues became a women-oriented idiom which often capitalized on lyrics that were explicit in their sexual connotations. Although the records were aimed toward the race market and were heavily purchased by Blacks, they were bought by Whites, too. The image of the Black woman is thus again projected as in the bordellos and previously on plantations as a sex object, alluring and suggestive. Though her own feelings of depression, misery and heartbreak were aimed toward her Black men, she was being exploited by Whites for economic reasons and purposes.[7]

Black music today is heavily exploited by the White record industry. Popular Black artists, females and males, may attempt to produce songs that can be identified with various segments of the Black population and with a resistance to and struggle against oppressive conditions. However, recording corporations mainly produce a music whose role as a social conditioner is more of a sexual stimulant than anything else.

The role of religion figures prominently in the sexual socialization of most Black women. The rich gospel life with its Baptist moans, sanctified bounce, and spirited strutting was and is as rich and emotional a part of certain Black women's upbringing as blues and jazz was to other young women. In the "puritanical" homes, sex was spoken of as "sinful," and "nice, decent" girls didn't attend functions that featured "sinful ways."

The messages from their mothers and older females about the sinfulness of sex, though not totally unheeded, did not stop the young girls from engaging in sexual explorations with young males at church-related events and activities (Sunday school, church outings, etc.). Here again one sees the ambivalence: an unmarried teenage mother's baby would be welcomed and handled by all of the women parishioners, including the minister's wife—that is, sex was "sinful," yet the product of "sinfulness" was welcomed.

It is interesting to note the results of a comparative study of premarital coitus, religion, and the southern Black. Data was gathered from a southern Black college, a midwestern White university, and a Swedish university. Church attendance was a factor considered in the comparisons since, in previous studies, the researchers had found religion to be a most important factor operating to restrict variant sexual activity. They cited Kinsey, who reported little difference among the denominations, but considerable difference between the religiously active or devout on the one hand, and those less active or devout on the other. The former showed up with lower rates on virtually every type of disapproved sexual behavior that Kinsey studied, and this was especially true of premarital sex.[8] This relationship did not hold for the data gathered in the study of the southern Blacks. The conclusions reached were: religiosity as measured by church attendance had more effect in controlling premarital sex among the Whites than among the Blacks in the samples.[9] (As a matter of fact, for the Blacks in three of the four comparisons, coitus incidence is greater for the frequent church attenders, contrary to expectation.) The conclusion in the study is in harmony with a similar conclusion reached by Reiss and based upon analysis of attitudinal data. For the Blacks in his sample, Reiss found little difference between frequent and infrequent church attenders in the acceptance of premarital coitus. In contrast with White society, he explained, Black communities generally have lacked strong ecclesiastical authority over sex, with their churches serving more as a source of tension reduction than as enforcers of a puritanical code of ethics.[10]

In a curious light it can be said that historically religious expressions and sexual expressions played similar roles in the survival experiences of Blacks. Religion, it is often said, provided a source of hope, and escape from the horrendous realities of slave and post-slave life. It offered faith as a healer, a balm, that renewed the spirit and soul, enabling the worshippers to continue with their daily hardships. At the end of grueling and bitter work weeks, thousands of Black folks have historically flocked to churches to have heart and soul restored and replenished, to experience joy and pleasure, religious fervor and zeal, which frequently culminated in "gettin' happy" or "gettin' in the spirit." Also on weekends, thousands of Blacks headed for the Chicken Shack, the Bucket of Blood, or Lil's Bar, or would go stompin' at the Savoy, or doing the do at Minton's Play House, or boogeying at Rockland Palace or the Audubon. These places, too, served as meeting grounds where spirits were elevated and restored, the soul was replenished and hopes ran high. Joy and pleasure were experienced through dancing and other sexual expressions and encounters, which frequently resulted in deliciously heightened emotions. Opiates of the masses? Or survival activities? It has often been said that religious leaders could lead their flocks to the sea or off a mountaintop. Great blues or rhythm-and-blues singers could also lead their audiences dancing and swinging to whatever destination they chose.

Young Black females growing up in homes with strong or weak religious influence, Catholic or Holy Roller, were cognizant of an ambiguity associated with sex. Sex was sort of a "desirable no-no," an "attractive nuisance." How this ambiguity was resolved was largely dependent on what was learned from messages and behaviors of significant persons in the families and from the community and peer ethos. This included information about heterosexuality and homosexuality. For example, young girls were aware of the admiration bestowed on the minister by adult females. They were also aware that occasionally the ministers had a sexual preference for younger boys.

Homosexuality among men in Black communities was considered a dubious distinction. (This, too, is prior to the gay activist movement and does not apply to those in the "fast life"—entertainers, celebrities, etc., during the Forties through the Seventies.) The male homosexual was not categorically ostracized, nor did he become totally invisible. The extent of derision and/or acceptance depended to a great extent on how he manifested his homosexuality. Those who were extremely flamboyant in mannerism or dress were targeted for taunts, ridicule, and occasional physical abuse. Those homosexuals who went about their business without an ostentatious display of what were considered to be female characteristics and behaviors, and who were discreet in their sexual encounters, were more or less "tolerated" and "accepted." The popular explanation was that these men acting sort of "sissyish" were "mama's boys" who had never grown out of *that* stage (whatever *that* stage was supposed to be)—that they had never been able to "cut their mothers' apron strings." The attitude toward male homosexuals reflected a curious tendency to recognize and even overemphasize a positive quality in spite of the gayness. For example, a male who acted kind of "sissyish" was also a *good* cook or a *good* artist or a *good* hairdresser. Young males, however, were warned by their families to "stay away" from Mr. So-and-so. The young males implicitly understood that the reason for "staying away" from Mr. So-and-so was because he might "do something funny" to them—and that this "something funny" was somehow connected with sex. It is important to note here that, with males, sex was a very definite part of the definition of being homosexual.

A curious combination of intrigue and fear concerning male homo-sexuals developed in the minds of young Black males. At later stages of development it was not uncommon for groups or gangs of young Black males (ages thirteen to seventeen) to extort money from the local neighborhood homosexuals. One or more of the group members would volunteer or would be elected or designated to be-come sexually involved with the older man for a monetary reward. The money would be used for alcoholic beverages, drugs, or food, or put to whatever use was deemed necessary and desirable by the group. The prevailing attitude surrounding involvement with a ho-mosexual adult male was, "it's no big deal. You just let him get his rocks off for a while, and then you get paid for doing nothing. It's a quick way to make some dough."

If the youth was passive rather than active in the sex act, that kept him "honest" and "innocent" of being a homosexual. In cases where the young male was the active participant, he maintained his male-ness, or macho-ness, with his peers on the grounds that he was play-ing the male role.

In the case of the young male being passive, an analogy can be made to male/female, active/passive roles in heterosexual sex. The young male is playing the role of the female. He can "just be there" while the older male gets his pleasure. Being used is equated with being female in the sex act. The young males, however, demand and receive pay. If the female demands and receives pay, she is labeled a whore. The double standard is working and, what's more, the young males are being socialized to view females as sexual objects that pro-vide the sources for their pleasures. As they grow older, they learn from females and occasionally are informed by older men that women can and do play active roles in the sex act and also can show them a trick or two or three.

The fact and idea of homosexuality among women as an issue in the sexual socialization of Black women is a story with silences and denials as its most salient features. Female homosexuals (the term "lesbian" was not a popular one in Black communities prior to the current gay activist movement) were viewed as "something that wasn't supposed to be." Lesbianism was considered "unnatural." The female homosexual was seen as a "man" and it was said "it's not nat-ural for a *woman* to be a *man!*" The expression "to be a man" is key to comprehending the attitude toward female homosexuals in Black culture. The female homosexual was spoken of as if a biological condition existed. "Now, a woman is not supposed to be a man, and anyone who was what they weren't *supposed* to be was a sort of freak, an oddity, going against 'nature.'" Consequently, that person was to be pitied and one felt ashamed of or for "it" (her). "It" was an embarrassment. In Black communities, homosexuals were referred to as "it," not "he" or "she."

On the one hand, female homosexuals were denied "existence" by the community's refusal to openly acknowledge their lifestyle. On the other hand, when references were made to female homosexuals, it was most frequently in terms of an image of woman-as-man. The predominant image was of a rough, tough-looking woman with short hair, wearing men's clothing and shoes, capable of drinking and swearing "like a man." It was said that lesbians "acted like men" and were "capable of cutting with razors"; one kept one's distance from these women. Young Black females in beauty parlors would hear remarks being made about "bulldaggers" or "funny women." The victims were so designated largely on the basis of superficial appearances. "You could tell one of them by the way they looked."

An interesting and important point to mention is that the dominant theme of ideas expressed about female homosexuals did not relate to their sexual encounters. Certainly a percentage of the Black female homosexuals had sexual involvements with women (some had involvements with men), and somewhere in the recesses of the minds of adult Black women there was an awareness of this fact. The question of why they chose to emphasize the so-called "unnaturalness" of these women and to downplay the sexual preference, since sexual contact between Black women was and is a reality, calls for further research and analysis. What we are concerned with here are the attitudes transmitted to the young Black females concerning sexual patterns and values.

The types of messages that young females received about homosexual females seldom included explicit factual information. The primary message was simply to "stay away from *them*." (The denial of their existence was so thorough that older women were essentially in the ludicrous position of warning young females about something that didn't exist.) The combination of the mystery and denial surrounding the Black female homosexual created an indigestible image for young Black women. This resulted in their being grossly ignorant about homosexuality and fearful of the "bulldagger," which in reality was little less than the stereotypical image of a crude male. As previously stated, explicit connections between sexual relationships and female homosexuality were rarely mentioned in the presence of young girls. The idea of a female wanting to define and express herself along nonheterosexual lines was not considered. The concept of a patriarchal society, wherein women were oppressed and therefore would logically want to break out of old patterns, was not considered as part of the psychological composition of the female homosexual. The image excluded having any mental process other than the desire to be like a man. The concept that young Black females developed concerning female homosexuality was an image of a man-woman— that is, a mannish, rough, tough, heavyset, tall, or super-athletic-looking female. Central to this idea is the fact that there is a prohibition against usurping the prerogatives or the appearance of the male.

The present-day, highly discussed homophobia in Black communities must be regarded in the context of this background. Young Black females—whether they are on college campuses, on city streets, in Westchester suburbs, or in Manhattan penthouses—who react negatively to lesbianism are reacting to a set of ideas and notions that differ markedly from the concepts and ideologies that surround the progressive-minded, politically astute, White and Black lesbian cultures. Present-day political lesbians speak of a feminist/lesbian politics and ideology. They are redefining women's lives in light of a raised consciousness which enables women to see their roles as women under patriarchy as oppressive and therefore to see a need for radical change. What the Black community and, in particular, Black males are reacting to are a combination of facts, myths, and old notions coupled with a resistance to change. Black feminists and/or lesbians are seen as identifying with White culture, despite references in many accounts of life in African cultures to women identifying with or relating to other women. The resentment is partially located in the "fact" that Black women are identifying with White. (The attitude is that, regardless of what benefits it may bring, "White" behavior is not for Black women.) There is also resentment of the idea of Black women becoming lesbian because the old, highly negative image of female homosexuality is still actively asserting itself.

Furthermore, the open association of sex with lesbians is a reckoning that cannot be denied today. When one recalls the belief that same-sex erotic love has its locus in the "unnatural," it can be seen that the idea of Black lesbianism is a highly unpalatable one for the Black community. There is a reluctance to seriously address the inequalities and exploitative practices that exist in Black female/male sexual relationships, as well as a resistance—indeed, a refusal—to consider lesbianism as a sexual politic. To do so might readily and logically result in Black males being displaced as number one on the sex scene. Black males fear another rejection of them, this time by lesbians. Consequently, they defensively focus on attacking those aspects of female homosexuality (lesbianism) that they know will ensure support from the overwhelming majority of the Black community. They focus on the myths: (1) it's unnatural for a woman to "be like a man"; (2) lesbians *hate* men, but Black men and women need to work in concert against racism. Here they are using the myth of lesbians as men-haters in conjunction with a positive truism; this serves the purpose of further alienating lesbians (and heterosexual Blacks); (3) lesbians really want and need a man, but since they couldn't get one, are competing against men, and if they succeed, our race will suffer from lack of reproduction (chauvinistic thinking and gross ignorance about who wants and can have babies).

On another level, homophobia in Black communities can be analyzed in terms of psychological defense mechanisms. This is particularly applicable to Black males. It would seem logical that since Blacks are racially oppressed, oppression for other reasons could be understood by them. Yet, there is an extremely hostile homophobic reaction, particularly among Black males. The issue of lesbianism is used as a red herring to avoid reexamining and redefining Black female/male relationships. Many Black males refrain from examining lesbian politics in fear of having to relinquish some of their treasured male privileges. A reaction to lesbianism on this level represents a form of homophobic attitude. Black males who may be progressive-minded, extremely intelligent, very astute, and articulate become emotionally blind, irrationally stubborn, unnecessarily hostile, and downright reactionary when it comes to the topic of lesbianism. They will cling to a stereotypical definition of female homosexuality rather than considering and accepting a current, enlightened definition.

For example, the definition of lesbianism that follows can hardly be interpreted as being a disruptive or damaging factor in Black communities. "Lesbianism—an intimate relationship between women on the conscious level, elements of this intimate relationship being: sensitivity, spiritual nurturing, validation of self, emotional and psychological growth. Expression of physical love may or may not be a part of the relationship."[11] However, the idea of a proliferation of Black women adhering to such a definition would cause much consternation, confusion, and anxiety among most Black males. They would interpret it, and rightly so, as meaning that Black women no longer were concentrating primarily on defending and nurturing the male ego. They would also feel that they were being rejected as Numero Uno in the love lives of Black women. In actuality the Black woman who rediscovers her womanhood—"colored girls who no longer consider suicide because the rainbow is enough"—will be better able to develop strong female/male relationships.

It is unwise to talk about the Black community as homophobic unless the homophobia is analyzed within the socio-psychological context of Black dynamics. As has been reiterated, the Afro-American culture and the societal pressures of racial and economic oppression have indeed constituted a society with two distinct cultures—one White and one Black. Therefore, a phenomenon that appears to be similar for both racial groups requires a historical analysis in order to attain an accurate and valid perspective. Black maleness and White maleness have similarities and differences. It is the differences that are critical in discussing Black males and females and their relations, of which lesbianism is a part.

There unquestionably is a strong negative reaction to Black lesbians within the Black community. However, the reason for this must be analyzed within the historical framework of intraracial sexual attitudes. This will enable a strategy to be devised that will deal with the causes of the problem as well as with the manifestations of the problem. This is not to say that reactionary behaviors such as name calling, physical attacks, and sexual harassment stemming from homophobia can be sanctioned. By no stretch of the imagination can cruel, insensitive, ignorant, violent behavior be justified. There are a growing number of Black lesbians whose voices are being heard on the Black political scene. Their roles will be incorporated into the sexual socialization of young Black females.

An analysis of Black feminism, such as "A Black Feminist Statement," which was produced by the Combahee River Collective, unmistakably reveals a political, scholarly, and progressive-minded perspective which, not surprisingly, is threatening to those males who fear and resent giving up some male privilege and having to rethink their attitudes and behavior toward women and child raising. The following passage comes from "A Black Feminist Statement" and is taken from the section on "What We Believe":

. . . Although we are feminists and lesbians, we feel solidarity with progressive Black men and do not advocate the fractionalization that white women who are separatists demand. Our situation as Black people necessitates that we have solidarity around the fact of race, which white women of course do not need to have with white men, unless it is their negative solidarity as racial oppressors. We struggle together with Black men against racism, while we also struggle with Black men about sexism.

We realize that the liberation of all oppressed peoples necessitates the destruction of the political-economic systems of capitalism and imperialism, as well as patriarchy. We are socialists because we believe that work must be organized for the collective benefit of those who do the work and create the products and not for the profit of the bosses. Material resources must be equally distributed among those who create these resources. We are not convinced, however, that a socialist revolution that is not also a feminist and anti-racist revolution will guarantee our liberation. We have arrived at the necessity of developing an understanding of class relationships that takes into account the specific class position of Black women who are generally marginal in the labor force, while at this particular time some of us are temporarily viewed as doubly desirable tokens at white-collar and professional levels. Although we are in essential agreement with Marx's theory as it applied to the very specific economic relationships he analyzed, we know that this analysis must be extended further in order for us to understand our specific economic situation as Black women.[12]

In looking again at the sexual socialization of Black females prior to the influence of the current women's movement and the gay activist movement, consideration must be given to those post-adolescent females who felt sexually inclined toward other females while growing up, yet preferred the company of males to females after adolescence. It is known that a society develops and produces the types of individuals it needs and feels are necessary for the maintenance of that society at a particular time in history. So it can be speculated that the Black community did not nurture female relations that exceeded the prescribed lines for female friendships. There is a strong history of friendships between women—women gathering together in beauty parlors; women meeting in the kitchen over a cup of tea, coffee, or soup; women talking on the stoops; and women congregating at church meetings. However, these relationships are considered as platonic: loving but not sexual, affectionate but one doesn't fondle.

In an interview, Adrienne Rich talks about unconsummated relationships and the need to reevaluate the meaning of intense, yet supposedly non-erotic, connections between women. She asserts: "We need a lot more documentation about what actually happened. I think we can also imagine it because we know it happened. We know it happened. We know it out of our own lives."[13] The question must be raised as to what happens when there is the desire on the part of women to love sexually, to fondle, to caress, and to spend inordinate amounts of time together. The close childhood friendships with holding hands and later walking arm in arm and staying overnight at one another's homes, the close-knit adult friendships—both must be channeled along purely platonic lines in order to be "acceptable" and "respectable." The erotic feelings and expressions have had to be "put on hold" or indulged in and not named.

The young Black female enters adulthood with a fixed idea about homosexuality. That fixed idea does not give her latitude for expressing her sexuality along any other lines than heterosexual ones. The concept of heterosexuality (forced as it is) is easily incorporated, given the Black female's background of her linkage with men, and the messages she received about men and sex: men are the barometer for good times, happiness, glad times, sad times, troubled times; the other half of a partnership; the ones women can't live with and can't live without; the sharers of hard times and the good life—the vicissitudes of life. She has been socialized to believe that sex is equated with man, not woman—not even a woman who "looks like [is] a man."

Black heterosexual males and females must become knowledgeable about the concept of lesbianism as a political measure, as a force against sexual oppression. Lesbians should not be viewed as being "sick," simply because they are not. Wife-beating, battered women, child abuse, the proliferation of pornography involving the young and innocent, enslaving young women (and men) in prostitution—these horrendous corruptions, heinous crimes, and inexcusable behaviors do not generate the phobic, hostile reaction that lesbianism does. The question must be raised: Does heterosexuality exempt behavior from being viewed as "sick," "abnormal," and an object of derision to the Black population?

An understanding of lesbian politics will help all Blacks feel less defensive. Black lesbians and all other thoughtful Blacks must continue to define and clarify the lesbian position in terms of a serious politic that deals with patriarchy under capitalism, racism, and classism.

Myths and stereotypes other than those related to homosexuality also play an insidious role in the young Black female's sexual socialization. Black mothers frequently overreact in response to the old myths and stereotypes about Black women being licentious, loose, immoral, and promiscuous. This overreaction takes the form of the mother being doubly strict with the rules of behavior she sets for her daughters in their dress and deportment. There may be an excessive concern about looking "decent" in public to offset stereotypes. Again, it must be emphasized that there is no monolithic Black female group. There are prostitutes among Black women, but the reason has absolutely nothing to do with a gene for licentiousness or any other such irrational explanation.

Historically, the sexual conduct of Blacks has been misunderstood and misinterpreted. The respected and well-known historian John Blassingame is guilty of this infraction. "Many of the plantations," writes Blassingame as late as 1973, as quoted in historian Herbert G. Gutman's *A Black Family in Slavery and Freedom* "were so large that it was impossible for masters to supervise both the labor and sex lives of their slaves. Sexual morality, often imperfectly taught (or violated by whites with impunity), drifted through a heavy veil of ignorance to the quarters. Consequently, for a majority of slaves sex was a natural urge frequently fulfilled by casual liaisons."[14] Herbert Gutman straightforwardly addressed this incorrect analysis:

The misunderstanding on which such an analysis rests is not a new one. Prenuptial intercourse among slaves was noticed and misunderstood by most non-slave contemporaries, too. Such behavior had been relatively common in the society in which the parents and grandparents of mid-nineteenth-century observers of the slaves had lived, but was later harshly censured by a shifting moral code. Many mid-nineteenth-century observers believed that prenuptial intercourse was evidence of the absence of sexual standards and even indicated "savage" or "natural" behavior. Pro- and antislavery biases and mid-nineteenth-century Victorian beliefs, such as the belief that marriage and hence the "family" required positive legal and contractual sanction to be "real," that "sex" had to be subordinated absolutely to marriage, and that sexual "restraint" (the ideal of chastity) had to be imposed upon all inferior and dependent classes and races distorted the perceptions of most observers. . . .

Toombs and others discovered that "fewer children are born out of wedlock among slaves than in the capitals of the two most civilized countries in Europe—Austria and France."[15]

As Gutman commented,

That many slaves distinguished between prenuptial intercourse and "licentiousness" and believed prenuptial intercourse and pregnancy compatible with settled marriage escaped the notice of all but a few observers.[16]

The slaves did not consider intercourse an evil thing, and marriage regularly followed prenuptial slave pregnancies. Males clearly showed a sense of responsibility for their progeny; mutual respect and understanding existed between couples. This phenomenon of attitudes toward sex among Blacks has been similarly described by Bessie Head, the African author:

People's attitude to sex was broad and generous—it was recognized as a necessary part of human life, that it ought to be available whenever possible like food and water, or else one's life would be extinguished or one would get dreadfully ill. To prevent these catastrophes from happening, men and women generally had quite a lot of sex but on a respectable and human level, with financial considerations coming in as an afterthought.[17]

Present-day society still reinforces certain myths about Black women. The young Black female experiences directly, indirectly, and vicariously hostility, violence, and sexual abuse, which are the symptoms of economic, sexual, and racial oppression. The battered woman, childhood sexual abuse, incest, sexual harassment and extortion, rape, unwanted pregnancies, butchered abortions—these are the types of onerous, destructive, detestable experiences that become part of her socialization as a female and, as such, influence and affect her adult sexual attitudes and behaviors.

The following composite discussion represents a freewheeling conversation among a group of Black women reminiscing about their experiences as young girls growing up. It dramatizes salient dimensions of their sexual socialization. The conversation is based on numerous tape-recorded sessions involving groups of women, all of whom were close friends. The following five personalities were selected: Kay, age 41, college graduate, master's degree, divorced, no children, social worker; Terri, age 30, attending college part-time, married, three children, temporarily unemployed; Sue, age 32, secretary, separated, two children; Edith, age 28, college graduate, teacher, single parent, one child; Rose, age 31, high school graduate, divorced, one child living with grandmother in another state, saleswoman in a department store.

KAY: Terri, you said that without a father you don't know how men are supposed to treat you?

TERRI: The strange thing about it is I had a stepfather, and yet I always say, "I never had a father." He was a stepfather, but he was just thrown in there. He was in the house, but he was just passing through and coming back, he was never *there*. You know, my real father died when I was five and everybody who knew him said he was a real nice guy. I never knew my stepfather. I lived in the same house with him from the time I was six until I was seventeen, but I don't think we ever spoke ten words to each other. He was a quiet man, he wasn't very verbal and he didn't know how to deal with me.

KAY: Didn't you learn from your mother how a woman is supposed to be treated?

TERRI: My stepfather's role in the home was support.

SUE: But did he ever mistreat your mother?

TERRI: He kicked her ass a couple of times, but when I got over the initial shock, I began to see that she needed it. I mean she really deserved it.

KAY: Really? You think some people deserve to be treated that way?

TERRI: Some people like getting their ass kicked.

SUE: That's true!

EDITH: Yeah, I know that's true.

KAY: But liking and deserving are different.

TERRI: That's a matter of opinion. I could say, deserving, liked . . . No! She *must* have liked it, she let him keep on kicking her, she never left him so she must have liked it. She used to taunt him. I think she *wanted* him to do it because she did something she *knew* a man would kill her for. And she would do it and slyly

throw it in his face and he'd get worked up—"I don't like that"—
(*imitating a man's voice*). He'd start beating her ass and the next
thing I knew, they'd be coming out of the bedroom smiling—I
couldn't figure it out. (*laughter*)

SUE: Ah, ha, ha. I like that!

TERRI: When I was older I asked her why. I said, "Mommy, why
did you stay with him so long?" and you know what she said? She
said, "He was a nice man." And I said, "Ma, he kicked you down
the stairs, don't you remember, and all the neighbors knew." And
she said, "Well, you know I did some things that hurt. There were
a lot of things." And I said, "Son of a gun. Here I am screaming
all the time, 'Don't hit my mother!' and you liking it all the time!"
But it's true, if you're in a home and there is no male, how do you
know how he's supposed to treat you, except for what you see on
TV. And if the people next door got no father—and if they do,
their fathers are kicking their asses—how do you know?

KAY: Because it's just a question of plain humanity as to how people are treated.

TERRI: Honey, if everybody on the block is doing it *that's* humanity! That's your source of reference.

EDITH: Different men treat women different ways. And all women
are different.

KAY: But in some ways I think they're the same.

SUE: Okay. Then tell me what is it that all women have in
common?

TERRI: Pussies. They have pussies. (*laughter*)

SUE: That's it?

EDITH: I don't know if women have anything in common except
they can have babies—biological features. But women have similar
experiences at one point or another. They're treated different. Like
I feel united with this group. I feel a part of something here. But
what is it? I don't know. I guess that's what you're asking.

ROSE: Hmm. I don't know. I'm just thinking about it. I never gave it any thought before. (*There is a lull in the conversation as the women reflect on what has been said.*)

SUE: I think there is an emotional understanding that women can relate to. Like I can understand Terri's experiences even though I may not agree or haven't experienced it all myself. I don't think a man could relate to that.

(*At this point a male visitor comes into the room.*)

ROSE (*addressing the man*): What do you think is the one unifying factor among women? Or what unifies women all over?

MALE: They're lazy!

ALL: Lazy? What? You're crazy! Hmm.

EDITH: You think it's similar experiences, like the Black experience, it's the women experience? They go through similar things?

MALE: Okay. I guess similar experiences that create loneliness.

ALL: Loneliness?!

MALE: Am I right? I'm leaving.

ALL: Yeah, you'd better. Bye now! Later! See ya!

EDITH: How about that—loneliness! (*in amazement*)

SUE: We're not lonely!

TERRI: That sounds like a male problem.

ROSE: There are a lot of men that don't have nobody.

EDITH: "No One Knows the Blues Like a Lonely Woman." Did you ever hear that song by Laura Nyro? I wish I had that album right now.

SUE: Kay, do you know the answer?

KAY: I don't know *the* answer, but I certainly have an answer. It's because people react to us like we're second-class citizens. I think that women play roles, especially with men, and I think that the common knowledge that there is so much role-playing going on creates a bond. It's like a common knowledge that as second-class citizens, we're not going to be considered equals to men no matter what.

TERRI: You know, my professor told me a woman's never going to be equal to a man. I said why? He said because women have periods. Your glands are juggled up. We're difficult, he said. That's why we'll never be equal.

SUE: We're just different, but not inferior.

EDITH: I'm gonna tell you all what I think now. I feel in fact that women are superior.

ALL: That's right! Why? In what way? I think so too.

EDITH: You know why I feel women are superior? We're emotionally stronger whereas men may be physically stronger. I mean the shit that we go through being all we have to be. You can't just be successful and a woman, you have to break the shit that men put up there for you. To be a successful woman you have to have more than a successful career. For instance, I just can't be a teacher and a woman—being a good woman means I must adequately sustain my family, be spiritual mentor for my friends, be able to deal with a man, be able to deal with other men, hold a household together and a million other things. I dare say a man, any man, would have broken beneath the strain—any man who would have gone through what I have gone through in my life, age eighteen to twenty-eight, would have copped out. He couldn't have taken the weight, the strain, and come out smiling. They would have been a junkie—a drunkard—couldn't have took the weight! Couldn't have come out smiling.

ROSE: I think you're right.

SUE: I think men recognize that women are emotionally stronger.

TERRI: Better equipped.

SUE: They fall on that physical thing. That they can pick up boulders.

TERRI: A machine can do that! Now what's your claim to fame? *(addressing males in absentia)*

SUE: You know what I mean? They always fall on that physical strongness. They don't ever attempt to fall on their emotional or mental strongness.

EDITH: I don't even think they do that. I never had a man come to me from that point of view—where he's telling me where his strength is coming from—his physical strength, like in his arms. But because he was a *man*. Somehow he never said, "I have a dick, so I'm stronger," but you know he feels it. That's where he's coming from. They sort of think that the dick makes them superior.

TERRI: I think we're superior by virtue of having compassion.

SUE: Huh?

TERRI: I think we're superior by virtue of having compassion and empathy.

SUE: So you're falling back on the emotional. Women are emotionally and mentally stronger. But when you go down with a man and have a bout, they'll say, "We're physically stronger." That kind of stuff.

EDITH: That's stupid, because they just developed that area. If you were trained you could be a boxer—you could box a man.

SUE: I could *never* box a man. I would never attempt to.

EDITH (*emphatically*): If you were trained you *could* box a man. You could be *trained* to box a man!

SUE: Oh, with training.

TERRI: You could karate him to death. You may not be able to box him, but you could kick his ass.

EDITH: But you know, it's a degrading thing. You know, it's been bred in our homes that males are special. Let me tell you a story. Just from my own experience. I see a lot now. Do you know that even in my house the men at the table had their plates served first? Even though I didn't never really check it out till later. We were trained to want to please your brother.

SUE: I wasn't.

EDITH: I know—that's why I'm telling you about this. My brother was going out with girls. And I'd take pride in ironing his shirts and when he came home, I'd ask him, "What did you do when you were out?" We [girls] were raised to act certain ways. We weren't supposed to be tomboys. We were taught to live our lives through our brothers. They [adults] would say, "You're a girl, you don't do that. A girl doesn't do that. You're a lady! A lady doesn't do that."

SUE: Oh yeah, yeah.

ROSE: That's true. I remember that.

SUE: Did I tell you about when I first got my period? My grandmother scared me when I got my period. I was nine years old and I thought I just hurt myself and they [mother and grandmother] thought I had played around and lost my virginity. And they brought out my panties that I had just thrown in the hamper. My mother and grandmother sat me down and demanded to know what it was. "What happened? What did you do?" Then they told me from now on you can't jump rope and you can't play with boys.

EDITH (*screaming with the memory*): That's it! That's it! You couldn't jump rope! (*laughter*)

SUE: No, they wouldn't let me go near my brother, man.

ROSE and EDITH: Right! That's right! You got to be careful with boys.

SUE: It was a trip.

EDITH: You got to be careful with boys.

SUE: You *got* to be! Not why. They didn't tell you why you gotta be careful with boys. I didn't know what the hell they were talking about. She never explained nothing to me. Everything I learned in the street. Anyway, she just told me you can't jump rope and you can't play with boys. And I'm saying, what else is there? You know, what the hell is there to live for!

EDITH: Oh, God, what else is there?

TERRI: Well, I learned you didn't jump rope when you had your period for a single reason. I had my period and a big old sanitary pad and no belt.

EDITH: Oh, no, baby!

ROSE: Oh, that's a bad experience!

TERRI: I was jumping double dutch.

(*Comments on jumping double dutch were made. The group exploded into hilarious laughter reminiscing about jumping double dutch. They all joined in chanting, in rhythm and cadence, the double dutch count: 2-4-6-8-20-2-4-6-8-30-2-4-6-8-40, etc.*)

TERRI: When your mother tells you don't jump rope, *listen to her!* (*All laugh.*)

ROSE: My virginity was broken by the super when I was five years old. I never had a father and the super was nice to me. One time he said, "Come downstairs to the basement," and he ate me for three hours. It felt pretty good. Afterward he said, "You're a very nice girl. What would you like?" I said the most money I could think of—I said seventy-five cents. Something told me not to tell my mother.

KAY: Didn't you feel ashamed?

ROSE: He didn't hurt me and I didn't know what shame was. I was raised that you were never supposed to touch yourself. (*Everyone expresses understanding.*)

SUE: That's the worst sin of all. Lord, you'd liable to get the whole rosary. (Saying penance after confession.)

TERRI: My nun said, "Do not touch thyself in any enviable place," and that was an enviable place. I was sinning left and right and I'd go to confession thinking this is the worst sin of all. And he'd ask me, "How many times?" and "Are you going to do it again?" Then I tricked them. I got a little towel and I could go ahead without touching myself, and I said, Lord, I got it now. So when he asked me, "Did you touch yourself?" I said, "No, Father," 'cause I hadn't touched a thing—I learned the trick.

SUE: Catholic school was a trip. They favored the Irish girls. They used to get to play the part of the Virgin Mary in the plays. I had to be Mary Magdalene, the whore . . . That's right. I was going to be stoned to death for prostituting myself and Jesus came in and said: "He who is without sin will be the one to cast the first stone." And they made it very clear that I was a prostitute.

TERRI: Well, don't feel bad—I only pulled the curtain.

(end of session)

There is no mistaking the fact that racist, sexist, and economic deprivations have seriously influenced the socialization of the five Black women. Also made obvious was the absence of constructive, knowledgeable information about sexual matters in the lives of the women during their growing-up process. They all had been ignorant about their bodies. It was also seen how they had to cope/deal with sexist attitudes and behaviors and sexual abuses coupled with the harsh realities of growing up in average, not-rich-not-the-most-poor Black neighborhoods. The five women, who were from lower- to middle-class families with high educational aspirations, were all familiar with certain experiences common to young girls growing up in a society where sex is the dominant commodity for monetary profit, personal gains and gratifications, and human exploitation. The experiences of the young girls included sexual abuse from adult males, psychological abuse from the school system, exposure to wife-beating, experiencing male preference and privilege within the family, socialization to "act like a girl," and Black female/male conflict concerning penis power.

Their conversation also revealed a recognition of female strength and solidarity based on the knowledge of a common fate stemming from sexual oppression both from society and the Black male—the former on an institutionalized basis, the latter on the personal level. The knowledge of Black male oppression does not seem to seriously interfere with the sexual intimacy among Black men and women. The reasons for this are manifold. The word oppression may be somewhat inappropriate, since its popular usage implies systematic overpowering or imposition by abuse of power and authority, and in the case of Black men and women such domination/overpowering is not automatically transferred to other areas of social living. In addition, there are numerous Black women who neither act nor feel oppressed or overpowered in their intimate sexual relations with men. What cannot be denied is the fact that, as was pointed out by one of the women in the group, Black men in general place their number-one claim to manhood in the locale of the groin palace, the home of the dick.

The growing awareness that their roles as women in Black society are in need of some revising was apparent in their discussion. The emergence of a different attitude toward males, one that is more demanding of equality in sexual and social areas, is addressed more specifically in the following discussion among four Black women: Dot, age 25, college graduate, social worker for Welfare Department, separated; Jean, age 35, two years of college, clerical worker, married; Betty, age 28, high school graduate, beautician, serial monogamy, no marriage; Sadie, age 40, dietician in a public school, twice married, now single.

DOT: I have just entered a new phase in my attitude toward sex. Between the media and the way I was socialized I came to look at sex as a romantic ideal. Now that's all different.

JEAN: How's that?

DOT: The way I see sex now is—it's politics, it's cash, it's economics! I'm at the point where I see it as an exchange, but not a romantic exchange.

JEAN: I'm afraid I'm beginning to hear you.

DOT: In other words, no more sex in exchange for sex alone. Because the way I feel, he's getting and I'm giving! He's feeling "good" and I'm feeling tired and used.

SADIE: So you mean you're going to use sex specifically as a means to obtain other things?

DOT: Well yes, and it's not my idealistic view. I wasn't raised like that, but I've become that way.

JEAN: When did you get rid of your idealistic views?

DOT: Well, within the last three relationships I had. The past three years.

BETTY: That sounds kind of interesting.

DOT: Yeah, I would say that from my experiences I've adopted this view. Not from what Mom and Dad taught me, but from the politics that males and females play. Sexual politics. You know, I got taken off. I was trying to be nice you know, romance and all that ha-di-ha-di-da.

JEAN: When you say "sexual politics," just what do you mean?

DOT: Sexual politics between a man and a woman. Games.

JEAN: Games, huh?

DOT: Yeah, X and Y, me and him, racking up points or trying to rack up points against one another.

BETTY: And who came out ahead?

DOT: Well, the last three—*they* came out on top.

BETTY: They *did* you in?

DOT: Did me in! But no more. It's an exchange from now on, but on *my* terms!

JEAN: And what are those?

DOT: I love to have the pleasure of sex, but he's got to give me something first. I have to put it on that level because when I was giving out of my heart, I didn't get nothing in return. I was giving but I didn't get.

BETTY: I hear you. I hear you.

DOT: And I don't necessarily like that policy, but I can't just, you know, be used for the American dream of romance.

BETTY: That's right. I'm with you, sister!

DOT: Sex is pleasurable. It's pleasurable. But it just ain't gonna be only pleasurable. It's gonna be pleasurable and something else. Dig it. Just being pleasurable ain't enough. Those days are over for me. 'Cause it can be pleasurable and I still ain't got no food in the 'fridge. That does not add up. Economics, you know. You've got to look at everything these days in those terms. The thing of it is that I don't like being like that 'cause I really care. It's like splitting myself, I feel like I'm splitting myself, you know.

JEAN: Well, tell me this now. If you go out with a guy and he really appeals to you, would you want to go to bed with him because he's him? No economics attached.

DOT: Well, I don't know.

BETTY (*laughing*): You could be persuaded.

DOT: Yeah, but I mean, you know, that does not necessarily excite me anymore. That kind of just physical stuff. It's gotta be more than just you look good, or when you talk your words come out a certain way.

BETTY: But you *could* be persuaded.

DOT: Yeah, well, I could be persuaded. But I find it very, very difficult to get down and stay on the sexual level alone.

BETTY: I prefer flirting. Holding hands, walking through the park. That's physical and could be considered sexual.

DOT: I don't consider that sexual at all! That's kid stuff!

SADIE: It really doesn't pay to be involved with men just to be involved. The way men are, I don't trust them no more. You know. (*Agreement expressed from others.*)

DOT: And they lie about everything. Generally.

SADIE: That's why you can't trust them. You know, it takes a while for men to be truthful.

JEAN: You all sure are putting down the Black men when you say those things.

DOT: No, I just don't want to operate with him at *his* level. Lying and cheating. They can't understand *why* we as women want to do the things we may be into—like health awareness. Abortion rights.

JEAN: Let's be more positive and analytical. Men are important in our lives, right?

BETTY: Oh, that's obvious.

SADIE: It's not so obvious to me anymore.

DOT: There's a lot of things that I like about them and a lot of things that I don't like about them.

SADIE: It's what I don't like about them that I feel needs to be changed.

BETTY: You think you can change a man?

SADIE: No, but if we change, they'll *have* to change.

JEAN: I like the idea of meeting a man, starting a relationship and both of us going forward with it.

BETTY: I enjoy a man's company. It's fun. I like the physical difference. I like the mental and emotional difference.

SADIE: Too often all you get is mental and emotional *stress!*

JEAN: Yeah, but we women still put up with them.

SADIE: I'm at the point now where I don't accept the man's role as the way it's been defined. You know, I don't believe in double standards where they hogwashed me all my life. Don't expect of me what you can't expect of yourself. Forget the double standards. Do you hear what I'm saying?

DOT: All I'm trying to say is I don't like the idea of men being able to do, like Momma used to say, "Well, a man can go and get drunk and . . ." Did your Momma ever used to tell you that? "He can get drunk and lay in the gutter and the next day he gets home and puts on his suit and he's still a man. But if a woman does it, she's a slut and all that." I don't think that should be. If she wants to lay in the gutter, you know, she should be able to get up, just like a man, get up the next day and go on about her business. And nobody say nothing except, "Sally was laying in the gutter yesterday." Or, "John was laying in the gutter the day before." You know. It's not so much a male/female thing as they make it.

BETTY: Maybe you should check out that gutter.

DOT: Yeah, you know. Check out the people that's in it.

BETTY: Take me to the gutter and drop me off. That's cool. I'll lay in there myself. It might be cool. Everybody has to have a thing.

DOT: But my main concern is where his head is, how he acts, you know. What are his beliefs, what kind of culture does he come from? Is it on the map? (*laughter*)

SADIE: And where you come from sometimes also determines the kind of sexual activities you get involved with.

DOT: Right. If you don't have communication somebody who may seem very nice and do all these things that you want, then when it comes time for the sexual they may be very cold, or they may be very macho. You know, they may be very quiet, and you like a screamer.

BETTY: That's the cutest thing. Being in bed and trying to explain, like, "Ah . . . sweetheart, you know, that wasn't getting it. (*laughter*) Like you're trying to ram my, you know, my gizzards through my elbow. Don't do it like that. Have a little tenderness." You know a lot of men have to learn that it's not so much the heavy jamming as the communication involved. And so, you know, it would be easier to get together sexually if your communication is in "synch." And then bring that communication right on outside with you—to the kitchen after you done finished with the bedroom.

JEAN: Establishing that communication can be a trip. Sometimes it hardly seems worth the bother.

DOT: Well, they're going to bother you anyway. Virtually not a day goes by when they don't bother me, you know. Also contact with men helps me to write good poetry—to bother with them also helps me to be creative about dealing with them. And so since they are here, they have to be dealt with. 'Cause you know, we can't leave them alone. They couldn't survive and where would we be?

SADIE: In my last relationship I was making an effort to do right. I suggested that we compromise on certain things. Not always do things his way. Well, he thought I was trying to prove something to him. He got an attitude. I said, "Let's deal with things like two adults. I'll give some leeway on some things and you on others," because he might be more cool in some areas, and I might be a little more cool in another. But we're going to do things fifty-fifty, I said. You know, like if you want me to massage your feet, you've got to bathe me too. I'll lotion you down one night, you lotion me down the next night. Why I always got to be lotioning you down? Goddammit, you know, I work too. When I want to get lotioned down, I got to go to a masseuse. I got to lotion you down, take a course on how to do it, to please you. Well, the upshot of it all was he split.

BETTY: Well, you know, it takes a lot of doing to get a man to accept a fifty-fifty relationship. You have to do it in a way so that you don't intimidate him because he is emotionally weaker than we are. He doesn't want to admit it, but he is. So we have to carry a lot of the weight in the relationship.

JEAN: But you know, women carry the heaviest burdens, and for years we have been putting up with an unequal exchange. And we continue to put up with them in the same old ways.

BETTY: It's not so much of a burden. I don't look at it so much as a burden. 'Cause I ain't going to let nothing be no burden, now. If you have to be a burden, go on your way! But we have to work it out together because we're in a tough situation together. It's a tough struggle for all Black people.

DOT: If it was all women, you'd have to put up with the same thing.

JEAN: No, you can't say that. It wouldn't be the same with women. Since women carry the burdens, you'd have all burden carriers. There would be more sharing of loads. What do you get in exchange for the heavy load you're carrying?

DOT: I see it more as a mission than a burden.

JEAN: Okay. We can call it a mission.

BETTY: Yeah, it's a mission and a challenge. It's a mission and a challenge just like everything else. Black men represent our mission and our challenge. Because I think if Black men and Black women—and this is my one political reality of the day—if we don't somehow soon get together it will be catastrophic. I feel that one of the personal satisfactions in dealing with Black men is reinforcement as a person. You know, trying to do what's supposed to be the correct thing to do as an individual. Now I can say that I get my reinforcement as a woman by sticking by Black men.

SADIE: It's never been easy for Black women. It's been real difficult. It's my nationalism coming out now. I'm for helping all of us Black people get together. And it's also a learning experience, I would say. A learning experience in working toward a closer perfection of unity.

BETTY: I get a lot of nationalistic satisfaction, too. You know, it's somewhat of a burden, but it's with *him*. It ain't with White Joe Blow over there. It's with *him*. So we'll know that the species will continue and you get some personal satisfaction out of knowing that. Not necessarily as a woman, but as a person dealing with another person and coming to some compromise together.

DOT: Yeah, I *used* to feel strong about the continuation of our nationalism. About his Blackness.

JEAN: What do you mean *his* Blackness?

DOT: I mean the fact that Black men have been fucked over and are fucked up and we can't desert them. I wouldn't go out with a White man. I'm just going to make the Black man pay a price. No one gets a free lunch anymore.

JEAN: *You* may not go out with a White man, but they damn sure go out with White women.

BETTY: That's why I like the fact that we are maintaining the Black family. I feel very strongly about that. I'm doing my little piece by sticking with Black men.

SADIE: Maintaining the Black family?

BETTY: Black male and female relationships—yes, yes, the Black family. That's the mission. Besides you get personal gratification, you know, the fact that I made the effort within the Black family structure. You know what I'm saying? 'Cause I wouldn't want to go through that mission with another woman.

JEAN: But you already do.

BETTY: I wouldn't want to in the same sense!

JEAN: You're in a household family structure with women and they constitute a major part of the Black family.

BETTY: I mean just pertaining to Black male and female relationships. Hey! My mother and father, case in point. They've been together for thirty-two years and they're always constantly accentuating one another. Mom carried the heavier burden, but my father hung in there. They maintained their relationship with all their burdens.

JEAN: Okay, okay. I hear all these reasons for maintaining relationships with our Black men—like personal gratification, a learning experience for working toward unity, and maintaining the Black family, but on a really personal and intimate level, what do you receive from the relationship?

DOT: We receive *nothing!* (*laughter*) We receive nothing!

BETTY (*in mock tones*): We got nothin'. You know (*in a loud tone*) to all you Black men out there in the sound of my voice, if you're in the sound of my voice put your hand on the radio. *We got nothing!* (*laughter*)

DOT: You give that call to arms and watch some bitch come and hit them with a frying pan, and pick up her thirty-eight with her other hand, you know, in a southward direction, and let 'em have it. Years of reparation are due. Oh, God, (*laughter*) we can't let them die like that. We just can't.

SADIE: Now let's get back to Jean's question. I must say that I did get certain satisfactions from both of my marriages, but sexual intimacy wasn't the main source of my satisfaction.

BETTY: Let me say this. I like to fuck as much as anybody, and as long as Black men are around there will be fucking.

DOT: If you're going to fuck anyway, why fuck for free? It's a physical need, so you might as well go and get some and like I already said in the beginning, get something else with it! Just a commitment to him ain't enough.

JEAN: It's only a physical need because you and society *made* it a physical need. People are conditioned to want sex.

DOT: Getting horny and wanting a man is natural! *You* must have been conditioned to think that it's *not* natural.

JEAN: Feeling horny may be natural, but *wanting* a *man* is conditioning! And that's a fact!

SADIE: Dot, at one time I thought the same way you did, now I'm beginning to wonder what it really was that gave me satisfaction, pleasure, in those relationships. What was it, really?

BETTY: Listen, you all. I *got* to say this—the dick is good! (*laugh-*

ter) The dick *is* good. And for me, I'm just the sweetest thing he done had. I *know* this is the sweetest thing he ever done had. So if I don't get something for it, he'd probably think I'd give it to anybody free. I don't want him to think that. Shit! So I just collect a little rent and get me some threads now and then, you know, it's like that.

DOT: It *does* make you feel good.

BETTY: Oh, when you be coming ain't nothing like coming! It's the best.

DOT: It's nice, it's good exercise. You can run track, but it just ain't the same thing. I think sexual intercourse is the best relaxer around other than the sauna. 'Cause if I can't get no sex, ain't nobody giving up no money, I go to the sauna and exercise and come home and masturbate and feel real good.

JEAN: But you'd rather have the man!

DOT: If there's a choice, yes. But sometimes you don't even want the damn choice for the hassle. It ain't worth the hassle. And it's not like you can say after you've had intercourse, "Okay, get up and go home. I came already, did you come? Now you can get up and go home. I've got some work to do." You can't do that.

BETTY: Personally I prefer a small dick.

JEAN: Size isn't supposed to matter.

SADIE: You couldn't prove it by barber or beauty shop talk.

DOT: Now you know what's a real joke, an embarrassment? A big two hundred and fifty pound dude with a three-inch peter. Peter is dick's little brother, you know. And you're supposed to act like it's all right.

BETTY: Well, you have got more chance to get clitoral stimulation with somebody with a small penis usually. For my build anyway.

SADIE: My final comment is, we got some problems to work out. You hear me, women? (*Doing take-off on Betty*) "Listen, all you Black women out there in the sound of my voice. If you're in the sound of my voice, put your hands together and listen. We Black women have to consider some serious changes in our relationships with Black men, because we've had enough! And we *know* they can do better! Amen." (*Group laughter and approval*)

The Black women's comments reflect an experienced view of the effects of institutionalized heterosexuality on their relationships with men. The direct sexual feelings expressed would be termed lewd, dirty, unnecessary, or shameful only if viewed from the lifeless puritanism of Anglo-Saxon Protestant ethics. The remarks of the women also represent a focus on both the precarious sexual relationship between Black men and women and the strong counterforce of uninhibited and unrestricted joy to be found in sex. The women are direct and explicit in expressing their feelings. At times they seem to vacillate; such is the actual case. There are serious problematic aspects in their relationships with men and, in trying to think through their problems and develop new strategies and tactics, there are uncertainties in their decisions, unsure and compromising behaviors. The reality of Black females linking their existence to males as part of their socialization process was unmistakably reflected in their conversation. Equally represented was a showing of their independent spirit. What was likewise obvious was the infiltration of consumerism with sex as the commodity. We can thus see how people can be molded by environmental factors that override customs, beliefs, and behaviors that at one time were hard and fast enforcers of moral, spiritual, and emotional boundaries.

The conversation also revealed an openness and willingness on the part of the women to talk about their dissatisfactions, likes, and desires about sexual relations. Heretofore many Black women were fearful of losing their man if they did not please him sexually, so they did not disclose dissatisfaction. Black women understand that the Black male has had little opportunity for economic advancement. They have therefore provided ego gratification to the male in the area of sexual relations. In attempting not to further damage the male ego, women sacrificed their feelings. In the long run, this created more problems for both partners.

What must not be overlooked in the four women's conversation is the fact that Black women as well as Black men truly enjoy sex and view orgasm as the ultimate in pleasure. This is a positive factor and should be used as a positive reinforcer for relationships. It should *not* be used as a reward or a lure. Females should not withhold sex if *he* doesn't behave, or promise him some if he acts right. Males should not feel that they are holding all the aces in the deck and if *she* doesn't conform to his desires, he'll just keep withholding those aces or play them elsewhere.

In their conversation, these Black women are not only questioning their insights on their own sexuality, they are simultaneously trying to historically analyze and assess the realities of the conditions that have contributed to the present state of affairs between Black women and Black men. The orientation toward males as part of the sexual socialization of Black women is a cause of ambivalence. The manner in which the Black woman defines her womanhood is central to a discussion of the attitudes toward Black males produced by the sexual socialization process of Black females.

A California study which had Black female graduate students for its subjects dramatizes how socialization processes account for the Black woman defining herself as an independent being, while simultaneously always defining herself in relation to "man." The following passage describes the women in this study collectively.

. . . During most of the formative years, she [the daughter] had observed her mother [or the adult female of the house] leave home for work. It was at the outside employment that many hours of the mother's day were spent. With increasing awareness, the child [student] realized that her mother's outside employment had a meaning of its own. She had another life, which was somewhat independent of but co-existed with their family life. Concurrent with the mother's maintenance of her job was also those manifested concerns for the man of their house. Given her mother's model of an outside independent life, integrated with an actualized concern and relation to her man, the student matured assuming no inherent contradictions between these two entities. Consequently the Black woman was defined as having a "life of her own" and also as "always" being in relation to man.[18]

The following passage demonstrates the formation of female attitudes that carry over into adult years. The family's concern for the welfare of the adult male in the house is graphically articulated.

. . . Whether a father, stepfather, grandfather, or mother's boyfriend, he was a focus of consideration in determining to "cook pork chops instead of liver, 'cause *he* like 'em," or not to "put too much starch in that shirt, 'cause *he* don't want no stiff collas," or to "clean your room, 'cause *he'll* have a fit if he see it filthy." Likewise it was the man who could also alter many previous decisions: "You can't bring your friends over this evening 'cause *he's* comin'." It was from this kind of emphasis within her family background that the Black female graduate student more than likely formed her definition of "Black woman" in relation to man.[19]

Another example of attitudes expressed by older females that contribute to the formation of attitudes toward males can be seen in the following passage from *All Our Kin*. Pride in sons and brothers is demonstrated. The setting is a very economically deprived household, but the sentiments hold true for millions of Black families.

. . . Alberta introduced me to her nineteen-year-old son, she pointed to him and said, "He's a daddy and his baby is four months old." Then she pointed to her twenty-two-year-old son, Mac, and said, "He's a daddy three times over." Mac smiled and said, "I'm no daddy," and his friend in the kitchen said, "Maybe going on four times, Mac." Alberta said, "Yes you are, admit it, boy!" At that point Mac's grandmother rolled back in her rocker and said, "I'm a grandmother many times over and it makes me proud," and Alberta joined her, "Yes, and I'm a grandmother many times over." A friend of Alberta's told me later that Alberta wants her sons to have babies because she thinks it will make them more responsible. Although she does not usually like the women her sons go with, claiming that they are "no-good trash," she accepts the babies and asks to care for them whenever she has a chance.[20]

Females have to learn at early ages (12–13) to cope with young males who emulate older Black males in their attempts at sexual conquests. Thus, the styling, profiling, and pretending begins on the part of both females and males. The young males preen, prance, profile, sweet talk, Bogart, or otherwise participate in the illusionary eroticism and conspicuous paraphernalia of romantic love. The females overdress, underdress, feign attitudes, fight other females over males, and "fall in love" with "tight pants," "pretty eyes," "attention being showered on them," "recognition," "peer understanding," and "comfort contact." Once the male sexual conquest is made—or, on some occasions, the female seduction—lack of information about sexual matters frequently results in unwanted pregnancies. The sex act itself often becomes a perfunctory act. The ambivalence surrounding the sex act is particularly complex for the young female. She hears about the joys and "goodness" of sex from adult women, songs, and literature, and she also dreads/fears getting pregnant or losing her virginity. She soon realizes the games, "sexual politics," that are going on.

An older woman, middle-class, age 35, put it this way:

Sisters have been socialized to believe that involvement with males is a real true relationship—a sincere commitment. The brothers, on the other hand, know that they have to "rap" to get over. So they bring wine, flowers, pizza. "If I make her *think* I care, I can get over." [So they imagine.]

"Getting over" means initially the fuck and then the repetition of it whenever the male feels like it. It is a "false" relationship in the sense that the play is to *get over*, not to establish a true relationship. (As Dot said in the conversation, "The sexual politics, the games, it splits me in two.") It is an exchange of services. For the female the game-playing is face-saving. If she gives in without the "games," she is considered a whore. Males play all sorts of games to keep the female believing that she is the one. For example, when they go away they will remind themselves to call So-and-so at a certain time to demonstrate how much they care. Notes for a trip: blue suit, shoe brush, *call Millie*, Brut, toothbrush, *call Marie*, comb, deodorant, *call Sally*. She is just another item that is needed for his care. He may make the call in between fucking rounds, but that doesn't matter. The female will feel cared for. Of course, there are occasions when the females discover the game and resort to some form of violence in retaliation—a slashed waterbed, cut-up suits, a smashed-in car window. But usually the male "gets over" for quite a while.

These games allow the woman to feel that she is not totally unrespected. She can point out to others and to herself, "See, he brings me flowers and records, pizza"—and, later in the game, groceries. Of equal concern is the situation when the male "talks politics"—that is, he is politically serious—and you have an intellectual relationship that doesn't necessitate his bringing flowers. Well, it is not considered disreputable to have this type of open relationship. But if a male starts talking *sex* right away, with no rapping or presents, it's not considered respectable. So in most cases, games are played to keep the image of respectability (an important necessity for the woman) and games are played to keep women on the string (an important notion for men). It may take three weeks or more or less for the fuck to be achieved—then good-bye. Conquest is the thing. Black women feel, in many cases, that they "need" a man and it is "unnatural not to have a man." They can "only go so long without one." Should the games be stopped and the women simply say, "I'm in this for a good screw just like you, so let's stop with the games," we would have a new situation. But the male trip is so ingrained and the female role is so ingrained that it is very, very difficult for both parties to change. (Sadie's statement during the conversation, "If we change, they'll have to change," is instructive here.)

Black women are faced with a reality today that demands changes ranging from a slight shift in posture to a complete about-face as they come to grips with their sexuality and relationships with Black men. The women's movement has provided a renewed interest and impetus for Black women to formally organize around issues of feminism and sexual equality, and to informally voice their opinions and attitudes about Black female and male relationships with far less reluctance than in the past. Sex for procreation still has importance for both Black females and males, but the idea of choice is equally as important. When to have children and how many to have are decisions that females figure in more prominently than in the past. A major reality that Black women face is the shortage of Black males. "Black women 25 years old and over are more than twice as likely as white women to remain never married. The situation grows far more grave among the college-educated where—within the urban population 19 to 44 years old—for every 100 males there are 54 extra females without a mate or forced to share somebody else's."[21] It is a well known fact that there are more Black males in jails than in colleges. Drugs, war casualties, interracial marriages and homosexuality increase the scarcity of available males. The problems Black women face in relation to this scarcity, their attitudes and opinions on the topic, their uncertainties, conceptions, ambiguities, and possible solutions are put forth in two witty and serious, insightful, candid discussions among four Black women. The views expressed are based on comments of Black women speaking out in 1979.

> Who's that a writin'? John the revelator.
> What's he a writin'? He's a writin' revelations.
> Who's that a writin'? Jane the liberator.
> What's she a writin'? She's re-writin' his revelations.[22]

A Group Discussion: Challenges to Traditional Patriarchal Paradigms, Round I

Four women, gathered in the home of Sandy in July 1979, were talking about men in their lives: Ellen, age mid-30s, married, two children, ages 5 and 7, living with husband; Sandy, age mid-40s, divorced, single, no children; Althea, age 28, never married, one child, age 5; Margie, age 31, married, two children, ages 7 and 9, with husband.

ELLEN: If I hit the lottery I would have another child. (*The group reacted initially as though her statement was just another casual comment about winning a lottery with no real serious intent.*)

SANDY (*responding lightly*):   What? Hit the lottery, have a child? What's the lottery got to do with your having a child? The lottery doesn't make babies.

ELLEN: I mean *my* child this time, not *our* child.

SANDY: You mean you'd pick out a father? Not your own husband?

ELLEN: That's right!

MARGIE (*entering the conversation, fully aroused now*):   Hold on a minute. You're saying that you would pick out some dude that would suit your fancy and have this child? What kind of man would you pick? What would he look like? Muhammad Ali or a young Harry Belafonte?

ELLEN: Characteristics. Characteristics are most important. In general, good physical characteristics, teeth, eyes, etc., and intelligent. I wouldn't have to live with him.

ALTHEA: Ellen, you been holdin' out on us? Is there a new man on the scene? If so, let me know, 'cause I ain't seen nothin' worth dressing or undressing for in months. And you know, with the shortage of men and all they're saying about the new Black woman and her new consciousness, and sisters supporting and *sharing* with one another.

MARGIE: What "they"? Who's saying all that?

ALTHEA: Oh, you know all that shit Sandy's always talking about. Black women writing about the *new* Black women, *contemporary* Black women, *together* Black women. Feminism. We're all of that. Didn't you know? (*laughter*)

MARGIE: Yeah, I'll bet whoever or whatever Black women are writing that stuff sure ain't sharing their man.

ALTHEA: That's if they got a man. Got to have before you can share.

MARGIE: I hear a lot of feminists are lesbians. Into women. Can't imagine that.

ALTHEA: Don't knock it if you ain't tried it.

SANDY: You two cool out. I want to hear Ellen. I want to hear more about this "lottery child."

ELLEN: No, seriously, I believe a woman should have as many children as *she* can afford, not as many as "we" can afford. My husband is out of state now, taking a course for five months (if he lasts), and I am glad to be free. Glad that he is away. I know two women whose husbands died recently, and they weren't glad that they died, but they were glad that they no longer had to put up with them. Now you know that is *sad* that you have to be glad that your husband is dead so you can feel free and good. I think the reason that marriages are so unsatisfactory is because in our society boys are raised one way and girls another and then they put them together at a certain age and they are supposed to fit together. Get along with one another, understand one another. Boys are raised to be strong, tough, not compassionate, earn money; girls are taught to be compassionate, gentle, understanding, have feelings, empathy; and then they get married and they don't receive what they have been experiencing.

ALTHEA: But you can't have women marrying one another.

SANDY: In some states it's legal now. I read that someplace.

ALTHEA: Well, the other night I was at the disco and this White chick came over and asked me to dance.

SANDY: What did you say?

ALTHEA: She was nice about it, said she had noticed me and would like to dance, so I was polite and told her "no thanks." She teaches at one of the elementary schools. I've seen her around.

MARGIE: Oh, Lord, they done took our men and now they're starting on our women. What's next. Our children. Hold on to your children! They're already trying to adopt them and the kids end up all messed up.

SANDY: There *is* an increase in lesbianism, and among Blacks, too.

ELLEN: I'm not quite ready to go that way, but I can understand why a woman will live with another woman. If you are sick a woman will fix you a cup of tea and not tell you to "get up and fix yourself a cup of tea." And if you say you have cramps another woman will understand it. I don't think men know anything about empathy when it comes to women. Like when I was married and we were both working, I would come home for lunch, both of us would be home for lunch, and I'd be rushing around the kitchen and fixing his lunch and mine, and he'd be there sitting watching me and talking. After lunch I'd rush back to work and he'd be calm and my job was rough, and I became pregnant soon and worked until eight months, so there I was still fixing his lunch. So I said, "Look, in five years I want to look like your wife, not your mother," so I quit working. But I'm working now and really enjoying it without him being here. You see, too many women are tied down to their husbands, to marriage, due to economic reasons. They have four or five kids and need their husband's support. They say when the kids get old enough I'll go out and get a job or go on my own, but that's like fifteen years of living under those kinds of conditions—living like that for fifteen years. If I had to do it over I wouldn't. I would, say at age eighteen, select the type of job I wanted and pursue that and once economically prepared I would have as many children as I could afford. A woman should be allowed to have as many children as *she* can afford.

ALTHEA: Well, in my case I'd still be waiting because I certainly couldn't *afford* to have any children. But once they're here, somehow you manage. And I don't get any child support from his father.

MARGIE: What you get is a lot of help from other women. Mothers, neighbors, sisters, babysitters, friends. Look at all the children Ma Gregory took care of. (A neighborhood woman who has taken care of babies and children for generations.)

ELLEN: Women should live with other women because they understand one another better, are more compatible, have empathy for one another, are more considerate. Women should have children if they can afford it and should be allowed to select the husband. Boys and girls should be trained more along the same lines. Marriage shouldn't be a lifetime contract. Like now, my husband is trying to be more considerate—the perfect father and husband—but I couldn't care less. In all this time I have grown sort of indifferent now. It really doesn't matter what he does. I just don't care now. Maybe marriage should be on the basis of a five-year contract, renewable if desired after five years.

ALTHEA: Hmm. Ellen, sounds like you been doing a lot of thinking about all of this.

SANDY: Yeah, sure does. I'm going to give it some serious thought myself.

MARGIE: Okay, Miss Serious Thought, Sandy. Bring on Chapter Two. Tomorrow. Same time, same place, only this time please have something a little stronger than iced tea.

Round II

The group has convened at Sandy's with wine instead of the insulted iced tea.

SANDY: I'm prepared for you all this time. But don't go drinking so much that you start talking a lot of foolishness, 'cause I've been thinking a lot about our last conversation and want to hear some sober thoughts.

ALTHEA: If you want us to be real mellow, you should have brought us some smokes.

SANDY: I said I wanted to hear sober thoughts, not stoned thoughts.

MARGIE: We'll be stone(d) sober. How about that!! (*Much laughter from Althea and Margie in particular.*)

ELLEN: Sandy, they're ignorant! Let's get on with our conversation about men, no men, marriage, no marriage, and children, no children.

MARGIE: Right! (*in mock tones*) The Black women's consciousness-raising session is now in s-e-s-s-i-o-n. (*turning to Sandy*) That's what this is, isn't it?

ALTHEA: We're just telling it like it is. You soothe me, I'll soothe you. Or we can call it constructive gossip. Hey, we're the Black women's answer to NOW. We'll call ourselves WOW, Women on the Warpath! They'll know we're women of color because who else been on the warpath except them bad Native American Indians! (*laughter*)

ELLEN: Make that plural [warpaths] because we have plenty of battles. I was thinking the other day that my problem is deliberately wanting to live free of the bonds and binds of marriage and men, but most women have the problem of getting a man. That Black male shortage is for real!

ALTHEA: I propose that the Black female move in on the White woman's territory like she has moved in on ours.

SANDY: *You* advocating Black women going with White men! Miss Black nationalist of the Sixties, am I hearing correctly?!

MARGIE: White boys! You talking about going with gray boys. Out! Scratch that!

ELLEN: It *is* an alternative.

SANDY: Not really. Alternative implies a choice between things. If the Black men aren't there, going with White men is not an alternative. It's taking leftovers. It can be called a challenge to the traditional, unwritten, but well-followed practice of Black women going with Black men only.

ALTHEA: Listen. Things are changing. And quiet as it may be kept, I know for sure that more and more Black women are going out with White men. They wine you and dine you in style! Some "leftovers" can be pretty good!

MARGIE: Yeah, and with everybody staring and glaring at you with something much less than style. And thinking you're an easy lay.

ALTHEA: Why worry about that? Everybody's an easy lay today.

ELLEN: Wrong!

SANDY: Celibacy is a choice that many women follow.

ALTHEA: A choice for who? Girl, you're a trip. What kind of women follow celibacy other than nuns and even they are getting closer and closer to being human, what with coming out of those habits and all. And you even got gay nuns now.

SANDY: Celibacy is a choice for those who choose it. The other day on one of those talk shows I heard of women who were "coming out of the closet" in terms of admitting that they were by choice celibate. You know so many women think that you got to have a man all the time or something's wrong with you, that your life just can't be fulfilled and satisfied unless there is a man that you are involved with sexually.

ALTHEA: Do y'all hear our choices? Do you hear them? Celibacy, gray boys, or White women! (*in disgusted tones*)

ELLEN: White women?

ALTHEA: Yeah, ain't no Black women going with another woman.

SANDY: Althea, don't be ridiculous. Black lesbians exist. Responses to them in Black communities make them less visible, but they are there and more are coming out with each issue of feminist/lesbian magazines.

ALTHEA: What kind of magazines are those?

SANDY: "Heresies," "Off Our Backs," "Matrices," "Conditions."

ALTHEA: Never heard of any of them. Must be White magazines.

MARGIE: Well, a choice between White men or women is no choice at all! I'd rather share a real man with five other women than have any cracker, low-life White boy.

ELLEN: That polygamy thing doesn't work either. I know several Black women who were into that and at first it seemed fine, but after a while, they found out that the males were still the king of the roost but this time with *several* hens under their direct command.

ALTHEA: Okay, let's add polygamy and as far as I'm concerned, scratch that too. Let's see, now, we have celibacy, polygamy, White men, and other women.

SANDY: Now I think we should make a distinction between "other women" and lesbianism. Friendship with other women is a must, a desirable must. We offer each other support, "an ear to listen and a shoulder to cry on." And lesbianism has proven to be very satisfactory for many Black women.

MARGIE: Yeah, but on the other hand we have a lot of women fighting one another, usually over men, talking behind one another's back—catty, real bitchy. And trying to outdo one another in clothes, cooking and lies about how well their husband treatin' them, and half of the time the ones who talk the loudest are the ones whose men beat the shit out of them.

ELLEN: How did we get that way? How come women are such contradictions? How come? Men aren't that bitchy.

MARGIE: No, because they're the reason we're bitchy. They spend their time relishing in our behavior over them. They feel all supreme because some women are fighting over them. Check it out and see if every time women are into some kind of mess, a man is responsible.

ELLEN: The women ought to get together and have a rebellion. Not so much because we're oppressed but because we're not being treated right. You know, those White women keep talking about being oppressed about this and oppressed about that, and how men oppress them sexually. Well, I don't feel oppressed at all when it comes to sexually dealing with men. Lots of times I could teach them a thing or two, but you know with their weak egos (*in mimicking tones*) I let them feel good about themselves, so it ain't about feeling oppressed sexually. But there is something wrong in relationships when both people can't be honest. But if you're honest you'll lose your man 'cause there'll always be several women waiting in the wings to please him no matter how much of her act is pure "D" lies.

ALTHEA: Preach, sister, preach. Get in the pulpit Sunday morning and tell it all!

SANDY: Black women should truly get their act together. We need to. I read a recent statistic which said that there were over two million more eligible Black women than Black men. That makes us more vulnerable than ever unless we do something about it. This same article mentioned the growing number of older women going with younger men, and the women had some positive things to say about it.

ALTHEA: Well, that won't help the numbers game, but it will provide male company. The younger men have less hang-ups, are less possessive, are into newer ideas. Health foods, yoga. In a way they're more interesting, less demanding. The only thing you have to watch out for is their using you like a reverse sugar daddy. A sugar momma, I guess.

SANDY: We have to learn, to *realize*, that singlehood is and can be a totally self-rewarding decision. Our professional and personal aspirations, our close friendships, leisure time activities, travel—building our own self-esteem—those are the things we need to start doing. We've been trained and taught to nurture, care for, everyone but ourselves. It's time for some reciprocity. And if that's not in the cards, then we must "do for self," as my mother always told me. And it's not about us ruling out men. Quite the opposite. They and society have ruled themselves out of our lives. Or the terms that they want to enter our lives are just not acceptable. Not workable. Not in our best interests.

ALTHEA: I think we're going around in circles. Simply put, and this is my way of thinking, there aren't enough Black males and even those who are eligible need some training about dealing with women. My choices include men of other color. There are Hispanic men and even some Asians might do—especially the tall, karate types. And we could check out those Arabs and Iranians. Younger men can add a little diversion now and again. Women, well, as close as I am to some women I think that's enough. The relationship is fine without the sex, but if it should happen, that's cool. Who knows. Several years ago I wouldn't think of touching a White man, much less sleeping with one. Let the Africans keep their polygamy, and you know, even women with men need to learn to appreciate and deal with being alone, constructively. Like singlehood within marriages.

MARGIE: I feel a real challenge. A new challenge for Black women. I'll be able to tell my grandchildren about how the Eighties was when we Black women shifted gear into different life options.

(end of session)

The Eighties offer the Black woman the challenge of taking a giant step into a region called "her own rights" without divorcing herself from Black culture, which embodies care, concern, and nurturance for the Black community. She must do so without negating her own sexuality, which in many instances she must redefine for herself. She must come into her own being, in relationships with and to men, but ones that do not disallow her personal freedoms, personal happiness, and the opportunity to pursue her personal and private aspirations.

In the Eighties the challenge to the Black woman is not to negate or neglect Black men, but to define herself in terms of her needs, her desires, and her psychological and emotional makeup. Her expressions of sexuality are indeed a very personal matter, and unless her sexuality is inextricably connected to a politic of liberating options, it need not be the most salient aspect of her personality or person. That is to say, whether a woman defines herself as a traditional wife in a monogamous marriage, a lesbian, a celibate, a polygamous wife or a single woman, those decisions in and of themselves tell us very little about her political aspirations or political commitments or ideology. They simply tell us who she may or may not be sleeping with. In the case of traditional monogamy, we would know in general terms that she is in a situation with male dominance as a given. So it is incumbent upon Black women to start defining themselves in terms of a politic that may or may not incorporate their sexual preference.

A woman's sexuality and sexual preference should be a complement to her well-being, not the locus of her well-being. It is neither the dessert nor the main course. It could be either, or it could be neither. Black women need to learn to deal with their sexuality. The old notions and myths and stereotypes must be done away with analytically and systematically. Women always have gained strength and support from other women; this practice should be embellished and drawn upon to help women further their self-development. Women's support groups, organized and run in constructive ways, can provide an excellent source of new ideas while helping to break down old barriers and reestablish warm, rewarding female friendships. A compassionate, erudite, introspective analysis of the relationship between sexuality and politics is needed. As Black women, we have for years been strong and indestructible, as Mari Evans so eloquently put it in her classic poem, "I Am a Black Woman":

> . . . I
> am a black woman
> tall as a cypress
> strong
> beyond all definition still
> defying place
> and time
> and circumstance
>   assailed
>   impervious
>   indestructible
> Look
>   on me and be
> renewed.[23]

The Eighties find the Black woman still strong, still defying definition and time. She is faced, however, with a complicated new set of circumstances, as previously examined: the women's movement, the shortage of Black males, and an America whose corporations are reaping bigger and better profits while the deleterious effects of racism and economic oppression go on, unabated and worsening. The Eighties will be the time for Black women to be renewed as well as to provide the model, symbol, and image for others who seek their own renewal.

NOTES

1. Carolyn M. Rodgers, *How I Got Ovah*. Garden City: Doubleday & Co., Inc., 1968, p. 15.

2. Amilcar Cabral, "Guardian Voices of Revolution," *The Guardian*, January 1980, p. 17.

3. Adrienne Rich, *Of Woman Born*. New York: W. W. Norton & Co., 1976, p. 182.

4. Carol Stack, *All Our Kin*. Harper/Colophon Books, 1974, p. 47.

5. Michelle Russell, "Slave Codes & Linear Notes," *The Radical Teacher*, March 1977, p. 2.

6. AC-DC Blues (Gay Jazz Reissues), ST-106, Stash Records, Inc., P.O. Box 390, Brooklyn, NY 11215.

7. Sharon Harley and Rosalyn Terborg-Penn, Daphne Duval, "Black Women in the Blues Tradition," *The Afro-American Woman—Struggles and Images*, p. 71.

8. Harold T. Christensen and Leanor B. Johnson, "Premarital Coitus and the Southern Black: A Comparative View," 1980, unpublished paper, p. 2.

9. Ibid., p. 3.

10. Ibid., p. 4.

11. Nacemah Shabazz, "Homophobia: Myth and Reality," *Heresies*, Vol. 2, No. 4, Winter 1979. New York: Heresies Collective, Inc., 1979.

12. Zillah Eisenstein, ed. *Capitalist Patriarchy and the Case for Socialist Feminism*. New York: Monthly Review Press, 1978.

13. Barbara Smith, "Towards a Black Feminist Criticism," in *In the Memory and Spirit of Frances, Zora and Lorraine*, ed. Juliette Bowles. Washington, D.C.: The Institute for the Arts and the Humanities, Howard University, 1979, p. 39.

14. Herbert G. Gutman, *The Black Family in Slavery and Freedom, 1750–1925*. New York: Vantage Books, 1977, pp. 61–62.

15. Ibid.

16. Ibid., p. 63.

17. Bessie Head, *The Collector of Treasures*. London: Heinemann, 1977, p. 39.

18. Jualynne Dodson, "To Define Black Womanhood." Georgia: The Institute of the Black World, p. 17.

19. Ibid., p. 19.

20. Carol Stack, *All Our Kin*. New York: Harper/Colophon Books, 1974, p. 120.

21. *"Where Have All the Black Males Gone?"* *Black Male/Female Relationships*, Vol. 1, June–July 1979. San Francisco, California: Black Think Tank, Inc., p. 5.

22. This improvisation is based on two lines recalled from a camp song.

23. Mari Evans, *I Am a Black Woman*. New York: William Morrow & Company, 1970.

VIII

The Subject of Struggle:
Feminism and Sexuality

so why dont we go on ahead & be white then/ & make everythin dry &
abstract with no rhythm & no reelin for sheer sensual pleasure/ yes lets
go on & be white

—Ntozake Shange

> I reach through the dark, groping
> past spines of nightmare
> to brush the leaves of sensuality
> a dream of tenderness
> wrestles with all I know of history . . .

—Adrienne Rich

> The past leads to us if we force it to.
> Otherwise it contains us
> in its asylum with no gates.
> We make history or it
> makes us.

—Marge Piercy

Central to the political energy of the Women's Liberation Movement has been an urgency to understand and question sexuality and
the effects of the social organization of sexuality on the lives of
women and men. In the dominant White, bourgeois culture of a capitalist society where sexuality is fetishized in specific patriarchal
forms, it is a pivotal distinguishing feature of today's feminism that
it has been built out of the problem of sexuality and out of the irrec-

oncilable dilemmas of the institution of heterosexuality as this society has shaped it. Yet although sexuality is central to contemporary feminism, there are all kinds of difficulties in the ways of discussing sexuality that feminism has evolved. These strategic problems and difficulties are as important as the "content" of what feminism "says" about sexuality itself.

My project here is threefold. First to assess, from my own socialist-feminist perceptions, the nature of the dilemma and paralysis around developing the politics of sexuality within the women's movement. This has to entail examining the conflicts and disagreements between radical feminist and socialist-feminist method and approach to the question of sexuality. Secondly, I find it crucial to discuss some of the aspects of the further complication within feminist thinking on sexuality which has emerged, confusedly but consistently, around the polarization of heterosexuality and lesbianism—and the theoretical and political dilemmas this continues to generate. I want to raise the issue of this polarization and the controversies it harbors, since the perception of feminism and sexuality by those not immersed in the movement, and by many Black women and men, is in fact acutely affected by it, in any case. I address it here with no expectation of "solving" the dilemmas it poses, but to highlight the important paralyses, silences, and assumptions within the *interpretation* of sexuality which this lesbian/heterosexual polarization has produced. The polarization has all kinds of political necessities and even inevitabilities in it, but its terms *have* to be reconsidered, I believe, if the sexual political imperative of the women's movement is to sustain a relevance and enabling force for women whose lives are complexly enmeshed in the real fabric of our society. Thirdly, stressing both the theoretical political and personal political angles from which I am writing (which are not synonymous, nor mutually determining in any simple way), I want to discuss briefly some of the ways of looking at the problematics of sexuality which the women's movement has provoked.

I wish—for the sake of readers new to the terrain of White feminism—that there was a simpler account to offer about "sexuality" and what the women's movement has to "tell" about it. The political debates internal to the Women's Liberation Movement, with the diversity and divergence of positions and analyses they offer, are perhaps, however, the most important aspect to comprehend about White feminism. Nowhere do they emerge more intensely than around the question of sexuality itself. These differences within feminism are part of its ongoing energy and challenge. At the same time they are of tremendous political import to the progress and strategies of contemporary feminism. It is important to stress to begin that there is no *one* feminist way of analyzing sexuality, there is no *one* central position within the women's movement from which to characterize and interpret sexual oppression and sexual politics. There is only an ongoing struggle and attempt to explore, reconceptualize and strategize, in the face of both indisputable realities of sexual discrimination and overt oppression of women, the complex mechanisms which sustain women's lives as circumscribed by both blatant and subtle forms of sexual exploitation and abuse.

Given that sexuality is central to the contemporary feminist struggles, it is an ironic fact that the feminist sexual agenda is fragmented and in some ways has hardly begun to be developed. Feminists come to consciousness through a seething fabric of criticism, anger, accusations and "speaking bitterness" out of personal experiences, to confront a culture which has, within its network of sexual discriminations and inequalities, *denied* women's sexuality. The feminists of today have an ongoing struggle to dismantle that denial, and evolve radically new ways of understanding the interwoven processes in our cultural, ideological, and institutional histories which have produced the different levels of our experience of sexual limitation and oppression. Yet the denials, restrictions and coercive definitions which the dominant White, Western culture invests in women's—and in men's—sexuality, haunt our very political endeavor. We speak about, and we speak out of, a heritage which is part of us. We carry its contradictions and terms of reference right into ideas and activities which we think are the most "different," the most oppositional. We dream of a society (often without images) which would be radically different, where sexuality would not carry with it certain normative assumptions of power and violence along gender lines. However, feminists continue to live out in our real lives sexual relations which are permeated with the oppressive ideologies, psychology, and institutional assumptions which simple "consciousness" cannot simply eliminate. Nonetheless, the clashing and explosive perspectives feminism offers on sexuality—however fragmented—do shift the ground and possibilities for disrupting the passive reproduction of oppressive sexual lives, and for beginning to imagine and negotiate *some-*

thing else on the intimate and social terrains where sexuality is lived out.

Within the patriarchal fabric of the daily workings of this society, feminism struggles to find ways of imagining how to transgress and disrupt the cultural codes which inhibit, repress, and express our sexuality through patriarchal forms which reinforce the disempowering of women. The White feminist imperative has turned searing searchlights onto the practices in women's lives where women are used and abused by men in the realm of sexuality itself. Through the initial practice of "consciousness-raising," it was realized that White women share a context in which heterosexuality perpetuates women's dependence on men and embodies practices and attitudes which undermine and inhibit women's sexual and social sense of themselves. Through "consciousness-raising," feminists from diverse backgrounds, with varying histories of passions, romances, and investments in relationships with men, accumulated a confessed inventory of crises, humiliations, repressed communication, and unsatisfactory terms of social collaboration with men, which permeated their intimate connections with them, and often ritualized lack of control and absence of negotiation within sexuality itself. These recognitions of the dilemmas in heterosexual relationships were not easy to evolve—given that all women have complex means of idealizing and repressing ambiguous features which are inevitably present in *any* heterosexual connection, given the distribution of social and sexual powers that the larger framework of male dominance and the sexual division of labor invests in it. The evidence presented from different women's sexual histories was not an exceptional account, although the media and antifeminist sources attempted to imply that these were women with "special" problems, blighted with "unlucky" personal tragedies of sexual unhappiness. What emerged was an account of recurrent features of sexual relationships with men which made it possible to realize that it was not a collection of random personal problems, but that there was a social and political problem having to do with sex, gender, and society which was inevitably acted out in a myriad of ways in the bedroom and the kitchen, as well as in the laws, economics, and cultural forms of our society. The dilemma of sexuality, at the heart of the White feminist project, was not incidental to social injustice. It was seen to be deeply enmeshed in the sustaining of power relations at the most personal and private level. New ways of understanding this, and new ways of subverting the disabling syndromes that sexual relations were seen to produce and reinforce for women, within the larger context of sexual inequalities, were needed. Only the women's movement began to seek them.

The first waves of indictment, anger, disbelief, and recognition brought to the surface by consciousness-raising were very important and necessary to provide survival mechanisms for many women. They allowed reassessment of the taken-for-granted terms of relationships that were disabling and of situations that were immediately and potentially sexually oppressive. They provided new beginnings for rethinking and renegotiating the sexual dilemma. For the surges of anger, the listing of evidence of the ways that male sexual power and violence are institutionalized in the "normal" practices of our society and implicate *all* men (and therefore *all* women, until the social relations between the sexes is radically transformed), gave feminists provisionally adequate means of drawing back from the "normal" rules which organize us as women into systematic dependence on men. For the normally anticipated dependence of women on men, which the distribution of gender roles in our society underlines, becomes too easily the coercive site of women's appropriated, exploited, and disallowed sexuality. The claimed privacy and immunity of the personal dynamics of sexual intercourse were disrupted by the feminist intervention, which called for a resistance by women to the rituals of sexuality and the forms of social relations that sustained these rituals, which reinforced uncontested male power and male definition.

However, certain of the methods of communication which feminism developed about sexuality in this way were from the start problematic. The contexts in which men did and do exploit their dominance and power through the use of women's sexuality were, and are, all too real. It is also indisputable that the nature and extent of male sexual violence is systematically neglected and silenced in our culture, and thus provokes the incantatory intensity which often characterizes the facts that radical feminists bring to the witness stand. But this listing of sexual abuse and violence by men is usually disconnected from the complexity of historical social and psychological factors which provide the relentless contexts in which men are prone to this violence and women, with minimal social options for resisting it, accommodate it and perpetuate the conditions which produce it. The method of "inventories," which is still central to the radical feminist tendencies in feminism, implies that the accumulation of evidence, the naming of the points of enactment of male power—and most especially in the flesh of women's sexuality—is enough spontaneously to produce some kind of cross-cultural (for the evidence is always cross-cultural evidence), universal understanding of men as oppressors. Implicit in this is the inferred priority and necessity for strategies by which women can remove themselves from personal and political collaboration with men, as if, faced with "true" knowledge of the nature and consequences of sexual conflict, the automatic conclusion is a radical feminist position. The clearcut inventory of male abuse is drawn from real social contexts, but not explained in terms of those social, cultural, and historical contexts nor of the social relations necessary to sustain them, with all the implicit contradictions and twilight zones they imply. The inventory-and-indictment technique in fact builds only toward a statement of the absurdity and insanity of any conscious woman choosing to remain in sexual proximity with men, or ultimately in any relations with men, whether personal or political. By oversimplification it also discounts the nexus of pleasures, desires, affirmations, and positive intent which also mediate individual women's relations with men in our society. The problems of "adapting" the implicit thinking behind these forms of radical feminist method to the situation of Black women and men highlights what, I would argue, is already an inadequacy in these strategies for *White* women and men.

It has been important to elaborate these elements of radical feminist technique, and now to go on to contrast them with socialist feminist theoretical frameworks and methods, since the feminist discourses on sexuality among most of us White feminists have more often than not been inspired by radical feminist approaches. These not only have oversimplified and overpurified the language of anger and outrage, and thus oversimplified the problem, but have had a moralistic ability to inhibit less "pure," but often more complexly realistic, formulations of the many complicated angles on sexual experience that many feminists both personally and theoretically perceive. The already enormous difficulty feminists have had in finding ways of talking about sexuality effectively has been reinforced. One result has been a paralysis and silencing within the women's movement itself concerning the development of analysis of the conditions of heterosexuality—which, whatever the exploitative, abusive, and intolerable terms of bonding it still embodies, *still* has to be transformed in its economic, ideological, psychological, and sexual structures if the aims of ending sexual oppression are to be achieved.

The implications of radical feminist method do present acute dilemmas for Black women. The encounter of Black women with its discourses may indeed be highly instrumental in transforming the landscape it delineates, for radical feminism either urges an escalation of a kind of feminist consciousness which condemns men, or on the other hand does not enable means of understanding and transforming the sexual dilemmas and dynamics between men and women in specific cultural, material, and historical contexts. The imperative to indict men as simple agents of oppression does not develop analytical methods and critical tools for understanding the diverse social and political factors which produce and necessitate this power division and its eventual violent consequences. There is therefore no way of transforming existing power relationships—only an oppositional rhetoric which one can either adhere to passionately, or respond to with stunned helplessness or disagreement.

Socialist-feminism, which is a contrasting grouping of tendencies within the women's movement, has been concerned with developing theoretical analyses which can enable political engagement with the contradictory realities of daily lives across the wider political formations which shape them. While radical feminism has sustained its intention of breaking with frameworks evolved by male political thinkers (especially Freud and Marx), and has evolved its own traditions claiming to resist "contamination" from male thinkers, male politics, and male language, socialist-feminism has been less linear in its analysis of gender causality. In the last twenty years there has been an explosive reassessment, within the New Left in the United States and Europe, of the erroneous and inhibiting traditions of reductionism and essentialism which had accumulated in the Marxist heritage. These new socialist imperatives, intersecting with critical elaborations of the inquiry into the social formations of the unconscious and of language, have opened up new approaches to the understanding of oppression and the complexities which sustain, reproduce, and reinvent syndromes of oppression. In particular there has been a concern to find new ways of conceptualizing the Marxist and psychoanalytical modes of inquiry. This is leading into radically new ways of understanding the nature and functioning of ideology, the state, social relations, culture, and language; the subjective enactment of complex power relations, which inhibits these power relations from being easily displaced or transformed; and the reassessment of history and of its ideological production. All of this political inquiry "outside" of feminism informs and provokes the feminist imperative of socialist-feminists. The interaction of new socialist ideas and methodologies with autonomous feminist inquiry and strategy is engendering rethinking, criticism, and new analyses of the system of patriarchal capitalism and of patriarchal socialism which is, in contradictory ways, of urgent interest to socialists and socialist-feminists. Socialist-feminists are concerned, as expressed by the British lesbian socialist-feminist Beatrix Campbell, with "political interventions in the real contexts of lived-out social relations." This implies an ongoing commitment to analyzing the basic forces that structure social relations—the various ideological, state, psychological, and economic forces that cause and sustain the production of class, gender, and race relations.

As far as sexuality is concerned, socialist-feminist thought has so far stressed the need to understand the complexity of the social relations of gender, recognizing the ambiguities and contradictions that are necessary to patriarchally determined relations. During the long, intricate history of the organization of reproduction, sexual ideologies have evolved and have been consolidated to protect this organization of reproduction and the interwoven economic organization, which itself has sustained simultaneously a class, race, and sex hierarchy. Where radical feminism names the oppressor, invokes spontaneous revolutionary feminist consciousness confronting the "facts," and infers obvious oppositional strategies, socialist-feminism, as in the new currents of the Marxist tradition itself, already stresses the illusion of the victim/agent-of-oppression model, where overthrow of the ruling class is only a matter of enlightened consciousness and time. Where radical feminism has tended to list and indict the coercive and oppressive conditions of reproduction and mothering, socialist-feminists are attempting to evolve a more adequate understanding of how gender is produced through the social relations involved in having children, and how the masculine/feminine polarity is psychologically produced and elaborated in our culture. Where radical feminist method tends to explain women's desire for men, sexually, as "false consciousness" (in contrast to the "correct" consciousness, which radical feminism provides), socialist-feminism has more interest in attempting to find ways of understanding the contradictory mechanisms by which, in spite of the patriarchal contours separating and opposing men and women, women do still desire and even celebrate sexual pleasure with men, and men still can renounce some of the fetishized and oppressive sexual practices which the sexual power divisions of our society produce and encourage in them.

One of the problems in the feminist approaches to the dilemma of sexuality is that, on the one hand, socialist-feminism tends toward theoretical abstractions in its exploration of gender relations at all the different levels of social, economic, and psychological organization, and in so doing has all kinds of mechanisms for actually not talking about sexuality. On the other hand, radical feminism provides graphic and gruesome accounts of the details of rape, battering, clitoridectomy, murder, incest, sexual slavery, etc., and limits the angle of approach to heterosexuality to this kind of account, without envisaging any real mode of transforming the social relations of gender which produce them. It is hard to find, among the various feminist discourses, positive accounts of desire, sensuality, and erotic experience. Recent writings about lesbian experience do affirm these lived-out sexual realities. The accounts of heterosexuality are still mostly along the lines of proof of failure of relationships, because of the patriarchally oppressive terms which confine the sexual practice.

The further complication written into the feminist discussions on sexuality is the polarization of heterosexual and lesbian women, and the assumptions which often extend from sexual self-definition into political interpretation. The logic of such extensions is, however, not clear at all. Heterosexuality, the sexual involvement of women with men, does invoke the privilege of the institutional form of sexual connection which patriarchal formations in our society condone, encourage, and enforce. It does, in the "normality" it can evoke, perpetuate the taking for granted of a relation which, based on the "normal" sexuality it is meant to enact, is in fact in many ways, both subtle and obvious, coercively programmed into women's social, economic, and psychological survival. Yet women have many ways of strategizing both their survival and sexuality with men, so that no matter what individual conflicts the institution of heterosexuality necessitates, they can and do still affirm the struggle of that connection. Sexual attraction and the terms of sensual and erotic arousal are not "voluntarily" chosen nor merely programmed into us, and often are even contradictory to the cultural stereotypes which surround us. The relationship between an actual individual relationship one lives out, the sexuality enacted within it, and the emotional contours which define it are never simply aligned with intellectual and political "knowledge." All kinds of personal and cultural histories, family relations, and individual encounters make certain individual paths through sexual interaction possible or not possible, provisionally liberating and challenging in certain ways, and destructive and oppressively "normative" in others. These observations relate equally to lesbian and heterosexual relations.

What is difficult as regards feminism and sexuality is that the lesbian presence and strength in the women's movement represent in fact a wide span of sexual-political positions.[1] Lesbianism on the one hand invokes a radical challenge to the normative structuring of women into dependence on men by positing women's autonomy from men in terms of the most symbolically threatening dimension— that of sexuality. At one level it affirms quite simply the pleasure women can and do experience together, and the desire and intimacy women can enact. It can imply a basic sexual preference, which may or may not be elaborated into a political analysis that confronts social and sexual behavior that heterosexuality enacts in our society. It can embody a political refusal to participate personally in the power structures which are institutionalized between men and women. The term "lesbian" is also sometimes used to designate activities, community relations, cultural practices, modes of living and the organizing of survival and support which are women-centered, and which imply lesbian sexual preference but are not organized merely around sexual activity. Yet sexual practice has to remain, in some way, pivotal to any definition of lesbianism and lesbian traditions. It is *feminism* which has in all kinds of ways made White women in the movement irrespective of sexual practice, conscious of becoming centrally important to each other out of the patriarchal heritage of sexual oppressions, and has generated myriads of women-centered activities and collaborations. It is sexual interest in women, along with sexual disinterest in men, attraction to women and/or decision to withdraw from sexual experience with men, which distinguish the lesbian modes of living. Even at this level, however, the sexual and cultural decisions and preferences cannot spell out an obvious "correct" political theory and strategy to deal with sexual oppression. There are lesbians who work in all kinds of collaborations with women who have sexual connections with men, and with men themselves, as well as those lesbians who take radical feminist positions or believe in various degrees of separatism.

The insistent resurfacing of homophobia haunts the women's movement and the feminist modes of thinking it evolves. It also produces forms of guilt and reactions of oversimplified moralism which, each in its own way, inhibit the development of feminist analysis, as well as forcing it to challenge the too-easy patriarchal molds which haunt feminism itself. As the women's movement moves on—and it is continually moving on—its discourses about sexuality are having to change and are having to go into crisis. The internal tensions and divergences within the movement are as important to that momentum as are its celebrations, agreements, and support. The tendencies complement each other because of the different emphases and angles they stress. The forms of entrenchment, the impasses, and the irreconcilable strategies produce crises in the movement, which in turn generate imperatives to reconsider in new ways the sexual political dilemma that the women's movement is committed to confront.

The political problematic of sexuality permeates all the political formations of our culture, the psychological landscape of our gendered and economically defined "families," and the sexual ideologies that are pervasive in our daily lives and interactions whether we like them or not. The problem of the *positioning of women in sexuality* in our society is complex beyond the too-easy pointing of fingers at a cardboard range of male oppressors. Yet most feminists, of whatever persuasion, have needed to use oversimplified ways of labeling the sexual political dilemma to gain ground and confidence in confronting it at all. New, more challenging ways of thinking about the social production of gender and the social relations of sexuality are beginning to emerge. The tactics and strategies are going to have to shift as the political thinking about sexuality finds new formulations and reassesses both the implications of the "evidence" in its specific contexts, as well as the "theory"—that is, the modes of interpreting, selecting, contextualizing and utilizing the "evidence" which has been invoked over the last decade. At stake in this are the new and ongoing forms of confrontation and debate caused by the wide range of positions and analyses held within radical and socialist-feminism.

Racism. Stereotypes. Sexism. Stereotypes. Heterosexism. Stereotypes. Lesbianism. Stereotypes. Homophobia. Stereotypes. White woman. Stereotypes. White man. Stereotypes. At each sentence I write, I must struggle against defense mechanisms which pressure what I *want* to say into rigid, self-justifying categories. Writing this section has been a demanding and anxious undertaking.

We affirm all of our transformations . . . We deny none of our transformations.[2]

Since the women's movement is made up of women of such diverse experiences—in which certain choices and realizations have been differently enabled or made necessary, while the larger political economy strengthens its ideological and material stranglehold—it is important to stress the different angles from which White feminists approach and affirm their concern with sexual power and exploitation, and the necessarily diverse tactics and strategies this entails. I cannot hope to do justice to the full significance of all of these sexual/political strategies. I can only situate myself provisionally, as of now, within the shifting, struggling, confrontational, and liberating dialogues which the women's movement opens up. But it is important that I do suggest what my angle into it all is. There is no completely objective position from which one speaks about feminism and sexuality. One's personal and political history influences the selection of certain things and not others—and so one's perspective becomes simultaneously insightful and limited. The specific experience of relationships, who to live with and how, family and social pressures around "normality," the emotional hierarchies programmed into our sexual, historical heads and the lived process of dislocation of these, the negotiation of commitments and respect, financial survival and political collaboration, passion, sisterhood, friendship, and their conflicts all interact and contradict, in relation to certain possibilities and impossibilities which each of us confronts differently.

The terms of my own thinking have been shaped in the simultaneous experience of Women's Liberation and socialist struggles, confrontations, dialogue. This has meant a lot of incompatibilities, yet has also made it possible and necessary to think about sexual oppression in capitalism as specific from sexual oppression in socialism and under imperialism. In addition, it has meant, and in part of my life still means, engaging in collaboration with men who define themselves as struggling against capitalist and imperialist exploitation and oppression. The feminist imperative, along with the male-defined socialist reticence to recognize (or perhaps even failure to imagine) the fundamental and far-reaching significance of that feminist imperative, means that a crucial part of my life is engaged with women and is constantly shaped by the challenges, thinking, caring, fighting, floundering, and demanding that the feminisms of the Women's Liberation Movement necessitate. Within that, I have found it possible to choose to parent a child with a man, which in itself is not an end, but the beginning of still more ongoing and difficult sexual-political struggles and all the social pressures, assumptions and crises these entail. Yet my life is centered in emotional and political relationships with certain men and women who meet (or do not meet) in an intricate network of the personal and political dimensions of heterosexuality and lesbianism. On my own journey I am specifically alerted to the reexamination of state power, ideology, cultural production, and the capitalist organization of profit, exploitation, and class hierarchies, which circumscribe and often delineate the terms of sexual political struggle individuals can engage in, and which the new socialist thinking addresses in ongoing ways.

I have drawn these strands of personal-political web together to make the point that there are significant men at different levels in my political landscape—as there are, similarly and differently, for most socialist-feminists. In fact, for the vast majority of White feminists, through our own experiences, those of women friends, political struggles, workplace situations, or the network of family—with fathers, brothers, sons, husbands, lovers, or friends—the ideas and experience of feminist struggle are lived out in a myriad of ways in dynamic and difficult relationship with men and the dominant heterosexist culture which sustains our form of patriarchy. Since the organization of sexuality embodies highly significant ideological, economic, and gender-role meanings in our capitalist culture, and is conceded particular importance in the personal and psychological organization of all of our lives, it is inevitable that the feminist project necessitates ongoing strategies, analyses, reevaluations, and demanding, if still fragmented, strategies concerning the politics of sexuality itself.

Various political strands of feminist lesbianism are evolving crucial space and contexts within which sexual preference and the social significance of sexuality can be gradually reformulated, with vital challenges to the heterosexism implicit at all levels in our culture. The feminist project also has woven into it various political strands of feminist politics engaging with heterosexuality. These struggle fragmentedly with the necessity of creating and politically inventing viable ways for men as well as women to begin to engage in transforming the limits of their socially and culturally constituted gender, and the power positions and related sexual practices this ritualizes. Men are being asked not only to incorporate in their political visions all the practical demands which would materially establish women's formal equality or radically new forms of social equality for everyone, but also to engage in the significant sexual-political struggles over the social relations of reproduction (masculinity redefined by the emotional and practical activities of nurturance and/or domestic labor) and the social relations of sexuality, with the forms of exchange and contract as well as power-related sexual practices which "normal" heterosexuality is meant to enact. Although the women's movement highlights the sexual dilemmas of our patriarchal society, the defense, survival, evacuation and indictment strategies which the first decade of Women's Liberation feminism evolved have been only minimally effective in enabling or even necessitating this form of sexual political engagement on the territory of traditional (male-defined) radical politics, let alone in the lives of individuals (men and women). Within the movement, certain groups of women have been able to develop women-only communities and cultural activities, which do not, however, always necessarily sustain feminist *sexual*-political struggle. The claiming of freedom of sexual preference and of a sexual space that is not intruded upon by males is a crucially important choice in a male-dominated society. It does not produce, however, a zone of immunity from patriarchal forms of social relations nor from the patriarchal constructions of sexual practice and sexual significance. Meanwhile, many other feminists have kept drifting ambivalently (if not apologetically or with feminist irritation, since, after all, were men not meant to be "The Enemy"?) across the non-neutral territory marked off by inspiring—but ultimately inadequate —radical feminist rhetoric. These feminists have not embraced the lesbian alternative, which, it has been implied from certain sections of the women's movement, was the crucial and evident strategic move in confronting the patriarchal dilemma women face. Questions still remain as to how the social construction of gender can be transformed; how the social relations between men and women can begin to be restructured; why patriarchal, male-dominated practices emerge in different forms in different cultures; what the levels of political struggle are which are going to confront those practices; and how men and women can decide to commit themselves to changing them in the institutional, interpersonal, and gendered psychological forms.

Mostly it has been individual men who, in the necessarily random contexts of personal relationships with feminist women, have agreed (at least provisionally) to negotiate disrupting the normative gender roles that society constitutes in them. Individual efforts, however, are inevitably limited, if not undermined, by the larger social-political odds against sustaining and developing this process. Relationships with feminist women end; easier options are always available to avoid the sexual-political confrontations. The question is always there: How do you disrupt the reproduction of oppressive gender roles anyway—how do you collaborate with someone to politically transform the context and activity of sexual pleasure? The effort by men to engage actively with sexual politics often remains parallel to, but separate from, other political, economic, and cultural practices and struggles that they engage in as men. What is interesting, however, is that the most complex and multi-layered engagement of men in feminist politics—as well as their resistance to it on all levels— often occurs when men are having to live out the stakes of their commitment to feminist transformations through their sexual practice itself. The breakdown of patriarchal behavior and patriarchal political imagining (for men and women) appears to go farther when the challenge to the normative ways of being deals with the emotional, psychological, and physical stakes that feminism questions within sexuality itself.

In saying all this, I am affirming the political necessity and the far-reaching political potential of feminist struggle *within* sexual and emotional relationships with men, as well as in contexts where men do not matter. I am arguing this against the positions held within White feminism which argue that the key transformations and most radical challenges will occur most significantly and exclusively in relation to women-only avenues of change imagined in opposition to a general category of "men." The transformation of patriarchal structuring of gender and power cannot, I believe, be changed only by women changing themselves—though it is also indisputably true that this structure will never change if women do not commit themselves to changing themselves and the social-sexual structures which confine them. These changes have to occur, however, within the real situations and possibilities that different women encounter and choose. This is why the various tendencies within feminism are of crucial importance in the variety of practices and necessary tensions they are constructing in different relationships between women and between women and men. The exploratory dialogues between Black and White feminism are bringing men back onto the White feminist agenda and calling for a profound rethinking of the too-easy rhetoric that White feminism has often had recourse to. It is too liberal and too racist a White feminist response to claim that *men* are the enemy, then "make an exception" for Black men because, under the conditions of racism, Black women claim solidarity with Black men. The problem lies in the initial White radical feminist entrenchment, which is illuminated challengingly by the contrasting perspectives that Black feminism is beginning to present.

As with racism, not only the institutions of oppression have to change—so do the attitudes and practices of those people who enjoy privilege from those oppressive institutions. This is not to say what is often proposed as a reason for not questioning heterosexuality as an institution and as a privilege: that feminists' energy should, a priori, be focused on some kind of self-sacrificial missionary quest to "change men." Rather, the transformation of the oppressive terms of patriarchal heterosexuality *within heterosexuality itself*—changing the forms of sexual practice and erotic motivation that have developed in our society—is of pivotal importance to the feminist project as a whole. The institutions, ideologies, gendered psychologies, and power structures that the capitalist exploitation of patriarchal heterosexuality has established in the White dominant culture determine the sexual imagination, the consciousness of the body, the "meaning" and anticipations elaborated from sexual involvement, and the investments, dependencies, and power tactics projected in relation to the terms of sexual pleasure. The ending of patriarchal sexism will not mean the elimination of difference, but a transformation of the social hierarchies and abusive power relations that have been systematically ritualized from biological difference. For feminism, this has to pose a radical dislocation of the relationship between sexuality, patriarchal eroticism, and patriarchal distribution of power, which at present permeates the context of *all* of our lives and is enacted in various ways, to various degrees, in all sexual relationships which women, as well as men, engage in.

The existence of males within the significant topography of my political landscape *by definition* places me marginal to and, in the recent climates of feminist sectarianism, in an ambiguous relationship to certain sources of "women's culture" and purely women-centered experiences and activities that certain sectors of the women's movement are committed to evolving. The energy and political understandings that these communities galvanize, in ways which the political connection with struggles that implicate men do *not* (or do against a different set of odds, from different angles), challenges and shifts my political vision in important ways. My feminism partakes in the Women's Liberation determination to refuse to accept the offensive conditions of the institutions of heterosexuality, the normative homophobia of our culture, the institutionalizing of every area of women's lives that is defined in dependent and inferior relationship to men. My love for certain men and women (and my conflicts with certain men and women) shapes my political commitment as one that has to struggle to create a feminism which, while seeking to resist and sabotage male dominance in its concrete and psychological forms, also caringly and dynamically urges, challenges, and welcomes my son into the possibility of his own journey of conscious struggle for the ending of every dimension of sexual oppression.

The position I occupy and affirm is nonetheless riddled with a politically significant unease and essential discomfort, which a willingness to engage in sexual-political struggle *with men*, under patriarchal conditions, always entails. Yet the political rethinking of the terms of personal interaction with men within the networks of social and economic restructuring that feminism requires, is, I believe, of fundamental importance to the Women's Liberation Movement as a whole. The questioning and renegotiation of sexual practice and the "meanings" enacted through heterosexual activity have to be one essential feature of the complex feminist endeavor. In a society where masculinity is privileged and has integral to it power over women, women's involvement and struggle with men is a risky affair—but then, all personal negotiations as we live them now, with the class-elitist, racist, and sexist connotations they invoke, are a risky affair. We cannot, just by so wishing, transform ourselves outside the limits of the society of which we are still part. The collaboration and struggles between women—highlighted in particularly severe ways by the interaction of Black women and White feminists—have many levels of political problems and understandings which have to be politically analyzed, understood, put at risk, and transformed. This will happen only if viable grounds for political engagement can be constructed. As Marge Piercy wrote:

> For us to be friends
> is a mating of eagle and ostrich, from both sides[3]

Features of the Sexual Landscape

It was the impossibility of trying to work politically with men whose sexism devalued the political and personal presence of women that galvanized the specific eruption of the Women's Liberation Movement.[4] The imperative was to be able to be a political person without being objectified because of your sexuality and relegated to marginality because of your gender. The quest was for self-respect and respect from others—to break away from a history of cultural dependency and systematic devaluing of women. The blatant surfacing of active sexist practices in daily interaction with men (especially for the White women who, because of their class- and race-privileged access to education, had somehow greater anticipation of their future as "equal citizens") generated a reassessment of and a revolt against the ways that women's gender and sexuality organized their lives in society. It was "the revolt against dehumanized sexual relationships, against the role of women as sexual commodities, against the construction and spiritual strangulation inherent in the role of wife."[5] The realization that the implications of being socially constructed as "woman" meant confinement, loss of control, a giving over of the self into dependency on men—that men, in *their* socially constructed gender, perpetrated this confining, controlling, and limiting of women, including the women they loved and slept with—put sexuality immediately into a state of crisis. The anger that resulted (results) was the anger of understanding how, just as White women have been limited *as subject* in White male-dominated laws, significant arenas of politics and skills, and sexually segregated areas central to the economic organization of capitalism—so we are limited *as sexual subjects* in our sense of ourselves and our interaction with men and with each other. Within the controlling ideological patterns of White, Western patriarchies, women are present as sexual objects for male control and appropriation. White women's sexuality has been repressively controlled or charged with menacing significance. This means that their lives are organized around what their *sexuality* is assumed to suggest and around reproductive inevitabilities beyond their control.[6] The feminist intervention occurs at the level of refusal to be oppressed because of gender, and resistance to a sexuality which consolidates female powerlessness and male dominance.

The White, bourgeois dominant culture stressed the male-centered nature of sexual energy and pleasure along with the "risk" of pregnancy which, if it did not bring shame, brought the social disempowering that White motherhood embodies. This heritage equated female sexual pleasure with feminine abnormality or indecency while demanding that women engage—whether "freely" or under direct coercion—with men in sexual activity on patriarchally shaped male terms. Through the Fifties and Sixties the conflicts and repressions of this cultural heritage were brought into new forms of crisis as Western capitalism expanded its consumer industries and media resources to project new manifestations of this sexual tradition as key, obsessive motifs of the capitalist economy. Women were to be seen as free agents of, free participants in, the terms of the patriarchal heritage. The capitalist development of technology, education, legal reform, and job options served well the development of patriarchal "democracy." Contraceptive developments (though a health risk, and though evolved within the racist and imperialist ideologies of population control), as well as legal and institutional liberalism brought shifts which at certain levels appeared to concede to women real kinds of new power over their lives. Birth control *was* of key importance in liberating the sexual potential of White women as sensual beings rather than purely as mothers. The significance of the "freedoms" it brought to White women's sexual sense of themselves is highlighted interestingly when compared with the traditions which affirmed Black women's sexual potential both in sensuality and in reproduction, apart from the issue of contraception.

An important feature of the sexual dilemma of the patriarchal culture in which White women participated was the polarization of female sexuality into oppositional and incompatible camps. It was either reduced to the capacity of fertility, where it had to be organized and contained in ways that protected male property rights in women (in other words, female sexuality was for reproduction, not pleasure), or it was equated with the underside of the patriarchal erotic imagination. In the latter case, female sexuality was seen as embodying powers of evil, indecency, and moral subversion when it was expressed illicitly, was not connected with motherhood, or was threateningly associated with women's autonomous pleasure. The modern form of this dilemma, which feminism is still facing, is the sustained polarization of sexuality—meaning marriage/motherhood/ confinement/exclusion and dependency on men or the patriarchal state—and sexuality meaning women's autonomy, their right to pleasure and the new-found freedoms this opens up—but in terms of child-lessness. New possibilities are opening up for women's gratuitous enjoyment of sexual pleasure, which the White cultural traditions have for centuries inhibited and denied. But these pleasuring freedoms are still imagined within the economic and ideological imperatives of patriarchal capitalism, and the consumer/erotic landscapes they sustain. Women have gained a freedom not to reproduce, not the freedom to have non-oppressive and non-exploitative relationships. Sexuality is not just composed of good technique and freedom to not have children; it is constituted in a web of psychological and emotional needs, which are socially produced, and sets of power relations which bring complicated options of abuse and of satisfaction. White feminism is still struggling with the oppositions of a patriarchal culture which defines nurturance and family as incompatible with women's autonomy, independence, achievement . . . and freely enacted sexuality. For White women, the attempt to claim our right to be sexual and autonomous beings contradicts many of the levels of male control and the disabling dependency on men that circumscribe our lives. The problem is how to find ways that both can affirm the gratuitous nature of women's sexual pleasure and also reconnect sexual autonomy with reproduction when desired, in the face of the patriarchal organization of gender and power through the activities of reproduction.

So for White feminists the point of enactment of sexual relations is at the heart of the larger patriarchal fabric. This is the recurrent starting point: there is no easy or relaxed collaboration with men, no mutual cultural support to be acted out in sexuality itself, for the sexual connection always occurs for us within the history and current reality of cultural, economic, institutional, and sexual male power. This means that every subjective sexual moment embodies the psychological and social formations of gender and the irreconcilable categorizations of men and women that our culture contains. As White women, we cannot live out our sexuality oblivious to that.

The recent explorations by Nancy Chodorow, Dorothy Dinnerstein, and Adrienne Rich stress the effect of sexual divisions of roles based on "mothering" and the social production of gender under patriarchal sexual division of labor. These resonate with the many feminist analyses of the economic, institutional, and cultural "separation of powers" and "allotment of suffering,"[7] which have been evolved and sustained throughout our sexual-political history. As feminist research examines new questions about the histories of White women's lives—as well as men's in context with women's—we are discovering the complexities of sexual conflict in White history and the censorship of women's relationships with each other that this heritage has imposed. We are learning that nothing is "pure" or "natural" when it is related to gender definitions and sexuality itself—that the social organization of sexual difference institutionalizes and legitimizes inequality and male dominance, which are inevitably embodied in heterosexual practice as our culture defines it. Sexual practice and the sexual imagination both celebrate the "differences" of men and women as "natural," which feeds into the perpetuation of that male dominance. The history of the social construction of gender has resulted in the coercive institutionalization of heterosexuality, which prevents women from being able to imagine themselves surviving without involvement in a structured relationship of "loving dependence" on a man. Meanwhile, paradoxically, it has resulted in the *incompatibility* of men and women in bonding patterns where power is unequal and the polarities of the definitions of masculinity (non-relational, achievement-oriented) and femininity (nurturant and low in self-esteem) are at odds with each other. Soaring divorce rates, the number of single-parent families, "an upsurge in incest and violence against women, an epidemic of tranquilizer addiction," the investment of male sexual culture in vast pornography industries, and high rape statistics are but a few of the salient symptoms of the crisis in heterosexual relations and the conflicts and incompatibilities being acted out in male-female units.[8]

What has been traditionally talked about as the "complementarity" of natural male and natural female characteristics has been rearticulated by White feminists, as the oppressive reality of the coupling of woman with man, where to be woman means to be contained and disallowed as a sexual subject and to be man affirms power in the world, being achievement-oriented, absent from nurturant roles, and culturally produced as an active sexual *subject* whose sexuality depends on objectifying women's sexuality.

I believe it is crucially important for White women to come to terms with the *specific* histories of White women and men within male-dominated, racist, capitalistically organized society. In particular, it needs to be recognized that when feminists talk about "men" and "women," they are referring to "man" and "woman" as they experience that polarity in their own historical and cultural context, within their own heritage's consolidation of male dominance and whatever forms of control or definition of women's sexuality that has entailed. This sexual heritage was reinforced by the racial and sexual codes of slavery. Black women have their own different tales to tell of specific forms of "womanhood" and "manhood" evolved under the brutalizing yoke of slavery with its very different ensuing distribution of power to women of different races. There is a culture of shared strengths and sensuality in collaborative survival for Black women for which the White dominant culture has no equivalent experience.

I am not claiming that "therefore" there are no sexual-political struggles to be negotiated in the Black community. Nor am I implying that sensual and sexual pleasure are absent in White experience. I am merely underlining the fact that the reference points of Black women and White women are in separate and opposed—yet for racist sexism, intrinsically complementary—cultures and in different angles of the same historical process, within which the sexual sense of self and of others for Black and White women has evolved in contrasting ways. The goal is to understand what has been enabled and what disabled in these opposed yet interdependent sexual histories in order to locate the terms of different struggles today.

The White feminist account relates to a history within the "normative" terms of capitalist patriarchal culture—with patriarchal traditions stemming from European origins and converging to be legally and institutionally reaffirmed in the economic and cultural patterns of the White dominant culture. The White feminist confronts the alienation of women within sexuality, as part of *the institutionalized negation of women as subjects*—whether in relation to the state, law, family, education, health care, or productive work, or in terms of *sexuality itself*. White feminist struggles should be able to make evident to Black women the systematic disempowerment of women which can follow from access to the dominant culture. The feminist imperative affirms and develops the struggle for women's autonomy as active subjects who are choosing not to invalidate their sense of self by situating their lives in immediate relationships with men *in the sexist conditions* built into this society. The politics of lesbian feminism and heterosexual feminism—though divergent and often conflicting in their recent political rhetorics—are both ultimately committed to challenging the disempowerment of women. They involve differing tactics for challenging the desexualizing of women in relational terms, the fetishistic sexualizing of women along patriarchal lines, and the psychological and economic dependence of women on men.

An article by the feminist historian Carroll Smith-Rosenberg provides one angle of exploration of the way female physiology and sexual development was interpreted in White male medical texts in nineteenth-century America.[9] She is looking at the medical and biological arguments that were put forward to legitimatize notions of "what women were"—what roles women were "naturally" destined for. She looks at the learned views which "reflected and helped shape social definitions of the appropriate bounds of woman's role and identity." The general concept of male sexuality in the nineteenth century focused on the man's *will* to indulge in or repress sexuality. The male was conceived of as maturing into strength, vigor, approved sexual impulses, and freedom. The woman was conceived of as maturing (if a *real* woman) into chastity, frailty, loving dependence, and sexual *duties* within wifedom. Woman's physiology explained her "nature" —her life was thought to be composed of a series of debilitating crises, from menstruation through pregnancy, childbirth and lactation to menopause. The male arguments "demonstrated" the "natural" weakness of women, and often embodied notions of shame and distaste at the functioning of the female body. They claimed that women should negotiate the crises of puberty and menopause by entering "a regimen of quiet, avoidance of mental activities, the shunning of new activities and a commitment to domesticity." As lashings and lynchings, field and domestic slavery, and systematized rape continued in all their extreme brutality, I don't believe these men considered that there was any connection between their stated ideas about female physiological maturation and the *Black* women and men who were objects of their sexual violence. The amazing (or perfectly ordinary) thing is that six years ago I myself witnessed a male psychiatrist presenting explicitly the same "biological" arguments justifying "normal" feminine roles and behavior to a group of five hundred high school girls.[10] He concluded his talk by stating that he hoped the young women present would not be led astray by the hysteria and "unnatural" demands of "women's libbers," that their duty was to accept the roles cut out for them in society and the family and make them function "properly"—not to challenge the societal structures that their elders, "who knew best," had set up for them. Our White patriarchal culture, though malleable enough to accommodate economic and ideological developments, has all kinds of subtle and not-so-subtle loyalties to its former historical assertions on sexism and misogyny.

When I began reading and compiling notes for this section, I was struck by the fact that, in many of the texts and anthologies that the women's movement has produced, there is a general sense of sexual anger and outrage, while in fact very few of them talk of sexuality itself except, in general terms, of its oppressiveness to women. It seems that the only way many White women have found to approach sexuality is through a nightmare maze of elaborate and necessary analyses of the process by which we were disallowed as sexual subjects and the ways in which heterosexuality has been institutionalized and made coercive in our society. Moving from the recognition that

A man proves his masculinity by going to bed with women, a woman proves her femininity by *not* going to bed with men. Masculinity equals sexuality, whereas femininity is opposed to it . . .[11]

feminist discussion of sexuality has had to engage, at a first level, in arguing that White women *were actually sexual beings*.

Modern feminist writers drew on Masters and Johnson and the Kinsey report to show that women's sexual capacity was as strong as men's and that the clitoris existed. The problem was *the nature of the heterosexual engagement itself*, and the myths it fed on, not women's predetermined biological/psychological condition. Other feminist explorations had to contextualize women's sexual experience in the "objective" evidence of sexual discrimination in society at large. They looked at myths, male-dominated cultural traditions, male-dominated language and argumentation. They had to address the profoundly sexist concepts sustaining all the "normal," "respectable" academies of knowledge; sexual images and the media; the history of patriarchal pyschological, medical, and literary interpretations of femininity and female sexuality. They had to question rape as part of the "normal" male sexual imagination in White culture; the norms of masculinity and femininity; male purchasing power over women's sexuality in prostitution, marriage, and pornography; legal rulings on sexual rights and abuses; women's lack of control over reproduction in abortion laws, sterilization abuse, and health care. They had to confront homophobia and other systems of "phobia" by which male attitudes and patriarchal ideologies retain control of and "normalize" women's dependence on men.

White feminism embodies an urgent, ongoing imperative to recover "*the evidence of damage*"[12] out of the "normality" of the patriarchal history and actuality of the dominant White culture, and to understand the various social and political factors that perpetuate this damage. As the fragments of evidence surface and fit together, as new questions, processes of inquiry and criticism emerge, the women's movement is laying ground for more adequate ways of understanding the systematizing, sustaining, and reproduction of sexual oppression in which White women's sexuality is embedded. Women need to understand the ideological and psychological mechanisms of oppression which weld into daily reality the injustices, power structures, and hierarchies of the exploitative society we all live in. By identifying the means of our oppression we build a significant basis for political resistance and struggle.

The "identifying" and recovering of repressed historical and contemporary inventories of male sexual violence does not, by itself, make understandable the coalescing social histories and imperatives which have produced gender in individual men and women—so that masculinity becomes rooted in male power over women's sexuality, and femininity embodies dimensions of complicity and often affirmation of the oppressive patriarchal divisions of power. The radical feminist tradition is in recent years accumulating a much-needed inventory of the statistics, as well as vivid accounts, of the condoned, organized and legitimized sexual violence men enact on women—most often on women they know. There are, however, problems in these inductive procedures, which often imply—by accumulative *naming* of the end results, within widely differing patriarchal cultures, of the male violence against women—that there is some kind of genetic, cross-cultural universality in the male of the human species, implicitly perceived as the unavoidable propensity, will, and ability to oppress women. The emotionally rousing effects of cross-culturally juxtaposing social rituals and individual acts of sexual violence do evoke symbolically the ongoing state of sexual crisis which makes feminism and women's liberation movements urgent and crucial. Yet such accounts do not open up, either politically or with newly conceived theoretical insight, the specific cultural, social, and historical understandings of the *processes* by which individual men and women come to be situated in relation to each other and to the codes of their society in terms of acceptance of and acquiescence to this sexual violence. The accumulation of the selected evidence of the violence of White racism, from which White feminists have implicitly gained their sense of self as *White,* cannot of itself posit the political strategies for the necessary political collaboration between Blacks and Whites in order to sabotage and dismantle the institutions and personal relations of racism and skin privilege. Nevertheless, this knowledge can enrich the basis from which we struggle for a society and culture which does not elaborate that racist heritage, for the evidence also confronts us with pivotal questions of *class* and with interwoven histories of resistance and refusals of both Whites and Blacks. The evidence has to be situated in the many dimensions of cultural, economic, ideological and historical complexities within which both the violence and struggles occurred. So, in unexpected parallel, the inventory of male sexual violence and criminal abuse of women can enrich a knowledge of the extensive stakes and urgency in the feminist endeavor—yet it in no way provides self-evident solutions or any inevitably "correct" positions for feminists to take as regards "the male sex" as a whole (babies, boys, and all men). Such facts must be used and developed knowingly, with new forms of political conceptualizing and from a richly complex range of angles on historically specific processes as well as in relation to the cultural evolution of economic and reproductive organization. If not, we run the risk of producing rigid and entrenched polarizations which in these years of right-wing ascendancy, haunted by new specters of fascism, will only aid the new wave of regressive exploitation of all aspects of women's lives.

Western Patriarchal Obsessions

> I get up, go to make tea, come back
> we look at each other
> then she says (and this is what I
> live through over and over)—she
> says: I do not know
> if sex is an illusion
> I do not know
> who I was when I did those things
> or who I said I was
> Or whether I willed to feel
> what I had read about
> or who in fact was there with me.
>
> —Adrienne Rich[13]

We begin by recognizing that sexuality with men and the patriarchal ideologies around all sexual activity in the White dominant culture confirm women's absence as sexual subjects. In contrast to the
ideologies of love and unique desire which attempt to suspend sexual
experience in a world of its own self-fulfilling needs, feminism refuses
to separate sexual experience from the rest of the social relations society embodies. We know that we are not present in sexual relations
with men as equals. Produced and gendered within patriarchal families, all women's sexuality is haunted by gendered, sexual divisions
and roles. Of course, this is true of men's sexuality as well. Sexuality
itself, then, is a site of danger, where the temptation to "escape" and
relish "abandonment" creates a high risk of undermining our struggle to avoid collusion in our own oppression.

The sexual involvements of feminists with men, and with women,
carry the gendered ambivalences and conflicts which the power relations and erotic imagination of our culture embody. Sexuality therefore becomes a site for struggle, of conscious critical questioning,
renegotiation of terms, and a political reimagining of the sensual and
sexual. The supposed bed of ecstatic abandonment (or resented ritual) becomes threatened and haunted by the feminist inquiry and
feminist fantasies of democratic (rather than tyrannical) eroticism.
The unconscious and "spontaneous" articulation of our sexual selves
is half illusory. Even in its "genuine spontaneity" our sexual practice
is sustained by and enacts forms of eroticism, rituals of real or acted-
out sexual pleasure, which are elaborated in a culture which is centered around a fetishizing of particular aspects of male sexuality,
which reinforce male dominance *through sexual interaction itself*.
The domain of heterosexuality will be problematical until the wider
context of sexual oppression, male dominance, and the gendered
polarities as we know them are radically transformed—a transformation which cannot be suddenly imposed from without, but
which must become internalized across the daily lives and social relations of both men and women. This is the feminist affirmation that
the personal is political. The lulling caress is paralleled with the
knowledge that:

> Millions of dead women keen in our hair
> for food and freedom.[14]

Or, as Marge Piercy writes elsewhere: ·

> If we do not build a new loving out of our rubble
> We will fall into a bamboo-staked trap on a lush trail.
> You will secrete love out of old semen and gum and dreams
> What we do not remake
> plays nostalgic songs on the jukebox of our guts,
> and leads us into the old comfortable temptation.
>
> . . .
>
> I fear being manipulated
> by that touch point between us
> . . .
>
> What feels natural and easy, is soft murder
> of each other and that mutant future.[15]

There is a political resistance to a nonproblematic "ease" that assumes the "naturalness" and the ensuing organizational principles of any sexual engagement. In terms of heterosexual relationships, this posits a difficult renegotiation of terms in personal practices, which is militated against by the social and psychological structuring of the gender polarities embodied in the sexual connection. The women's movement underlines the necessity of attempting to disrupt, at the most personal level, those attitudes, behaviors, and feelings that reinforce White women's negation as sexual subject, their passivity, their dependence, the lack of confidence and self-esteem which White women's sexual histories embody.

As Adrienne Rich movingly wrote:

> I reach through the dark, groping
> past spines of nightmare
>
> to brush the leaves of sensuality
> a dream of tenderness
>
> wrestles with all I know of history
> I cannot now lie down
>
> with a man who fears my power
> or reaches for me as for death
>
> or with a lover who imagines
> we are not in danger.[16]

The dilemma is not solved by simple decisions or conscious recognition. We all embody and reenact a social, historically determined unconscious which weaves complexity and contradictions through all attempts at sexual-political struggle. Whichever paths we take, our struggles are riddled with conflict and ambivalence because of the effects of the capitalist culture's consciousness industry and of the patriarchal, nuclear-family, father-mother-daughter-son context of our psychology. This is true for men too—since it is not by deliberate, calculating will that all men perpetuate the sexual negation of women. It is through a passive, "normal" positioning, through absorption and reproduction of the "normal" gendered assumptions and roles, that they reinforce and reenact the social relations of oppression. This occurs despite the fact that real emotional bonds link men and women out of the textures of their mothered childhoods and their establishing of interdependent relationships.

Moreover, the relationship of man to woman is like no other relationship of oppressor to oppressed. It is far more delicate, far more complex. After all, very often the two love one another. It is a rather gentle tyranny. We are subdued at the moment of intimacy.

—Sheila Rowbotham[17]

> No colonized people so isolated one from the other
> for so long as women.
> None cramped with compassion for the oppressor
> who breathes on the next pillow each night.
>
> —Robin Morgan[18]

The problem of woman's unique relationship to our oppression is greater than any individual experience. Our dependency ties us to those who have oppressed us or denied us by the bonds of love.

—Jessica Benjamin[19]

The women's movement has opened up dramatically the seething complexity of the ways ideologies are embodied in daily practices. On the one hand, the uncovering of the "damage" male dominance has wreaked on the female psyche and women's place in society activates angry and moralizing indictment of "men." The lesbian-feminist refusal to operate in the ongoing wake of this "damage" is politically and symbolically very relevant. At the same time, understanding the dimensions of women's oppression makes tolerance of certain expectations men often have of women as intimate companions wear very thin. As men fail to engage in the effort to understand sexual oppression and resist attempts to dislocate their "normal" practices, which are based on socially constructed expectations of themselves and of women, the tensions between these men (who are often political radicals) and feminists escalate. Certain feminist refrains haunt the heterosexual bedrooms:

> You are the sun
> in reverse, all energy
> flows into you and is
> abolished—
> —you demand
> you demand
> I lie mutilated beside
> you
> —How can I stop you
> Why did I create you
>
> —Margaret Atwood[20]

> When another year turns over
> compost in the pile
> last year's feast breeding knots of juicy worms,
> I do not want to be indicting
> new accusations to another ex-lover
> who has thrown off the scarlet cloak of desire to reveal
> the same skeletal coldness, the need to control
> crouching like an adding machine in his eyes,
> the same damp doggy hatred of women,
> the eggshell ego and the sandpaper touch,
> the boyish murderer spitting mommy on his bayonet.
> I am tired of finding my enemy in my bed.
>
> —Marge Piercy[21]

The consequences are conflict at the personal level with men, the challenging of the viability of heterosexual sexuality, and wariness of sexuality itself.

A group of men and women collaborating on writing about "The Politics of Sexuality in Capitalism" jointly acknowledged:

So sex became a divisive thing between us in its own right, though sex as such hadn't been the cause of it.[22]

It is in this context that sexuality as a specific ground of antagonism between men and women is understood; it is in this context that the White feminist resistance to heterosexuality is unavoidable. The feminist struggle is committed to understanding the history and processes of male dominance and women's oppression—so, until that dominance and oppression end, the relishing of "free" sexuality with men (given that feminist understanding) is highly problematic. As one heterosexual feminist wrote: "I have noticed that when I feel most militantly feminist I am hardly at all interested in sex."[23] This contradiction feeds ambiguously into the negation of female sexuality we each carry in our own personal and historical heritage. Since many White feminists still live out sexual relationships with and/or commitments to men, it situates sexuality as a difficult and explosive arena of sexual-political engagement. We can, however, still choose to negotiate, work, live, or sleep with men, but *only as a site of struggle*. If we do, it is only in the knowledge that if we do not engage in struggle with and against men, and with and against our socially, historically constructed *selves within that intimacy*, if we are not continuing the long necessary process of deconstructing the gender polarities we each enact, we are undermined at the deepest political levels.

Yet even to begin to understand this does not open up a comprehensive, clear-cut strategy which can voluntaristically transform and "liberate" the lives we lead as sexual beings. Apart from the diverse social, family, and particular psychological formations each woman and man is informed by, beyond the chosen codes of naming these, each of us comes into sexuality within the contours ascribed to it by the culture of our society. Not only the *forms* of sexuality (what you do, what you think you are meant to do, what is invested in the sexual interaction, what constitutes "doing it well," how you accommodate the needs, fantasies, and demands of the other, what the limits of communication about it all are, what is deemed erotic or is not, etc.), but the very significance sexuality is invested with at many levels in our social relations, are all highly problematic. In other words, our whole sexual imagination and practice is constituted across our lives not only out of the subtle rulings, prohibitions, and possibilities our culture has accumulated around male and female sexuality, but within the crude and reductive images of sex and the "meanings" acted out, promised, and fantasized in the narrow confines of Western capitalist notions of the *patriarchal erotic*. Sexuality itself is where (supposedly, but also in very real terms) consent is actualized to a whole series of complex sexual power relations, where the proof is in the *pleasure*. This pleasure, of course, may or may not be mutual, or may be contrastingly mutual in its sado-masochistic "normality" which the capitalist, patriarchal erotic calls for.

In the normative dichotomies evoked by this patriarchal erotic standard, sexuality is on the one hand dulled into the ritualistic, familiar, safe, "normal" (healthy) behavior associated with the socially affirmed bonds of normal marital status and its organization of sexuality around parenting. This behavior will be "erotically" disrupted from its taken-for-granted repetition and emotional rituals only by a sad "Total Woman" attempt to reenergize the male erotic powers now situated *outside* the relations of family and familiarity, or by the "turn-on" of the sadistic (physical and psychological) and variously displaced enactments of male sexual violence. Sexuality remains a realm suspended in the sub-worlds of the patriarchal erotic, where, blended with currents of male romantic nostalgia, it is fantasized out onto the fetishized bodies of women, shaped and positioned to celebrate the male-gendered subjects, as Western patriarchal capitalism necessitates.

How any one woman sexually interacts with any one man on this landscape poses risk, danger, problems, unresolved struggle, and a fragmented sense of progress and defeat. Yet patriarchal systems will not change through moral indictments or self-righteous angers. Rather the only real hope is that, within the "formal" feminist struggles to "objectively" change the external institutions of the society, there will evolve engaged and dialectical processes of men and of women, changing and having to change. These changes have to occur not just in ideas of formal political rhetoric, but in the minutiae of behavior comprising the social interactions where sexual difference and sexual activity highlight the sexist structures of the world in which we live.

The feminist intent is to question the social images and contours determining and defining sexuality in our culture. It is to question the desensualizing of human interaction, the incompatibility of tenderness with eroticism, the choice of an erotic standard based on objectification and alienation, the existence of blatant or latent syndromes of sado-masochism, the cultural production of images which ritualize sexuality within oppressive, fetishized obsessions. The tactics involved in this will be diverse and no doubt contradictory. But whatever the approach, questions have to go on being asked: what intricate levels of gendered power distribution are being celebrated and constituted through certain forms of sexual practice; what distinctions can be made between power *over* and exchanged, enabling power *with*; what are the disabling and enabling modes of interaction and discourse around transforming sexual practices emerging from the patriarchal erotic, which we all, whether lesbian or heterosexual, are deeply shaped by; what informs certain pleasures, however ambiguously, and how are the experiences of sexual exhilaration, enjoyment and even care—which are often affirmed by women with men—socially constituted against the sexist fabric of our culture; what exchanges are being made around and within sexual practice itself; what changes has feminism already influenced within the cultural terms of heterosexuality; what remains at stake at a multiplicity of levels in the social relations being acted out in the context and communication processes of this caress, that eye, this thrust, that body rhythm, this orgasm.

I was sexual only as a token, a symbolic expression of love.
—Red Collective[24]

So longing for love, so affected by discrimination.
—Fay Weldon[25]

Feminism has attempted to look at the ways in which the intimacy of sexual oppression is institutionalized and reproduced ideologically. On the one hand there is the propensity in our gendered unconscious, mothered into existence in the isolated, patriarchal nuclear family, to quest for the unique affirmation that one loving relationship can give. On the other hand, there is our imbibing of the "love culture," the conscious anticipations that our families offer (while sustaining strong taboos on female sexuality), and the social values we encounter in the romantic cult which the capitalist culture industry exploits and propagates in all aspects of its mass media. These and the social contents of the heterosexist nuclear family are material conditions which all women—lesbian and heterosexual—experience. While pornography consolidates its corporate stranglehold on the normative male erotic imagination, the love syndrome wins its profits among women.

In contrast to the Black daughters who received from their mothers explicit warnings about men and sex, the White daughter of the dominant culture is shaped in the anticipation and dream of "love and marriage." What we learn is: The right one will sweep you off your feet. He will be special, exceptional. Your feelings will transcend history, you will be united in universal human feelings. Love will somehow give structure and meaning to your life, whatever the social realities you live through (and the sexist terms of the union). These "yearnings, impotent strivings to project a new world,"[26] become pivotally structured into girls' and women's self-imaginings. Whatever else women may hope to achieve, our culture reinforces the longing for a unique, synthesizing, romantic connection (with a man) which should result in monogamous bonding and the institution of marriage.

The romantic love ideologies transcend the sexual—and offer no resolution to the dichotomy of the incompatible images which judge and condemn women's enactment of sexual freedom while fetishizing their sexuality. Emotion is emphasized and sexuality is represented in a mist. The emotions that are encouraged emphasize abandonment, loss of self, the pleasure of being uncontrollably overwhelmed by the male presence and redefining your whole world in terms of him. It is a celebrating of powerlessness. The pleasure is in the giving up of power and autonomy to become a part of what is made to appear as the "natural universality"—the male-centered unit. Whatever the circumstances women live out ("Dear God, preserve us from such love. Down here among the wage-earners—our love is less lofty. Money and law interfere."),[27] the images hover as yardsticks of failure and nostalgia. The accounts of the realities of women's lives within the configurations of romantic love are starkly represented in a variety of fiction and poetry by women writers. It is, in fact, in women's literature that the dilemma, disillusionment, yearning, and failure of the love syndrome is most powerfully articulated, as the following passages illustrate:

> The willingness to hang on the meathook and call it love,
> that need for loving like a screaming hollow in the soul,
> that's the drug that hangs us and drags us down
> deadly as the icy sleet of skag that froze your blood.
> —Marge Piercy[28]

This is how it is supposed to be. This is a man. This is loving. His possessing was a current that seemed to require from her that she only let go: then she would be held firmly in him without tension, without decision . . . It was a deep image, present from earliest adolescence, of the strong man who wanted her, who would be a world in which she floated, whose being would contain hers. This was what she had always been told would be the true center of her being, the central act of her life. A woman loving a man. Now it had happened. The more she loved him, the more she felt herself to be in love . . . This became the content of living. See, she would tell herself, it is an equal relationship for he does the cooking. But she knew she lied. He had too much heavy will for controlling her.

—Marge Piercy[29]

Love had brought her here to lie beside this young man: love was the key to every good; love lay like a mirage through the golden gates of sex. If this was not true then nothing was true . . . They made love. She was too tired to persuade herself that she felt anything at all . . . Rolling off her, he yawned and said with satisfaction, "How many hours have we slept during the last fortnight?" She did not reply. Loyalty towards love was forcing her to pretend that she was not disappointed, and that she did not—at that moment she was sick with repulsion—find him repulsive. But already that image of a lover that a woman is offered by society, and carries with her so long, had divorced itself from Douglas . . . Because that image remained intact and unhurt it was possible to be good-natured. . . .

—Doris Lessing[30]

The phantom of the man-who-would-understand,
the lost brother, the twin—

for him did we leave our mothers,
deny our sisters, over and over?
did we invent him, conjure him . . .

It was never the rapist:
it was the brother, lost,

the comrade/twin whose palm
would bear a lifeline like our own:

. . . It was never the crude pestle, the blind
ramrod we were after
merely a fellow-creature
with natural resources equal to our own.

—Adrienne Rich[31]

The conflicts and hostilities enacted in heterosexual intimacy because of the inequality and dominance it embodies are covered over by the impossible yearnings of the romantic love tradition, which is rooted solidly in Western civilization and in capitalist cultures. The realization of self is conveniently imagined at the site of individual relationships isolated from political and social contexts.

I do not want to live indefinitely in a world you dominate.

—John Berger[32]

The corollary of imaginings of a special, exceptional love is the institution of monogamy, which comprises the "obvious" sets of rules through which to live out the uniqueness and proofs of commitment. Monogamy, in its Western heritage, evolved within patriarchal codes of property rights, inheritance laws, and male rights of control over women's sexuality and fertility. The daughters and mothers, wives and sisters moved within the laws of the fathers, brothers, husbands, and sons. Today, however, the strong emotional propensity to invest in the institution of monogamy is developed by the contemporary nuclear family formation, shaped by the heritage infused into the marriage contract and the requirement of a unique female nurturance figure. The monogamous construct is the "normal" outcome of "real" love, and as such is embedded in the laws and culture in the patriarchal forms we know. It is a curious combination of social coercion and personal consent. Although it is meant to suggest, ideologically, proof of commitment and correct sexual morality and to affirm the essential meeting of one person's needs by another, in reality it proposes a redefinition of self as "fused with another" which is determined by specific rules and ultimatums. If these rules are broken or transgressed, the emotional construct is programmed to fall into chaos.

Monogamy and the marriage contract exist in patriarchal capitalist societies hand in hand with the sexual double standard, however. This sets the pattern for rigid male control of female sexuality within the monogamous unit, along with self-willed freedom for male sexuality to be enacted in a world of sexual duplicity, prostitution, and pornography. Yet the institution of monogamy, which embodies this heritage of male property rights in female sexuality, still structures normative, "meaningful" sexual relationships. It is ideologically situated as the significant hinge between romantic love's orientation of the central, "special" relationship and the anarchic violence of male sexual abuse and exploitation of other "objectified" women outside that relationship.

The emotional scenario of power and control, jealousy and violence, the definition of partners' limits of freedom, though rooted in the patriarchal institution of heterosexuality, affects the emotional landscape of lesbianism and male homosexuality as well. The psychological patterns and needs, the emotional imperatives of individuals, whatever their gender or their sexual preference, are formed culturally, ideologically, and economically in landscapes that monogamy consolidates and welds together. The ideological implications it holds for women—and which are highly significant given the sexually oppressive heritage we are all formed from—are that it marks out the context where "sacrifice of autonomous self"[33] (that is, the multi-layered giving up of independence and autonomy) is simultaneous to the "loss of bodily self-determination."[34] The institution of monogamy therefore constitutes the site where the fragility of the White female's sense of self and sense of freedom is consolidated in crucial ways. It confirms the elimination of a sense of a freely acting, self-confirming female subject, and concedes defining power, appropriation, and control to "the other." The feminist slogan demanding free legal abortion available to all women on request—"A Woman's Body Is a Woman's Right"—has got its particular contradictions in the lives of women who *for love* have implicitly and explicitly conceded sexual rights and prerogatives in their body to *one other person*. As subjects of monogamy, living within the sexual and emotional and social hierarchies it necessarily generates, we are actively constituting patriarchal values and meanings. It is not only marriage or heterosexuality which causes these problems. They are inherent in the configurations of monogamy as an institution that relentlessly situates itself between romantic failure and potential violence. The focus of the institution is defined through genital sexuality, although it has far-reaching emotional and social consequences beyond that.

> Loving not packaged in couples
> shivers cracks down the closed world, the nuclear
> egg of childhood . . .
> Can you imagine not having to lie?
>
> —Marge Piercy[35]

I have touched only briefly on certain aspects of socially constructed needs and cultural assumptions that contain and describe female sexuality and that are questioned by White feminism. By living out these and other needs and assumptions, we reenact and reproduce the very fabric of patriarchal organization. This realization does not lead to an easy list of strategies feminists should "directly" live

out. Our social and economic possibilities and our personal histories
are too complex to allow simple, one-dimensional solutions—but all
feminist questioning, any efforts at dismantling the existing historically and culturally developed organization of sexuality, open up new
angles of critical consciousness about the levels of struggle necessary.
The "natural" world of "instinct" and "spontaneous sensuality" is
intrinsically woven into our historical continuum of male dominance.

> Every act of becoming conscious
> (it says here in this book)
> is an unnatural act
> —Adrienne Rich[36]

In order to create an alternative, an oppressed group must at once shatter
the self-reflecting world which encircles it and at the same time project
its own image onto history.

—Sheila Rowbotham[37]

White women's experiences, interests, and histories emerge in
daily life in innumerable different directions. There are many centers to feminism and the struggle for women's liberation, not one. As
Black women, Third World women, and women from socialist and
liberation struggles enter the landscape of the movement, the movement changes, creates new centers, and finds old ones radically
changed. In relation to the problems, questions, and struggles, different women engage different issues in terms of sexual discrimination and make different choices about where and how to live out
the struggles involving sexuality itself. Many feminists reluctantly or
determinedly decide to engage actively in more or less satisfactory or
at least challenging relationships with men, which involve developing strategies with men against male dominance within the most intimate encounters. Many feminists defiantly or determinedly decide to situate their emotional, political, and sexual lives with other
women, and struggle with the specific dilemmas, discrimination, and
affirmations which the lesbian decision embodies.

The women's movement is the shifting, evasive, and ever-
reformulating ground on which feminist support, collaboration, and
necessarily confrontational processes intersect. Whether it involves
explicit sexuality or not,

feminist sisterhood is radical female friendship which frees woman to
bond and to retain and enhance her identity. To bring herself to her
community with women.

—Arlene Raven[38]

Out of the isolation, exclusion, and reconstruction that White women's heritage grows from, this is no mean task. Given the complex dilemmas of relationships with men, the exit of significant numbers of women from the arena where relentless odds favor coercion and failure which the heterosexist, patriarchal "tragedy of sex"[39] entails, is of vital political importance. The lesbian choice not only enables specific creative and cultural energies to emerge in opposition to the dominant White male culture, it also provides an affirmation of women's emotional and sexual autonomy, which in many ways is harder for women still connected to men to do. The lesbian existence, by its very self-contained affirmation of living, working, caring, and cultural/political activity not centered around men posits a defiance to the all-pervasive male-centered structures of the White dominant culture. The shared feminist imagining is of a woman who "would no more be prepared to suppress her sexuality than to suppress or subordinate herself in any other sphere."[40] The politically formulated lesbian argument is that women should not just "swim upstream against the currents" but also should "move the river, create new currents . . . to shape this torrent as it shapes us."[41] This imperative is crucial in any process of radical political transformation or revolution.

Consciously "out of line" with the all-pervading "normalities" of heterosexist prejudice, feminist lesbianism generates an imagining of different levels of challenge and terms of vision, which can nourish fundamental perspectives needed for the overthrow of male dominance. Because they situate themselves apart from the claustrophobic patriarchal rituals and gender polarizations that heterosexuality consciously and unconsciously always evokes, lesbian women have always had to invent a potentially different context for sexuality and sexual practices—in contrast to those women who slide unquestioningly into the usual roles that the institution of heterosexuality demands. Lesbianism as a sexual preference does not solve the patriarchal dilemmas, but it is nonetheless unquestionable that the refusal—and lack of desire—to act out heterosexually reinforced roles of femininity and submission in the immediate presence of men suggests new dimensions in the struggle for women's liberation. Equally important is the totally autonomous affirmation of women's pleasure in each others' company—socially, politically, economically, and sexually—which lesbianism affirms.

The question all feminists confront is "What social relation do we wish to make out of sex?" The personal struggles to invent a new social relation continue to follow their lonely paths of intimacy amid the political rhetoric of the women's movement. Ground is gained, lost, shifted; goals are provisionally obscured or possible. Each effort against the patriarchal coercions has to be an exceptional as well as a common contribution to the feminist processes of change. I have lingered around the sexual dilemma to retrace some of the feminist struggles into consciousness, into becoming not just sexual, but political subjects. In political passivity White women are reduced to collusion or localized subversion, perpetuating the terms of the dominant White, patriarchal, capitalist traditions and the racism, sexism, and class oppression these necessitate. As political subjects we can form strategic coalitions with groups of men and women from different racial and class experiences to sabotage and transform the well-oiled mechanisms of the system we would otherwise support. If the solutions and strategies are not yet fully with us, the questions are becoming clearer. As Sheila Rowbotham writes:

How can we mobilize the resistance of many different sections of society? How can we bring together in our practice the separations in ourselves which paralyze us? How can we connect to our everyday living the abstract commitment to make a society without exploitation and oppression?[42]

The conditions and experience of sexuality are enmeshed in the traditions, laws, attitudes, and institutions of a society and its cultural formations. White feminism confronts and attacks at many levels the terms of male dominance and control in the White dominant culture. The struggles to confront the sexual codes of behavior, to subvert the exploitative sexual images, to affirm as political the challenge to the patriarchal erotic, and to question reductive and culturally fixated assumptions about female sexuality—and male sexuality—which are rationalized and unconsciously woven into the normality of social life, are fundamental features of the Women's Liberation Movement. These struggles are symptomatic of a refusal to dissociate abstract political principles from the experiences and interactions of everyday life. The defiance and challenge that are sustained in activist struggles and reforms in public society—health care, reproductive rights, legal equalities, economic equalities, childcare, crisis centers, etc.—are integrally connected to various styles of ongoing questioning and defiance of the ideological, physical, and psychological forms through which White women experience themselves socially and sexually.

There is no ahistorical, trans-social, "liberated" sexuality out there for the taking. The thousands and thousands of individual confrontations, negotiations, and redefinitions of the terms of sexual interaction and the fragmented, but nonetheless essential, shifts in sexual imagination that the women's movement has begun to encourage are part of the overall struggle to oppose and subvert the complex system of hierarchies and exploitations of which American society is composed. It will be out of the ground prepared by these dimensions of struggle that White feminists come to consider the terms and consequences of racism and of their own complicity in that racism. As White feminists learn not to make, from a position of racial privilege, misleading generalizations and incorrect parallels into the sexual and social experiences of Black men and women, as well as those of men and women of different classes and other Third World cultures, we also have to confront the racist fabric of the sexism fought by feminism, and the racist perspectives of that feminism itself. The political framework evolved by the Women's Liberation Movement in its struggles against sexism, sexual inequality, sexual exploitation, and male dominance at all levels—especially in the formulations of sexuality itself—provides a landscape of political imagination for engaging with struggles against racism, racial inequality, and White dominance at all levels. This is, for Whites, unprecedented.

NOTES

1. For one of the most challengingly developed discussions of some of the political implications of lesbianism, see Adrienne Rich: "Compulsory heterosexuality and Lesbian existence," *Signs*, Summer, 1980, Vol. 5, No. 4, p. 631 ff.; see also Elizabeth Ettore (ed.), *Lesbians, Women and Society*. Boston: Routledge & Kegan Paul, 1980.

2. Adapted from Robin Morgan's theme in her poem "Network of the Imaginary Mother," in *Lady of the Beasts*; op. cit., she wrote in the first person singular.

3. Marge Piercy, "The Bumpity Road to Mutual Devotion," in *Living in the Open*. New York: Alfred Knopf, 1977, p. 54.

4. The magnitude of the sexist assaults sustained by White women political and social activists can be gauged by trying to imagine Angela Davis speaking to a mixed audience of Black men and women about the causes and conditions of the imprisoning of Blacks, or Billie Holiday singing "Strange Fruit" and, as a response, having men of their own constituency shouting, "Get her off and fuck

her. Women are only cunts." The parallel is for many reasons unimaginable, but the emotional images are mutually suggestive.

5. Marlene Dixon, "Why Women's Liberation," in *Liberation Now*. New York: Dell, 1971, p. 18.

6. Agnes Smedley's autobiographical novel *Daughter of Earth* poignantly articulates her struggle against her own sexuality and her refusal to freely engage in sexual relations with men, in order to retain a sense of control over her life and become a political activist.

7. Adrienne Rich, "From an Old House in America," in *Poems Selected and New 1950–1974*, p. 240.

8. Barbara Haber, "Is Personal Life Still a Political Issue?" in *Feminist Studies*, Vol. V, No. 3, Fall 1979.

9. Carroll Smith-Rosenberg: "Puberty to Menopause: The Cycle of Femininity in Nineteenth-century America," in *Clio's Consciousness Raised*, ed. Hartman and Banner. New York: Harper & Row, 1974.

10. A group of girls from four different high schools came together in Southampton, England, in Spring 1974, for a daylong conference on "Women in Society" and were addressed by a local male psychiatrist on "The Psychology of Women."

11. Ann Oakley, "Cultural Influences on Female Sexuality," in *Conditions of Illusion*, Allen, Saunders, and Wallis, eds. Leeds, U.K.: Feminist Books, 1974, p. 79.

12. Adrienne Rich, "Diving into the Wreck," in *Poems Selected and New*, p. 197.

13. Adrienne Rich, "Dialogue," in *Poems Selected and New*, p. 195.

14. Marge Piercy, "Phyllis Wounded," in *Living in the Open*, p. 104.

15. Marge Piercy, "Doing It Differently," in *To Be of Use*, pp. 53, 55 and 57.

16. Adrienne Rich, "From an Old House in America," in *Poems Selected and New*, pp. 241–42.

17. Sheila Rowbotham, *Woman's Consciousness, Man's World*, p. 34.

18. Robin Morgan, "Monster," in *Monster*, p. 87.

19. Jessica Benjamin, "Starting from the Left and Going Beyond," papers of conference on The Second Sex—Thirty Years Later, New York University, Summer 1979, p. 103.

20. Margaret Atwood, *Power Politics*. New York: Harper & Row, 1971, p. 47.

21. Marge Piercy, "The Homely War," in *Living in the Open*, pp. 60–61.

22. Red Collective, *The Politics of Sexuality in Capitalism*, London: Red Collective & PDC, 1978, p. 25.

23. Sally Kempton, "Cutting Loose," in *Liberation Now*, p. 39.

24. Red Collective, op. cit., p. 23.

25. Fay Weldon, *Down Among the Women*.

26. Ros Baxandall, Irene Peslikis, Alix Shulman, Ann Snitow, "Men Have Died from Time to Time and Worms Have Eaten Them, but not for Love," papers from "Second Sex" conference.

27. Fay Weldon, *Down Among the Women*, p. 62.

28. Marge Piercy, "Burning Blues for Janis," in *To Be of Use*, p. 39.

29. Marge Piercy, in her novel *Small Changes*.

30. Doris Lessing, in her novel A *Proper Marriage*. New York: New American Library, 1966, p. 36.

31. Adrienne Rich, "Natural Resources," from *Dream of a Common Language*, p. 62.

32. John Berger, in his novel G.

33. Baxandall, et al., "Second Sex" conference papers, p. 30.

34. Iris Marion Young, "Is There a Woman's World?—Some Reflections on the Struggle for Our Bodies," "Second Sex" conference papers, p. 44.

35. Marge Piercy, "Living in the Open," in *Living in the Open*, p. 46.

36. Adrienne Rich, "The Phenomenology of Anger," in *Poems Selected and New*, p. 202.

37. Sheila Rowbotham, op. cit., p. 27.

38. Arlene Raven, "A Theory of Sense, Sentiment and the Senses," "Second Sex" conference papers, p. 65.

39. Adrienne Rich, "Waking in the Dark," *Poems Selected and New*, p. 189.

40. Angela Hamblin, "The Suppressed Power of Female Sexuality," in *Conditions of Illusion*, p. 97.

41. Marge Piercy, "Phyllis Wounded," in *Living in the Open*, p. 102.

42. Sheila Rowbotham, op. cit., p. 43.

43. Marge Piercy, "Contribution to Our Museum," in *Living in the Open*, p. 75.

Conclusions

We have presented certain features of historical and cultural differences between Black and White women and have outlined important tactics that each group felt was necessary for the furthering of their struggles for equality and freedom from oppression. As we did so, insights and perspectives on Black women's consciousness and White feminism were revealed, allowing the reader to begin to rethink and reformulate the sites of political crisis in feminist and anti-racist struggles. We have stressed the role that capitalism plays in the politics of racism and sexism, since the web of class-controlled technologies, corporate and multinational interests, propaganda, and pervasive hierarchical and class ideologies which capitalist society institutionalizes, normalizes, and supports are key deterrents to struggles for liberation.

We have heard Black women's voices claiming that the struggle for women's liberation cannot be divorced from the struggle for Black liberation, thereby creating a situation wherein Black women have to engage simultaneously in two struggles. The racist upsurge currently sweeping the United States bears stark testimony to the realism of this attitude. Cases in point are the kidnappings and murders of Black children, women, and men in Atlanta, Boston/Roxbury, and Buffalo; the fact that the KKK has been operating openly and ran a Klan leader for Congress on the Democratic party ticket; the 27.2% unemployment rate for Black youths with a college education, compared to the 22.3% rate for White high-school dropouts. The newly empowered Reagan regime is already attempting to introduce measures such as the proposed $54.6 billion cut in federal funding, which will disastrously affect the already high level of poverty as well as the education and employment possibilities for Black and Third World people in the United States.

We have seen that the women's movement in the United States has had many accomplishments to its credit during the past ten years. It has set millions of minds into motion with gears churning and turning in the direction of change—changes aimed at disrupting and transforming oppression, exploitation, and power hierarchies based on gender. The movement has been directed toward changes in the treatment of women; changes in choices concerning children and birth; changes in the status of women; changes in marriage relations; changes in the laws concerning sexual harassment and abuse; challenging sexual divisions of labor and the oppressive assumptions patriarchy sustains in gender identity; criticizing and transforming the male-centered vision of society and the power relations based on male supremacy and control; and challenging the sexual divisions, roles, and assumptions concerning gender. The numerous organizations and groups to which the women's movement has given birth represent strategized measures to confront the multifaceted sexism and misogyny of the dominant White culture and to bring about changes within the social structures of this society.

Black women can look back and recall that the Black liberation movement set millions of Black minds operating with a raised level of consciousness toward the goal of liberation from the oppressive forces of racism. Many organizations were formed and developed strategies to bring about changes in the lives of Blacks in such areas as housing, jobs, education, medical care, and freedom from police harassment and brutality.

Yet as we look back over the years, we see that all the tactics employed did not result in any substantive changes in the social and economic welfare of Blacks and women. At the most basic economic level, little has changed in the relationship of gender and race to the distribution of income:

	WHITE	BLACK
Family Median Income—1978	$16,740	$9,563
Median Income of Year-round		
Full-time Workers		
MALE	$15,378	$10,602
FEMALE	8,870	8,290

Median of All Income for
  All Persons

MALE	$10,603	$6,292
FEMALE	4,001	3,455

Median Earnings of Full-time Workers[1]
  Less than High School

WHITE MEN	$10,544
OTHER MEN	8,413
WHITE WOMEN	5,932
OTHER WOMEN	5,384

  College (4 or more years)

WHITE MEN	$17,351
OTHER MEN	13,801
WHITE WOMEN	10,575
OTHER WOMEN	10,061

Black women's initial attitude toward the women's movement was one of distrust. Their peremptory responses were ones of sneering, jeering, ignoring, and dismissal. Eventually, but very gradually, some Black women (largely from the middle socio-economic class) formed organizations designed to bring about changes for the economic welfare and well-being of Black women. The negative feelings expressed by Black women in 1969 about the women's movement are virtually unchanged today. Most Black women still feel a sense of distrust: they believe that the White women in the movement are largely middle-class and exhibit racist mentalities, and they are convinced that the concerns of the movement are not relevant to their material conditions.

The White women's attitudes toward the Black liberation movement and toward the inclusion of Black women in their movement have been jolted during the last few years. Some few political strategies have begun to change, faced with Black women's demands and anger. Others have not—but a general unease and anxiety about racism now prevails *consciously* in the Women's Liberation Movement, whereas five years ago anti-racist consciousness bore little relation to the practices and emphasis of the movement.

It cannot be denied that Black women's situation in America, like the status of all Blacks, requires radical remedies. The political framework of America is moderate to conservative, and that too cannot be denied. Consequently, Black women (and all Blacks) are consigned to seeking radical ends in a system whose structure is extraordinarily well organized to prevent any real changes from taking place.

Blacks in Professions

Medicine	2.2%
Law	3.4%
Engineering	1.0%

Women in Professions

Physicians	12.8%
Lawyers and Judges	9.2%
Engineers	1.8%

Ninety-four percent of all Board-certified gynecologists are men.

Media

Two-thirds of the nation's newspapers still have no minority employees (1,772 daily, 7,553 weekly). Of "directing editors" of newspapers with 40,000 daily circulation or more, 97.3% are males.[2]

Black women have a long history that enforces their attitude that, "There ain't gonna be no real changes made for our benefit under this here present system." This belief is one of the reasons that Black women view the women's movement with suspicion. The strategies utilized by key sectors of the Black liberation movement and the women's movement were and are reformist in the sense that they either posit the need for a new society but stress subculture solutions, or else view the government as basically positive and amenable to "progressive change." That is, movement activists either attempt to develop their own insulated cultural modes of survival, or they try to ameliorate their oppression under the existing system, using tactics that the system deems legitimate.

It must be clearly understood that sexist or racist policies exist not simply because of White male leaders who are insensitive to the moral implications of the system's discrimination against women and Blacks. The replacement of those leaders with females or Blacks will not necessarily make things better. Change will depend on the nature of the person's political analysis and vision, not on skin color or gender. In other words, a few reforms and better politicians will not rule out the need for a complete restructuring of society, which would end the dominant role played by those with corporate (money) power, who have political and financial investments in military and technical developments serving their own profits, interests, and propaganda.

An analytical view of the failures of both movements should be instructive to both groups. It should inform them that sparring is not the answer. Nor is it a matter of questioning one another's oppressions, or comparing oppressions, or taking comfort in the commonness of oppressions, or wallowing in a sense of being victimized.

Rape is America's fastest-growing violent crime.

Black women are eighteen times more likely to be rape victims than are White women.

Two hundred women per hour are physically abused (battered) by the men they share their lives and homes with in the United States.

No White male in the history of this country was ever given the death penalty for raping a Black woman.[3]

It is necessary for Black women to understand—by listening carefully and with as open a mind as possible—the expressed oppressions of White women. It is not necessary for Black women to identify with White women or even to try to do so. Nor is it necessary for White women to think they have to identify with Black women. Similarly, it is not necessary for middle-class White or Black women to experience or identify with the oppression of the poor. What is needed is an understanding of the fact that both racism and sexism are used as political tools that are intrinsically related to the Established order. Both are political weapons created and maintained under the aegis of the existing system.

For rather obvious reasons, it has not been as necessary or as possible to institutionalize sexism as a repressive measure against Black women in the same way as it has been to use it against White women. Black women can be kept in their places via racism alone. Hence, Black women correctly state that they are affected by racism more than by sexism. However, the underside of White sexism and the modes of power and sexuality interwoven in its heritage use patriarchal codes in the racist attitudes toward Black people. The "threat" of sexuality—repressed, controlled, and appropriated among White women by the subtleties of White social codes and norms— is exaggeratedly exploited to set up Black people, because of the threat of sexuality they are supposed to embody, as victims of racial oppression. Black women must realize that sexism is an integral part of the dominant governmental, economic, educational, legal, and family institutions of this society—that this sexism surrounds them and is ready to impinge on their lives oppressively at every moment as they try to survive within a society run by capitalist White males. Black women also need to realize that if these White males felt it necessary to employ sexism as a means to further subjugate Black women, they would do so in the wink of an eye. In fact, through the mass media and the workplace, this is occurring in both blatant and subtle ways. White and Black women must no longer be fooled into thinking that by pressing their personal "most severe oppression," or making a pitch that "their" oppression is the severest of oppressions, they will achieve any substantive gains. To use single-issue politics will result in a Pyrrhic victory at best. Just look at the record. Look at the social realities of today. Neither group has made any definitive gains that will ensure future generations of Blacks and women freedom from institutionalized societal oppressions. Provisional gains are already being undermined and reversed in the new formulations of right-wing ideas and policies.

Fifteen percent of the U.S. population is Black, but more than 45% of the prison population is Black. More than 48% of women in prison are Black.

Minorities comprise 4% of the U.S. Senate. Minorities comprise 5% of the House of Representatives. As a result of the November 1978 elections, Congress included one female senator and 16 representatives. In 1977, women held 2.9% of the *top* federal jobs, compared to 1.7% ten years earlier.[4]

It may appear that gains are being made, but the system is prepared to counter such gains with new or tried-and-true tactics. Consider these cases in point:

1) *Brown* v. *the Board of Education* was a landmark Supreme Court decision bearing the name of Linda Brown, who was eleven years old at the time. This ruling made school segregation illegal in her hometown of Topeka, Kansas, and the rest of the nation. In 1979, Linda Brown Smith—the same Linda Brown, now a mother of two—went back into court to request that her old case be "reopened" because, after twenty-five years, the schools of Topeka remain segregated. Her oldest son, a high school student, stated, "I had a funny feeling when I heard the judge agree to reopen the case. I began to wonder whether my kids will be in this lawsuit too someday."[5]

2) In the town clerk's office in Wallingford, Connecticut, prospec-

tive brides and their grooms are given a free "Bridal-Pax." This is a plastic drawstring bag filled with detergents, shampoos, soaps, items for personal hygiene, aspirin, glass cleaners, instant soups, romantic paperback novels, magazine subscription forms and antacids. For thirty-two years, thousands of town clerks throughout the United States have been distributing these handouts. In 1979 the president of the company shipped 1.2 million Bridal-Pax to clerks' offices, bridal shops, and bridal sections of department stores. The town clerk of Wallingford stated, "It's so nice to give them exactly the things they really need when they're married."[6]

The idea that marriage transforms a woman into a housecleaner, a housekeeper, a sparkling clean, hygienic person who suffers from headaches and heartburn and has an intellect on the paperback romantic novel level, couldn't be expressed more clearly than through the contents of Bridal-Pax and the words of the Wallingford town clerk.

The juxtaposition of Black women's consciousness and White feminism sets the stage for the need to construct different political sites for challenging the unsatisfactory realities of the male-female polarities. The differences recognized in the sexual relationships between Black women and Black men in contrast to White women and White men relate to the question of power. Male dominance as a salient problematic factor in male-female sexual relationships cannot be considered as a universal trait applicable to all men. To categorically lump all men together and attribute the same sense of power to both Black and White men is racist in the sense that the crucial role of white-skin privilege in our society is being disregarded. It is incumbent upon White feminists to recognize the very real differences that exist between White men and Black men when their degree of power is considered. The white-skin privilege cuts across any categories of class in a racist society, as does male privilege in the White dominant culture. Yet the forces shaping and sustaining male privilege are not equally participated in by all White men—though all White men benefit from these privileges and define their sense of gender in relation to them.

Black women have a specific political relationship to Black men. Black men have played crucial roles in the lives of Black women in helping them to survive the violent and inhumane treatment afforded Black women, and Black women have played similar roles in the lives of Black men. The position of White feminists committed to confronting racism in collaboration with Black women and men is paralleled by the position of White men willing and committed to engage in anti-patriarchal struggle in collaboration with White feminists. There are separate fights to be fought within each category of the oppressed and of oppressors who are consciously opposed to the oppressions they benefit from. Skin privilege and gender privilege mean complicity and power in relation to the individuals and groups attempting to confront the systems of power they both face and embody. Yet coalitions to oppose the social, economic, and ideological realities that sustain and reproduce exploitation and oppression are more essential than ever.

For White feminists, the recognition of racism and the will to fight it do not exempt them from the blindnesses, the harshness, and the passivities of racism, which their culture, their daily realities, and their political vision contain. The liberal conscience, the clever self-censorship of the more obvious forms of racist response, the internalized guilt-syndromes only deal with the tip of the iceberg. If the struggle against racism is to move forward, the basic slogans, self-righteousness, and political investments of White feminism must be radically questioned. The question of men is somehow pivotal in this. One of the ultimate forms that White feminist racism or racist feminism could take might be to argue that all men are oppressors, therefore women-centered reality needs to oppose the universal category of "Men"—and then to exempt Black men. Such an attitude would not stem from an understanding of racism, but from a desire to "include" Black women in the women's movement. A more adequate way of conceptualizing the construction of gender, in its material, socio-economic, and cultural context, must be developed and used as the basis for new forms of feminist strategy.

Black feminism is the context for the development of Black-defined sexual-political struggles, examining the sexual tensions and conflict in the terms of Black culture and its shaping within and against the White dominant culture. It has to seek ways that Black women and men can politically negotiate sexual-political tension and abuse in a way that reinforces their collaboration against racism and the capitalist formulations that embody and sustain that racism. If Black feminism has a committed solidarity with men, if their alliance is with their men (even if struggle and conflict internal to that process of alliance have to be negotiated), then the anti-racist imperative of White feminism has to seek political visions and strategies that have men on the agenda, not just in terms of committed individuals, but also in terms of coalitions against the particular forms of patriarchal, racist, and capitalist organization of society. The all-women spaces will occur interracially on terms that Black women will also set and define, and which will therefore be different from the terms elaborated within the White women's movement. If this challenge is taken up, if the encounter between White and Black women struggling against racism and sexism can move White feminism onto new ground, it may be crucial in reactivating, in radical and effective directions, the energy galvanized by the Women's Liberation Movement—an energy that risks dissipation, co-optation, and sabotage in the right-wing climate of current American politics.

Black males, because they do not have powers or the kind of masculine dominance similar to White men, do not bring the same level of worldly dominance into the sexual domain. The problems that exist among Blacks are concerned with egos and continued internal conflicts about color. In a recent study conducted by Drs. Kenneth Clark and Mamie Phipps Clark, questions dealing with sex preferences among Blacks produced these results, which show the issue of *color* as a problematic one:[7]

Black women expressed a preference for the following as sexual partners:

> Black men (44%)
> Dark-skinned Black men (16%)
> Light-skinned Black men (15%)
> White men (1%)
> Not sure (16%)

Black men expressed the following preferences:

> Black women (32%)
> Light-skinned Black women (30%)
> Dark-skinned Black women (9%)
> White women (8%)
> Not sure (13%)

Even the serious crime of rape takes on an additional complexity when Black and White women are contrasted. Mary Helen Washington spells out this difference succinctly in her *Midnight Birds*.[8] She refers to rape as a blood-knot uniting women, Black and White —but rape is also a bond between Black women and Black men, because it has been used as an excuse for savage intimidation of Black men. The increasing violence against lesbians and gay males in both Black and White communities, and the facts about women as murder victims (one out of every four murder victims is a woman;

nine out of ten murdered women are murdered by men; almost three out of four are murdered by husbands or lovers) are not only physical phenomena. It is political, economic, and social repression perpetrated by persons from the underclass as well as those with power and privilege in our society. Capitalism needs racism and sexism to sustain its important internal hierarchies: to pit race against race, men against women, and one class against another class.

In trying to achieve their liberation goals, Black people and White feminists have used similar tactics: legal action such as court challenges; mass action, including organizations and demonstrations; and electoral politics—lobbying, campaigning, and voting. These tactics have not brought about substantive changes. We live in a society that has mastered advanced technology and productivity beyond our dreams, which underlines more than ever the lines of division between those in power and control, and those rendered powerless, unable to affect the terms of power. Yet, because it is a system characterized by poverty and oppression, discrimination and exploitation, it can't help appearing to its victims as barbarous and unnecessary. How we understand that system and locate our struggles within it— and how we change our struggles because of other oppressions—are of utmost importance. Black women and White feminists have their own historic responsibility in these tasks. The forms the struggles against racism and sexism take become crucial in themselves.

The changing consciousness of many Black and White women and Black and White men is encouraged by the tide of revolutions and struggles against exploitation in different parts of the world. The root causes of spiraling prices for food, energy, housing, and medical care, cleverly camouflaged under the all-purpose term "inflation," are increasingly being understood by more people as the products of expedient political decisions made within the corporate-government power structure. The increased consciousness about domestic and international exploitation can be effectively translated into action through the collaboration and recognition of key political questions and challenges posed from out of the heritages of both the women's movement and the Black liberation movement.

This book is one beginning for the long but vital journeys that must be made into the political lives of Black women, White women, Black men, and White men, highlighting the racial and sexual politics involved and the dilemmas which have to be more widely understood in new ways. Only by undertaking such journeys and beginning to confront in new ways the problems surrounding racial and sexual politics can there be a shift in the forms of stasis which isolated political oppositions have tended to produce. This process is necessary to identify the possibilities for collaboration—not on male, or White, or middle-class terms—by various groups of people whose interests necessitate fundamental change in the society as we know it. The contents of this book are intended to stimulate and encourage readers to begin to make such connections.

Through this book, we have attempted to present both our contrasting and our collaborative perspectives and methods of approach on issues concerning the social, political, and sexual relationships between and among Black women, White women, Black men, and White men. We have attempted to demonstrate the need for these issues to be examined historically and ideologically in new combinations of racial, sexual, and class terms, and the need to apply new concepts of what history and political vision must embody to enable vitally rethought forms of collaborative struggle to emerge from Black and White communities.

NOTES

1. Fact Sheets on Institutional Racism. New York: Council on Interracial Books for Children, October 1978, p. 2.

2. Fact Sheets on Institutional Sexism. New York: Council on Interracial Books for Children, January 1979, pp. 6 and 13.

3. *Rape-Race-Rapism*. Pamphlet published by local group in Amherst, Massachusetts, on women and violence, Fall 1979.

4. Fact Sheets on Institutional Racism. Council on Interracial Books for Children. New York: November 1978, pp. 12 and 22.

5. *Civil Liberties* newspaper. Number 331, February 1980, p. 6.

6. "They Get More Than Just a Marriage License." Fred Ferretti. New York *Times*, October 27, 1980, p. B-5.

7. "What Do Blacks Think of Themselves?" Kenneth B. Clark and Mamie Phipps Clark. *Ebony*, November 1980, p. 176.

8. *Midnight Birds*, ed. by Mary Helen Washington. New York: Doubleday/Anchor Books, 1980, p. xxi.

Bibliography

This bibliography gives detailed citations for the texts quoted in the chapters related to White feminism. It also serves as a list—for readers not already familiar with the range of feminist writings that have been produced and made accessible over the last twelve years thanks to the Women's Liberation Movement—of some of the important White feminist sources of analyses. More extensive bibliographies concerned with specific questions are available from women's bookstores.

Since I believe that literature—novels, autobiographies, plays, poetry, etc.—give a special nuance, flavor, and substance to the consequences and dilemmas generated by the sexual oppressions named and analyzed in feminist arguments and explorations, I have listed these separately. They will, for some readers, evoke dilemmas and dimensions of sexual-political struggle in particularly dynamic and moving ways. To the texts I have actually quoted I have unabashedly added a small number of my own favorites. I have also included a selective list of feminist journals and magazines that are important resources in the ongoing debates in the women's movement.

Allen, Sandra, Lee Saunders, and Jan Wallis, eds., *Conditions of Illusion: Papers from the Women's Movement*. Leeds, U.K.: Feminist Books, 1974.

Barker-Benfield, G. J., *The Horrors of Half-known Life*. New York: Harper & Row, 1976.

Barrett, Michele, *Women's Oppression Today: Problems in Marxist Feminist Analysis*. London, U.K.: Verso Editions & New Left Books, 1980.

Barry, Kathleen, *Female Sexual Slavery*. Englewood Cliffs, N.J.: Prentice-Hall, 1979.

Baxandall, Ros, Linda Gordon, and Susan Reverby, eds., *America's Working Women*. New York: Random House, 1976.

Beauvoir, Simone de, *The Second Sex*. Harmondsworth, U.K.: Penguin Books, 1972.

Berg, Barbara, *The Remembered Gate: Origins of American Feminism*. New York: Oxford University Press, 1978.

Birkby, Phyllis, Bertha Harris, Jill Johnston, Esther Newton, and Jane Owyatt, eds., *Amazon Expedition: A Lesbian Feminist Anthology*. New York: Times Change Press, 1973.

Brownmiller, Susan, *Against our Will*: Men, Women, and Rape. New York: Bantam Books, 1976.

CARASA, *Women Under Attack*. New York: Carasa, 1979.

Chodorow, Nancy, *The Reproduction of Mothering: Psychoanalysis and the Sociology of Gender*. Berkeley and Los Angeles: University of California Press, 1979.

Cluster, Dick, ed., *They Should Have Served That Cup of Coffee*. Boston: South End Press, 1979.

Cott, Nancy, *The Bonds of Womanhood*. New Haven: Yale University Press, 1977.

——, *Root of Bitterness. Documents of the Social History of American Women*. New York: E. P. Dutton, 1972.

Croll, Elizabeth, *The Women's Movement in China*. London: Anglo-Chinese Education Institute, 1974.

Daly, Mary, *Beyond God the Father*. Boston: Beacon Press, 1974.

——, *Gyn/ecology*. Boston: Beacon Press, 1978.

Delphy, Christine, *The Main Enemy: A Materialist Analysis of Women's Oppression* (trans. from the French). London: Women's Research and Resources Centre Publications, 1977.

Dinnerstein, Dorothy, *The Mermaid and the Minotaur*. New York: Harper & Row, 1977.

Dreitzel, Hans Peter, ed., *Family Marriage and the Struggle of the Sexes*. New York: Macmillan, 1972.

Dworkin, Andrea, *Woman Hating*. New York: E. P. Dutton & Co., 1974.

Ehrenreich, Barbara, and Deirdre English, *Complaints and Disorders: The Sexual Politics of Sickness*. Old Westbury, N.Y.: The Feminist Press, 1974.

——, *Witches, Midwives and Nurses: A History of Women Healers*. Old Westbury, N.Y.: The Feminist Press, 1972.

Eisenstein, Zillah R., *Capitalist Patriarchy and the Case for Socialist Feminism*. New York: Monthly Review Press, 1979.

Ellmann, Mary, *Thinking About Women*. New York: Harcourt Brace Jovanovich, 1968.

Ettore, Elizabeth, *Lesbians, Women and Society*. Boston: Routledge & Kegan Paul, 1980.

Evans, Sara, *Personal Politics: The Roots of Women's Liberation in the Civil Rights Movement and the New Left*. New York: Alfred Knopf, 1979.

Figes, Eva, *Patriarchal Attitudes*. London: Panther Books, 1972.

Firestone, Shulamith, *The Dialectic of Sex: The Case for Feminist Revolution*. London: Paladin, 1972.

Freeman, Jo, *The Politics of Women's Liberation*. New York: Longman, 1977.

Friedan, Betty, *The Feminine Mystique*. New York: Dell, 1975.

Goffman, Erving, *Gender Advertisements*. New York: Harper & Row, 1979.

Gordon, Linda, *Woman's Body, Woman's Right*. New York: Penguin Books, 1977.

Gornick, Vivian, and Barbara K. Moran, *Woman in Sexist Society: Studies in Power and Powerlessness*. New York: New American Library, 1972.

Greer, Germaine, *The Female Eunuch*. London: Paladin, 1971.

Griffith, Susan, *Rape: The Power of Consciousness*. New York: Harper & Row, 1980.

Hartman, Mary, and Lois W. Banner, *Clio's Consciousness Raised: New Perspectives on the History of Women*. New York: Harper & Row, 1974.

Howe, Florence, ed., *Women and the Power to Change*. New York: McGraw-Hill, 1975.

Hymowitz, Carol, and Michele Weissman, *A History of Women in America*. New York: Bantam Books, 1978.

Johnston, Jill, *Lesbian Nation*. New York: Simon & Schuster, 1974.

Kollontai, Alexandra, *Selected Writings*. London: Allison & Busby, 1977.

Lerner, Gerda, *Black Women in White America*. New York: Random House, 1973.

——, *The Female Experience: An American Documentary*. Indianapolis: Bobbs-Merrill, 1977.

Liberation Now! Writings from the Women's Movement. New York: Dell, 1971.

Millett, Kate, *Sexual Politics*. New York: Avon Books, 1971.

Mitchell, Juliet, *Psychoanalysis and Feminism*. New York: Random House, 1975.

——, *Women's Estate*. New York: Random House, 1973.

Mitchell, Juliet, and Ann Oakley, *The Rights and Wrongs of Women*. Harmondsworth, U.K.: Penguin Books, 1976.

Morgan, Robin, *Going Too Far*. New York: Random House, 1977.

——, ed., *Sisterhood Is Powerful: An Anthology of Writings from the Women's Movement*. New York: Random House, 1970.

Neidle, Cecyle S., *America's Immigrant Women*. New York: Hippocrene Books, 1976.

Oakley, Ann, *Sex, Gender and Society*. New York: Colophon, 1972.

——, *The Sociology of Housework*. New York: Random House, 1975.

——, *Women Confined: Towards a Sociology of Childbirth*. Oxford, U.K.: Martin Robertson, 1980.

Olsen, Tillie, *Silences*. New York: Delacorte, 1979.

Red Collective, *The Politics of Sexuality in Capitalism*. London: Red Collective and PDC, 1978.

Reed, Evelyn, *Problems of Women's Liberation*. New York: Pathfinder Press, 1970.

Reiter, Rayna, ed., *Toward an Anthropology of Women*. New York, Monthly Review Press, 1975.

Rich, Adrienne, *Lies, Secrets and Silences*. New York: W. W. Norton, 1979.

——, *Of Woman Born: Motherhood As Experience and Institution*. New York: Bantam, 1977.

Rosaldo, Michelle Zimbalist, and Louise Lamphere, *Woman, Culture and Society*. Stanford: Stanford University Press, 1974.

Rossi, Alice, *The Feminist Papers*. New York: Bantam, 1977.

Rothman, Sheila, *Woman's Proper Place*. New York: Basic Books, 1978.

Rowbotham, Sheila, *A New World for Women: Socialist Feminist Stella Brown*. London: Pluto Press, 1978.

——, *Socialism and the New Life*. London: Pluto Press, 1977.

——, *Woman's Consciousness, Man's World*. Harmondsworth, U.K.: Penguin Books, 1973.

——, *Women, Resistance and Revolution*. New York: Random House, 1974.

——, *Women's Liberation and Revolution: A Bibliography*. Bristol, U.K.: Falling Wall Press, 1973.

Rowbotham, Sheila, Lynne Segal, and Hilary Wainwright, *Beyond the Fragments: Feminism and the Making of Socialism*. London: The Merlin Press, 1979.

Rubin, Lillian Breslow, *Worlds of Pain*. New York: Basic Books, 1976.

Ryan, Mary, *Womanhood in America from Colonial Times to the Present*. New York: Franklin Watts, 1975.

Schneir, Miriam, *Feminism: The Essential Historical Writings*. New York: Random House, 1972.

Scott, Hilda, *Does Socialism Liberate Women?* Boston: Beacon Press, 1975.

Tanner, Leslie B., *Voices from Women's Liberation*. New York: New American Library, 1971.

Tax, Meredith, *Woman and Her Mind: The Story of Daily Life*. Boston: New England Free Press, 1970.

Thompson, Mary L., ed., *Voices of the New Feminism*. Boston: Beacon Press, 1970.

Vicinus, Martha, ed., *Suffer and Be Still: Women in the Victorian Age*. Bloomington and London: Indiana University Press, 1973.

Williamson, Judith, *Decoding Advertisements*. London: Marion Boyars, 1979.

Wittig, Monique, *The Lesbian Body*. New York: William Morrow & Co., 1975.

Wolff, Charlotte, *Love Between Women*. New York: Harper & Row, 1972.

Wollstonecraft, Mary, *A Vindication of the Rights of Woman* (1792). New York: W. W. Norton, 1967.

Women's Collective of the Birmingham Centre for Cultural Studies, The, *Women Take Issue: Aspects of Women's Subordination*. London: Hutchinson, 1978.

Zaretsky, Eli, *Capitalism, the Family and Personal Life*. New York: Harper & Row, 1976.

Fiction, poetry, drama

Arnold, June, *Sister Gin*. Plainfield, Vermont: Daughters, Inc., 1975.

Atwood, Margaret, *Power Politics*. New York: Harper & Row, 1971.

——, *Surfacing*. New York: Popular Library, 1972.

Berger, John, *G*. New York: Dell, 1972.

Bernikov, Louise, ed., *The World Split Open*. New York: Random House, 1974.

Broumas, Olga, *Beginning with Zero*. New Haven, Conn.: Yale University Press, 1977.

Brown, Rita Mae, *Rubyfruit Jungle*. Plainfield, Vermont: Daughters, Inc., 1974.

Chopin, Kate, *The Awakening*. New York: Hearst, 1972.

Fairbairns, Zoe, *Benefits*. London: Virago, 1979.

Fell, Alison, ed., *Hard Feelings: Fiction and Poetry from Spare Rib*. London: Women's Press, 1979.

French, Marilyn, *Bleeding Heart*. New York: Summit Books/Simon & Schuster, 1980.

Gilman, Charlotte Perkins, *The Yellow Wallpaper*. Old Westbury, N.Y.: The Feminist Press, 1973.

Ibarruri, Dolores, *They Shall Not Pass: The Autobiography of La Passionaria*. New York: International Publishers, 1976.

Kaplan, Cora, ed., *Salt and Bitter and Good*. New York: Paddington Press, 1977.

Kollontai, Alexandra, *The Autobiography of a Sexually Emancipated Communist Woman*. New York: Schocken, 1975.

Lessing, Doris, *A Proper Marriage*. New York: New American Library, 1966.

Millett, Kate, *Flying*. London: Hart-Davis, MacGibbon, 1975.

———, *Sita*. New York: Random House, 1977.

Morgan, Robin, *Lady of the Beasts*. New York: Random House, 1976.

———, *Monster*. New York: Random House, 1972.

Olsen, Tillie, *Tell Me a Riddle*. New York: Dell, 1976.

———, *Yonnondio*. New York: Dell, 1975.

Piercy, Marge, *Living in the Open*. New York: Alfred Knopf, 1977.

———, *Small Changes*. New York: Fawcett, 1978.

———, *To Be of Use*. New York: Doubleday, 1973.

Plath, Sylvia, *Ariel*. London: Faber & Faber, 1965.

Rhys, Jean, *Wide Sargasso Sea*. New York: Popular Library, 1975.

Rich, Adrienne, *Dream of a Common Language: Poems 1974–77*. New York: W. W. Norton, 1978.

———, *Poems Selected & New, 1950–1974*. New York: W. W. Norton, 1975.

Roberts, Michele, *A Piece of the Night*. London: Women's Press, 1978.

Russell, Dora, *The Tamarisk Tree*. London: Virago, 1977.

Sexton, Anne, *The Awful Rowing Toward God*. Boston: Houghton Mifflin, 1975.

Smedley, Agnes, *Daughter of Earth*. Old Westbury, N.Y.: The Feminist Press, 1973.

Wandor, Michelene, and Michele Roberts, eds., *Cutlasses and Earrings*. London: Playbooks, 1977.

Weldon, Fay, *Down Among the Women*. Harmondsworth, U.K.: Penguin, 1974.

———, *Remember Me*. New York: Random House, 1976.

Wittig, Monique, *Les Guerrillères*. London: Paladin, 1975.

Selected feminist periodicals

Chrysalis. 6355 Westlake Avenue, Los Angeles, CA 90057.

Conditions. A magazine of writing by women with an emphasis on writing by lesbians (No. 5 was a Black women's issue). P. O. Box 56, Van Brunt Station, Brooklyn, NY 11215.

Feminist Review. A socialist-feminist journal of feminist debate and analysis. 65 Manor Road, London N16, England.

Feminist Studies. A forum for feminist analysis, debate, and exchange. C/o Women's Studies Program, University of Maryland, College Park, MD 20742.

Heresies. 225 Lafayette Street, New York, NY 10012.

Off Our Backs.

Quest: A Feminist Quarterly. P. O. Box 8843, Washington, DC 20003.

Red Rag. A magazine of women's liberation. 207 Sumatra Rd., London NW61PF.

Scarlet Women. Newsletter of the socialist-feminist current of the Women's Liberation Movement. 5 Washington Terrace, North Shields, Tyne & Wear, England.

Signs: Journal of Women in Culture and Society. The University of Chicago Press, 11030 Langley Avenue, Chicago, Illinois 60628.

Sinister Wisdom. A journal of words and pictures for the lesbian imagination in all women. Box 30541, Lincoln, Nebraska 68503.

Spare Rib. 27 Clerkenwell Close, London EC1, England.

Index

relationships between Black men and
    women, 178–230, 280
    challenge of 1980s, 228–29
    facts about Black women's lives,
        180–81
    role of socialization, 181–228
    as victims of racism and economic
        oppression, 179
    styling, profiling, and pretending,
        178–230
Shabazz, Nacemah, 230 n
Shakur, Assate, 32
Shange, Ntozake, 231
Sheba, Queen of, 88
Shulman, Alix, 272 n
Simone, Nina, 185
Slavery, 32, 39, 162–63, 197, 239
Sloan, Margaret, 34
Smedley, Agnes, 139, 147 n, 272 n
Smith, Barbara, 36, 42 n, 230 n
Smith, Bessie, 183, 184, 185
Smith, Mamie, 185
Smith, Ruby, 183–84
Smith-Rosenberg, Carroll, 147 n, 253,
        272 n
Snitow, Ann, 272 n
Socialist-feminism, 55–56, 63, 232,
        236–41
    concerns of, 237
Socialist movement, 6
Southern Voter Registration Project, 2
Spirituals, 182
Stack, Carol, 181, 229 n, 230 n
Stereotypes, 28, 43, 106
    "helpless female," 28
Sterilization, 5, 30, 31
Stevenson, Karen, 111–12
Student Non-Violent Coordinating
        Committee (SNCC), 2
Swing Stompers (music group), 184

"Take Back the Night" (demonstra-
        tions), 64
Tax, Meredith, 70 n
Television, 167, 168, 175
    Black images on, 164–65
    commercials, 170
"Tell Me a Riddle" (Olsen), 133–34

Terborg-Penn, Rosalyn, 229 n
That's My Mama (television program),
        164
Thompson, Mary, 70 n
Thornton, Big Mama, 183
Tinubu, Madame, 88
Travolta, John, 162
"Tricks Ain't Walkin' No More," 183
Truth, Sojourner, 27, 32
Tubman, Harriet, 32

Ultra Sheen Hair Products, 157
Unemployment, 162, 167, 274
United Farm Workers, 60
U.S. Census, 129
U.S. Constitution, 46
U.S. Supreme Court, 279
Universal Negro Improvement Associa-
        tion, 1
Urban Research Review, 105

Varied Voices of Women, 36
Violence against women, 64–65
Viva (magazine), 152, 153, 154
Voices of the New Feminism, 38
Voight, Jon, 162

Walker, Alice, 80
Walker, Madame C. J., 160
Walker Method, the, 160
Wallace, Mike, 160–61
Waller, Fats, 184
Washington, Dinah, 185
Washington, Mary Helen, 282, 284 n
Watson, Mary, 36
Weissman, Michaele, 70 n, 71 n
Weldon, Fay, 132, 136, 147 n, 148 n,
        263, 272 n
Welfare, 31, 51, 104, 107
Wells, Ida B., 32
Welsing, Frances Cress, 37, 42 n
West, Hollie I., 42 n
White student movement, 52, 53
Wife beating, 5, 64, 168, 195
Wilkinson, Brenda, 80
Williamson, Judith, 176 n
Wilson, Flip, 164–65
Winship, Janet, 176 n, 177 n